EIGHTH EDITION

Business Records Control

Joseph S. Fosegan, M.S.
Mary Lea Ginn, Ph.D.

South-Western
EDUCATIONAL PUBLISHING
Thomson Learning™

Australia • Canada • Denmark • Japan • Mexico • New Zealand • Philippines
Puerto Rico • Singapore • South Africa • Spain • United Kingdom • United States

Project Manager: Marilyn Hornsby
Production Coordinator: Jane Congdon
Manufacturing Coordinator: Carol Chase
Art/Design Coordinator: Michelle Kunkler
Marketing Manager: Tim Gleim
Marketing Coordinator: Lisa Barto
Publishing Team Leader: Karen Schmohe
Internal Design: Elaine St. John-Lagenaur
Cover Design: Grannan Graphic Design
Production Services: Litten Editing And Production, Inc.

ISBN: 0-538-69340-1

1 2 3 4 5 6 7 8 9 WT 04 03 02 01 00 99
Printed in the United States of America

For permission to use material from this text or product, contact us by
• Web: www.thomsonrights.com
• Phone: 1-800-730-2214
• Fax: 1-800-730-2215

Chapter Opener Photo Credits: (Ch. 1) Systems Manufacturing Corporation; (Ch.2) Photography by Erik Von Fischer/Photonics; (Ch. 3) Photography by Erik Von Fischer/Photonics; (Ch. 4) Shaw-Walker is now known as Knoll North America, Inc.; (Ch. 6) TAB Products Co.; (Ch. 7) Borroughs Corporation; (Ch. 9) PRO/file Systems; (Ch. 10) © Charles Thatcher/Tony Stone Images; (Ch. 11) Esselte Pendaflex Corporation; (Ch. 12) TAB Products Co.; (Ch. 14) Schwab Corporation

Part Opener Photo Credits: Photography by Erik Von Fischer/Photonics. Props courtesy of Signal Office Supplies, Cincinnati, Ohio.

Preface/Contents Photo Credits: (p. iii) Photography by Alan Brown/Photonics; (p. iv) Kardex Systems, Inc.; (p. v) Eastman Kodak Company; (p. vi) TAB Products Co.; (p. vii) The Smead Manufacturing Company; (p. viii) InfoGraphix Corporation

Preface

Business Records Control, Eighth Edition, is about order and how to create it. Its purpose is to prepare office workers to manage records and information—the primary function of every office. Records and information management skills include storing and protecting records, organizing records, and retrieving them quickly when needed, tracking the movement of records to account for their location at all times, and finally, disposing of records no longer needed. These important office skills can be learned from this text.

Paper documents still make up over 90 percent of stored vital information. Nonetheless, office workers of the 21st Century need to be aware of the electronic- and image-based systems that currently help to control information in the modern office. Whether office records are paper, computer tapes or disks, optical disks, audio and video cassettes, or microforms, locating the records requires that they be arranged in some meaningful way. Basic filing methods are presented: alphabetic filing by name, subject, or geographic location, and numeric filing methods. Students learn how letters, numbers, dates, and more recently, colors function as the principal means of organizing records. Once learned, these skill can be adapted to organize office records of any varity.

Features

Text material and simulations in this edition reflect changing trends in records management. Manual filing systems are discussed thoroughly before automated records management activities are introduced. The ten alphabetic indexing rules presented agree with the simplified filing standard rules issued by the Association of Records Managers and Administrators, Inc. (ARMA) and are intended to serve as an industry standard. This edition includes current concerns of records and information managers, such as records retention and records disaster prevention. Also included are current trends in records media, technology, and office filing equipment, which have lightened and brightened the workday of

records personnel. Optional computer exercises in this Eighth Edition provide introductory practice in electronic records control. A template with file creation and data entry tasks completed is available for those whose class time is limited.

Learning Aids in the Text

Learning objectives used for directed reading open each chapter and questions for discussion and applications related to these objectives end each chapter. Self-help and self-check features include marginal questions, chapter review questions, chapter summaries, and terminology reviews. Marginal questions used generously throughout the text keep the reader actively involved with the text content. At least two reviews per chapter sharpen reader comprehension; the answers to these review questions are included in the back of this text and in the Teacher's Manual. Chapter summaries highlight the important chapter content. Terminology reviews follow the chapter summaries and list words that are defined in the chapter and printed in **bold** type. Full use of color illustrations and photographs dominates the chapters as visual enhancements to learning. Students benefit from the use of full color, especially in the chapter on color-coded systems and filing supplies.

Student Supplementary Items

Two filing practice sets accompany *Business Records Control,* Eighth Edition: *Office Filing Procedures,* Eighth Edition, and *Simplifile,* Fifth Edition. *Office Filing Procedures* provides a comprehensive experience in records control. Textbook chapters end with a specific job assignment from this practice set. Students apply the text material to practical filing jobs using alphabetic, numeric, geographic, and subject filing methods. Requisition, charge-out, and transfer procedures are included, and practical computer exercises have been added to *Office Filing Procedures,* Eighth Edition.

Simplifile, Fifth Edition, is a practice set in a file-box format. The student manual reviews the alphabetic indexing rules and contains worksheets for applying the rules. Practical filing projects make use of the alphabetic, numeric, geographic, and subject filing methods.

A test package is available for use with the textbook. The test package includes a pretest, five tests to be taken after Chapters 3, 5, 8, 11, and 14, and a comprehensive final exam.

Instructor Supplementary Items

The Teacher's Manual for *Business Records Control,* Eighth Edition, contains teaching suggestions, answers to questions for discussion, answers to review questions, and solutions to the end-of-chapter applications and computer exercises. The manual also includes the Manual for *Office Filing Procedures,* Eighth Edition, and answers to the seven tests.

Transparency masters for each chapter are available in the Teacher's Manual. Teachers may use the overhead visuals to highlight important aspects of each chapter. The pretest, five chapter tests, and a final examination are available as a separate packet.

About the Authors

We, the authors, bring to this text a blend of professional records management experience and teaching experience. Joseph Fosegan, former Chairman of the Office and Reporting Technologies Department at Alfred State College, has over 30 years' teaching experience in filing, records management, and other office and court reporting skills. Dr. Mary Lea Ginn has worked with records management professionals, served on the Association of Records Managers and Administrators, Inc. (ARMA) Filing Systems and Publications Coordination committees, edited records management materials, and taught in the office administration area.

Because we are in an information age, the revision of this text was an important and challenging task. Surely the content of this text should be a requirement of all prospective office workers in office support educational programs. It is our wish that this text prepare you well for controlling the records in the office where you will work and in providing a foundation from which you can grow as an office professional.

Joseph S. Fosegan
Mary Lea Ginn

Table of Contents

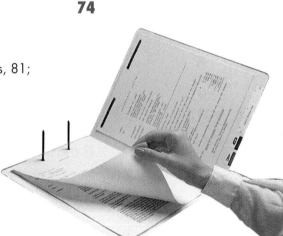

Part 3   Records Maintenance Procedures

Part 4   Other Filing Methods

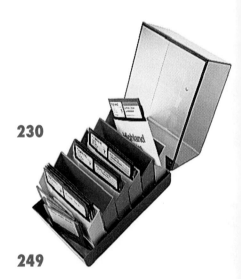

Part 1

Introduction to Records Control

Chapter One
A Preview of Records Control

Chapter One

A Preview of Records Control

Learning Objectives

After completing Chapter 1, you will be able to do the following:

1. Define a **record** and give examples of records.

2. Define **filing**, **retrieval**, and **records control**.

3. Identify other terms used to describe records responsibility and list the title of the person responsible.

4. Explain the four kinds (uses) of records.

5. List and describe the phases of the records cycle.

6. Identify the goal of a filing system.

7. Describe three records media—paper, electronic, and image.

8. Identify types of electronic and image records.

9. Define **micrographics**.

10. List job titles and write brief descriptions of jobs in the records area.

Introduction to Records Control

Imagine your frustration upon arriving at school to register for another term of classes and finding that none of your admission records or records from previous school years are in the files. What do you do? Or imagine that you arrive to renew your driver's license and all records of your current license and other personal information have been erased from the computer. What do you do?

Although we may tolerate misplacing a few items in our personal lives, usually we are very intolerant of office workers who misplace, lose, or accidentally destroy records. For an organization, failure to locate records can be costly. A bank may handle 500,000 or more depositor signature cards. An air-freight company may generate 150,000 shipping orders a month. An insurance company may process over a million policies. Even a small hospital may maintain medical histories on 5,000 or more patient admissions a year. Workers in these organizations are responsible for processing and maintaining these important records so they are not lost, misplaced, or accidentally destroyed.

In addition to the volume of records stored, records management is complicated by the different kinds of records kept by various organizations. Letters and memos, cards, blueprints and maps, reports, inventory and price lists, purchase orders, shipping receipts, newspapers and catalogs, sales and personnel records, videotapes, microforms (photographically reduced records), and computer disks and printouts are some familiar types of office records.

The variety and quantity of information and records managed in an office will vary from one organization to another. Workers in all job levels, from the factory floor to the executive suite, use records. (See Figure 1-1.) Factory workers check off the number of parts used in an assembly. Company presidents review financial reports. Building contractors constantly refer to architectural and engineering drawings. Common to all organizations, however, is the need to store and to protect these records and to find them when they are needed.

Figure 1-1
Records in Use
Source: *Photography by Alan Brown/Photonics*

Records Control

What is a record?

What are filing and retrieval?

A **record** is recorded information, regardless of media or characteristics, created or received and used in the operation of an organization. Records provide the memory or history of what has taken place in the past—even yesterday.

Filing is the action of arranging records in a predetermined sequence. **Retrieval** is the process of finding records and/or information. Learning and using alphabetic indexing rules are vital to accurate filing and retrieval of records. You will begin to learn the indexing rules in Chapter 2. In later chapters, you will learn how to file and retrieve records that have been filed in order by letters of the alphabet and in order by numbers. You will learn also that records filed by geographic location, as well as records filed by subject, make use of alphabetic order.

Records control is the set of procedures used to make filing and retrieval reliable and systematic processes. To control records, you must know why records are kept and which phases records pass through from creation to disposition.

What is records control?

In some organizations, the records responsibility is called *document management, records and information management,* or *records management.* The person responsible for the records management program is usually the *records manager.* Records management professionals have the ultimate responsibility for establishing records policies and procedures. However, everyone in the organization needs to have a basic understanding of records control. As you study *Business Records Control,* you will learn that controlling records is the basis for establishing an organization-wide records management program. Other important reasons for establishing a records and information management program are listed in Figure 1-2. These reasons are discussed in this chapter and in Chapter 7.

Figure 1-2
Reasons for Establishing a Records Management Program

1. To learn what records the organization creates and receives.
2. To ensure that records are kept as long as they are needed.
3. To retain records having business value or historical interest.
4. To store less frequently used records in less expensive space.
5. To destroy records that have served their usefulness.

Why Organizations Keep Records

Organizations depend on records for their daily operations, because they provide a memory of the organization's activities. Records are created to document specific actions and activities so those actions and activities can be substantiated and defended later if necessary. Employees come and go, but systematic records control ensures that records provide the information for conducting business. Generally, records are kept and used because they have administrative value, fiscal value, legal value, or historical value.

Records have *administrative value* when they are used in the performance of daily operations in a department or office. Policy and procedures manuals are used daily in some offices. A records manual provides records management guidelines and serves as a daily reference in a records management department or area. (See Chapter 14 for more on records manuals.) Also, correspondence and other records used for day-to-day decision making have administrative value.

Financial records have *fiscal value.* These records include tax returns, purchase and sales orders, invoices, and monthly and annual financial statements. According to law, many of these records must be kept by the company for a certain period of time.

Records having *legal value* provide proof of business transactions. Contracts, financial agreements, deeds, and titles have legal value.

Records have *historical value* when they provide evidence of the organization's accomplishments. Articles of incorporation, minutes of meetings that provide a history of operational decisions, and information about company officers have historical value. Historical records should be stored permanently in the most protected storage area.

Why are records used?

Review

1. Who uses records?

2. Why do organizations keep records?

The Records Cycle

Records have a life cycle that runs from creation to disposition. Records pass through a series of phases in a **records cycle**: creation, distribution, use, maintenance, and disposition. Study the records cycle phases illustrated in Figure 1-3.

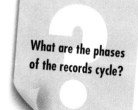

What are the phases of the records cycle?

Creation

Records are created inside a business through dictation, handwritten drafts, voice mail, electronic mail (e-mail), or by using computers and word processors. Records created outside the business are received through the mail, personal delivery, facsimile (fax) machines, voice mail, e-mail, and other communication delivery systems.

Distribution

To be useful, records must be distributed to persons requiring the data. Records may be sent to users within the company or outside the company.

Figure 1-3 Records Cycle

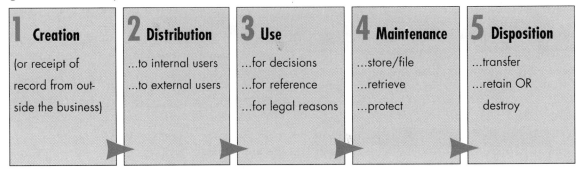

1 Creation	**2** Distribution	**3** Use	**4** Maintenance	**5** Disposition
(or receipt of record from outside the business)	...to internal users ...to external users	...for decisions ...for reference ...for legal reasons	...store/file ...retrieve ...protect	...transfer ...retain OR destroy

Use

Records are used for making and documenting decisions, for answering questions, for reference, or for tax or legal reasons. Records are used most often shortly after they are created. Usually, the older the records, the less they are used.

Maintenance

Filing and retrieving records occur during the maintenance phase. An organization selects a filing method (alphabetic, subject, numeric, or geographic) and designs a filing system for *efficient retrieval of records*. **Finding records after they have been filed is the goal of a filing system.** Throughout your study of *Business Records Control*, you will work primarily with the maintenance phase—filing and retrieving records. Transferring records from one location to another is also part of records maintenance.

Disposition

Records that are no longer frequently used are kept in long-term storage, discarded, or destroyed. You will learn how to follow a *records retention and destruction schedule* to move rarely used records and provide space for new records. Also, you will learn ways to dispose of records that are no longer useful. (See Chapter 7.)

The phases of the records cycle with which you will be most concerned in your records career are the maintenance and disposition phases. These two phases are extremely important for controlling records in either small or large companies. By controlling the number of records and where they are filed, equipment and employee costs can be reduced.

Review

1. What are the phases of the records cycle?
2. What is the goal of a filing system?

Organization of the Records Function

Records and information management performs a major function in many organizations. Because records and information management is a key component of administration and finance—primary organizational functions—it plays an important role in the successful operation of an organization. In your study of *Business Records Control*, you will learn how the records function is organized, what equipment and supplies are needed, how filing is done, and what records career opportunities are available to you.

Records are categorized into three media: paper, electronic, and image. Paper records generally are stored and retrieved manually (by hand). Electronic records are created through the use of computers and word processors. These records are stored magnetically inside the hardware (equipment) or on disks or tapes outside the hardware. Image records are created through optical or micrographic systems for storage on optical disks or microforms. The records media determine the equipment and the procedures used for filing and retrieving records.

What are the records media?

Paper Media

Even though the use of the computer to produce records and to assist in records control has increased, most offices continue to use paper records. According to a recent survey of 1,700 members of the Association of Records Managers and Administrators, Inc., conducted by The Olsten Corporation, paper filing systems account for 57 percent of records management systems in use.

The paperless office remains a myth. The more charts, tables, graphs, and reports that can be created from a computer file, the more paper copies of those charts, tables, graphs, and reports are requested and used. Paper records are stored in file cabinets or on shelves as shown in Figure 1-4.

Figure 1-4
Paper Media Storage Equipment
Source: *TAB Products Co.*

Electronic Media

Media used for storage and retrieval of electronic records are magnetic disks (3.5" and 5.25"), tapes, and computer hard-disk drives. Numerous types of storage equipment are available for computer disks and tapes. Two types of storage equipment are shown in Figure 1-5.

Figure 1-5
Electronic Media
Storage Equipment
Source: *Photo Courtesy of Counterpoint*
Source: *Fellowes Manufacturing Company*

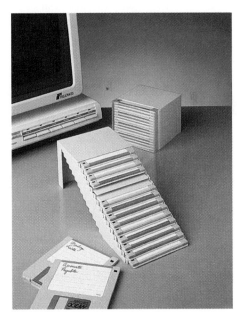

Image Media

Image media include micrographics and optical disk technologies. Microfilm, microfiche, and computer-output microfilm (COM) are examples of micrographics media. Optical disks use laser beams to read and write data. Examples of optical disks include the compact disk read-only-memory (CD-ROM) disk and the write once, read many (WORM) disk. Optical disks and CDs are *electronic image media.* Records are stored on optical disks and CDs in their full sizes. Records on COM and other micro-forms are stored in reduced sizes. Chapter 13 contains a detailed discussion of image technology.

Micrographics is the full range of services for creating, storing, retrieving, using, and protecting microimage records. Microimage records are created through a photographic miniature imaging process. Records are reduced in size when photographed. The microfilm is then formatted into rolls or flat forms—microfiche, jackets, or aperture cards, for example. A microform reader is used to enlarge records for use. An optical disk workstation and a microfiche reader and microfiche are shown in Figure 1-6.

Figure 1-6
Image Media Equipment
Source: *Photo Courtesy of Bell & Howell Co.*
Source: *Business Efficiency Aids, Inc., Skokie, Illinois*

3 Review

1. What three media are used for records?

2. Give one example of each type of records media.

Records Careers

Our complex technological society increases the demand for systematic records control and management. A career in records can be varied and exciting. Because the records area is broad, many types of career opportunities are available. The records function includes the total records and information management program, forms design and management, micrographics, and electronic imaging. Additional career opportunities are emerging for persons trained in records control and management.

What are four records management career areas?

Large organizations offer more specialized positions in records. They may have positions in all aspects of records, as well as separate records centers for processing and storing records. Often, large organizations provide opportunities for records staff to move into higher-level positions or career paths. Small businesses have more diversified tasks for each records employee and more involvement with records because only one or two people are responsible for the records. The records function in smaller organizations may be performed by secretaries, administrative assistants, or office managers.

Descriptions of common job titles are presented in the following paragraphs. Space limitations prevent listing all possible records positions.

Some of the more commonly used job titles for the records and information management and forms management areas are records and information manager, records and information systems analyst, records and information clerk, forms designer, and forms analyst. Brief descriptions and requirements for these positions are included in Figure 1-7.

Figure 1-7 Records and Information and Forms Job Titles and Descriptions

Records and Information Manager	The top position in the records program. Manages long-range plans for organization-wide records program and prepares annual budgets and reports for top management. Is responsible for protecting an organization's assets. Requires a degree, masters preferred, and six to eight years of related experience.
Records and Information Systems Analyst *Desktop Publishing*	Reviews current and potential systems and recommends changes, designs and develops manual and/or automated records systems, prepares retention schedules, writes procedures, and provides training. Requires a college degree or two years' college and specialized courses in records, or four to six years' records experience with automated technologies.
Records and Information Clerk	Assists in processing incoming information, sorts and classifies materials, retrieves information for users, and maintains logs and indexes. Requires a high school diploma or GED, keyboarding skills, oral and written communication skills, and ability to operate copy machines, reader-printers, calculators, typewriters, and computers.
Forms Designer *Desktop Publishing*	Provides technical expertise (including layouts and specifications for typesetting, size, color, type and weight of paper, and number of copies) of new forms or improvement of existing forms. Ensures that forms enhance and simplify manual and machine-processing methods. Prepares written instructions for use of forms. Requires two years' college in graphic arts or business administration and two years' experience.
Forms Analyst	Monitors existing forms for overlapping information, duplication, or inaccuracies and ensures that obsolete forms are omitted. Requires two years' college with courses in business administration, forms management, and systems analysis and two years' experience.

Source: Association of Records Managers and Administrators, Inc., Job Descriptions Guideline, Prairie Village, KS, 1991.

Common job titles in the micrographics area are micrographics operations manager, computer-output microfilm (COM) supervisor, data/document preparation clerk, and various equipment operators and quality control positions. Brief descriptions and requirements for these positions are included in Figure 1-8.

Job titles in electronic imaging include electronic imaging operations manager, image processing technician, and scanner operator. Brief descriptions and requirements for these positions are shown in Figure 1-9.

Figure 1-8 Micrographics Job Titles and Descriptions *image media*

Micrographics Operations Manager	Responsible for operation of micrographics center, including controlling costs of labor, supplies, and equipment. Requires three to five years' experience, including supervision, in micrographics production.
Computer-Output Microfilm (COM) Supervisor	Supervises all production operations, including scheduling, quality control, cost control, and equipment maintenance. Is responsible for programming and maintaining setup programs for customer jobs. Requires two to three years' experience in COM operations/camera operations, and job setup programming.
Data/Document Preparation Clerk	Prepares documents and materials for microfilming by removing holding devices, repairing tears and wrinkles, and placing documents in filming order. Receives, logs, and distributes incoming production jobs. Types labels, job information sheets, and headers; loads and indexes cartridges, cassettes, and reels; and edits film. Requires a high school diploma and keyboarding skills.
Equipment Operators and Quality Control	Rotary and planetary camera operator, duplicator operator, microfilm processing technician, quality assurance technician, and quality control supervisor positions require a high school diploma or GED and equipment experience.

Source: *Association for Information and Image Management,* AIIM Key Job Position Descriptors, *Silver Spring, MD, 1989.*

Figure 1-9 Electronic Imaging Job Titles and Descriptions

Electronic Imaging Operations Manager	The senior position in electronic imaging. Is responsible for equipment, staff, training, and reports and recommendations to top management. Requires a degree, masters preferred, and six to eight years' experience in electronic imaging operations.
Image Processing Technician	Prepares, scans, indexes, and verifies documents for transfer to optical disk. Commits image to optical disk and performs retrieval/printing operations. Verifies and indexes scanned images. Requires a high school diploma or GED and one year of experience in image processing or data entry.
Scanner Operator	Operates various scanners to commit documents and/or microforms to optical disk; prints documents; and performs basic preventive maintenance on scanners and printers. Requires a high school diploma or GED and six months to one year of related experience.

Source: *Association for Information and Image Management,* AIIM Key Job Position Descriptors, *Silver Spring, MD, 1989.*

The Association of Records Managers and Administrators, Inc. (ARMA), the professional organization for records and information professionals, publishes guidelines for careers in records and information management. The Association for Information and Image Management (AIIM),

What professional organizations serve the records area?

a professional organization for electronic and microimage professionals, publishes standards for electronic and image media and provides career information. A more complete listing of job titles and descriptions may be obtained from each of these organizations. The rapid growth in membership in both organizations in recent years presents strong evidence of the growth in careers in records and information management.

As you begin your study of records control, you are expanding your knowledge of another career option. Remember that in any career you choose, you will be using records. Knowing the importance of controlling those records will make you a more informed and valuable employee in any organization.

Review

1. What two records job titles interest you? Why?
2. What professional organizations serve the records area?

Summary

Records control is the set of procedures used to make filing and retrieval reliable and systematic processes. Organizations keep records because they have administrative, fiscal, legal, or historical value to the organization.

Records have a life cycle that includes creation, distribution, use, maintenance, and disposition phases. The maintenance phase, filing and retrieval, is the primary focus of *Business Records Control,* Eighth Edition.

Records are the memory of an organization and are useful in all types of organizations. Maintaining control over those records so that they are available when needed is an important function.

Records are categorized into three media—paper, electronic, and image. The majority of records continues to be stored on paper. The numbers and uses of electronic records (disks and tapes) increase daily. The use of image records—micrographic and optical—will continue to grow in the future. Keeping up with the advancing technology in the records field requires that various career paths be established for each records media.

✓ **Terminology Review**

filing	(p. 4)
micrographics	(p. 8)
record	(p. 4)
records control	(p. 4)
records cycle	(p. 5)
retrieval	(p. 4)

Questions For Discussion

1. What is a record? Give two examples of records that you used today. (Obj. 1)
2. Define *filing, retrieval,* and *records control.* (Obj. 2)
3. Name two other terms sometimes used to describe the records responsibility. (Obj. 3)
4. What is the title of the person usually responsible for the records management program? (Obj. 3)
5. Explain four uses of records. (Obj. 4)
6. List and describe the phases of the records cycle. (Obj. 5)
7. Which phases of the records cycle will you work with most often throughout your records career? Explain. (Obj. 5)
8. What is the goal of a filing system? (Obj. 6)
9. List and describe the three records media. (Obj. 7)
10. Which records media is used most often? (Obj. 7)
11. What media are used for storing electronic records? (Obj. 8)
12. Name two types of electronic image media. (Obj. 8)
13. Define *micrographics.* (Obj. 9)
14. List two job titles in each records management area. (Obj. 10)
15. Write a brief job description for two records job titles. (Obj. 10)

Part 2

Alphabetic Filing Procedures

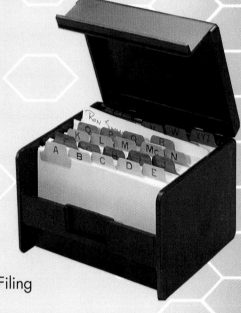

Chapter Two

Alphabetic Indexing and Card Filing

Learning Objectives

After completing Chapter 2, you will be able to do the following:

1. Define **indexing rules** and explain why they are needed.

2. Index, code, and arrange personal names, business names, and organization names in correct filing order.

3. List the uses of card files.

4. Describe the supplies needed to establish an alphabetic card filing system.

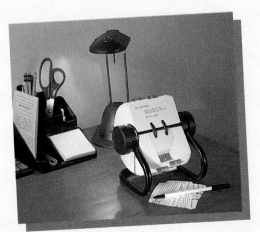

5. Describe the guide arrangement of an alphabetic card filing system.

6. Prepare cross-references for personal and business names that may be referred to in more than one way.

Alphabetic Indexing of Personal and Business Names

The office is sometimes called the mind or memory center of an organization because of the vast amount of information stored there. Information includes a variety of paper and paperless records. Office workers are responsible for sending, receiving, storing, and protecting the records that are necessary for operating the organization. In fact, storing records so that they can be located when needed is a primary office function. Just as people cannot function without the information stored in their minds, organizations cannot function without the information stored in their office files.

Why is the office the memory center of an organization?

Adopting Indexing Rules

Only when all office workers apply the same guidelines for storing and locating records can information be found quickly. **Alphabetic indexing rules** provide office workers with the necessary guidelines to arrange personal and business names alphabetically. *Index* means a pointer or indicator. A *rule* is an established guide for action. **Indexing rules** are established guides that indicate the proper location of a record in a file. Each indexed name has a special place in the file that makes that name distinct from all other names in the filing system.

What are indexing rules?

Over 90 billion documents are produced in this country every year; active office files grow about 25 percent every three to four years; and record-keeping costs double every year.[1] Why do office files continue to grow? Businesses need more information to be competitive in today's business world, and organizations have the computers to generate that information. Although computer technology has vastly improved information storage and retrieval, 95 percent of information is currently stored on paper.

Approximately 3 percent of stored documents are misfiled, and the cost to find each lost record is estimated to be $200.[2] This means that organizations spend billions of dollars every year trying to find misfiled records. Needless to say, all office workers need filing skills.

Records are stored most frequently by letter or by number. Letters and numbers are the only tools in our language capable of organizing information sequentially: A, B, C, etc., or 1, 2, 3, etc. When a filing task requires an alphabetic arrangement of personal and business names, a uniform set

Why are indexing rules needed?

1 John B. Dykeman, "Document Management Software: Make Sure What You Get Is What You Need," *Modern Office Technology*, April 1992, pp. 37-38.

2 Ibid.

of rules for alphabetizing those names MUST BE adopted and applied consistently and systematically by everyone in the organization. Otherwise, records will be filed in other possible locations, making retrieval difficult.

ARMA (The Association of Records Managers and Administrators, Inc.) has developed industry standards for records control systems. The alphabetic indexing rules in this chapter and in Chapter 3 are based on ARMA's Simplified Alphabetic Indexing Rules. ARMA designed the rules for use with both manual and computerized filing systems. Five of these rules are presented in this chapter. The remaining five rules are given in Chapter 3.

Indexing Names for Filing Purposes

Indexing is a mental process of (1) selecting the filing segment, (2) dividing the filing segment into filing units, and (3) determining the order of the units for filing. The following paragraphs give a more detailed explanation of the indexing process.

Select the Filing Segment

The **filing segment** is the *complete* name, subject, number or location being used for filing purposes. For the name *Helen L. Sanchez*, the complete name is the filing segment.

Divide the Filing Segment into Filing Units

A filing unit is part of the filing segment and may be a word, a letter, a number, or any combination of these. Filing segments are alphabetized by comparing the filing units letter by letter.

Alphabetic indexing rules help to determine the filing units and the order to consider the units. For example, the filing segment *Helen L. Sanchez* is made up of three separate filing units—Helen/L./Sanchez.

Determine the Order of Filing Units

A rule for indexing personal names is to consider the surname (last name) first. The filing unit considered first in a filing segment is called the **key unit.** When a name used for filing appears in a letter, on a printed or typed page, or on a signature line, the name is coded to show the key unit and the order of the remaining units in the filing segment. **Coding** is the physical process of marking the indexing units in the filing segment to indicate the order in which they are considered when filing. One way to code a filing segment is to (1) separate the units with diagonal lines, (2) underline the key unit, and (3) write numbers above the remaining units to indicate their rank in correct filing order. The name Helen L. Sanchez is coded in this way:

2   3

Helen/L./<u>Sanchez</u>

The coding process shows that the name is filed first under *Sanchez*, the key unit. If another surname *Sanchez* exists in the file, the given name *Helen* is used second to place the name in alphabetic order. Finally, the middle initial *L.* is used third if there is another *Helen Sanchez* in the file. In many offices, names on documents are coded by underscoring or highlighting the filing segment or the key unit. Throughout the text, however, you will be instructed to separate the filing units with diagonal lines, underscore the key unit, and number the remaining units. This practice helps to compare the filing units in names when alphabetizing questions arise.

Sometimes names are rewritten on a record in **indexing order**; that is, the filing units are written in the order that they are considered for filing purposes, in ALL CAPITALS, with no punctuation. The name *Helen L. Sanchez* is rewritten in indexing order in this way:

SANCHEZ HELEN L

What is indexing order?

Alphabetize the Names

Names are **alphabetized** by comparing key units and the remaining filing units letter by letter and placing the names in alphabetic order A through Z. If both last names begin with the same letter, compare the remaining letters in the names until one of the names has a different letter. Determine the order of the two names by the alphabetic order of the different letters. For example, file the key unit *Sanchez* before the key unit *Sanders* because the *c* in *Sanchez* comes before the *d* in *Sanders*. Study the indexing order of the following personal names. Note especially the two footnotes: (1) nothing is filed before something, and (2) a single letter filing unit comes before names that begin with that letter. The *underscored* letters determine the correct alphabetic order of the names.

What is meant by "nothing before something"?

Filing Segment NAME	Index Order of Units in Names		
	KEY UNIT	UNIT 2	UNIT 3
1. Stacy Ames	AMES	STACY	†
2. Stacy L. Ames	AMES	STACY	L††
3. Stacy Lee Ames	AMES	STACY	LEE
4. M. Lori Anderson	ANDERSON	M	LORI
5. Mary Anderson	ANDERSON	MARY	
6. Michael Anderson	ANDERSON	MICHAEL	

† NOTHING in Name 1, Unit 3, comes BEFORE SOMETHING in Name 2, Unit 3.
†† The single letter in Name 2, Unit 3, comes before a name beginning with that letter in Name 3, Unit 3.

Studying Indexing Rules

Study indexing rules in Chapters 2 and 3 until you know them well. They are used in some way with all filing systems you will study and practice in this text. First, read a rule twice to be sure that you understand it. Next study the order of the filing units in the names given in the examples below the rule. Finally, compare each name with the names above and below it. In this way, you will discover the unit or letter in a name that fixes its position above or below the other names in the list.

Although the names are real names, they do not necessarily represent a typical office file. The names are presented to illustrate the rules. Study the names to see how the rules have been applied.

RULE 1: Order of Filing Units

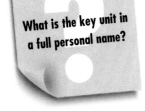

What is the key unit in a full personal name?

A. Personal Names Index full personal names in this order: (1) the surname is the key unit; (2) the first name or initial is the second unit; (3) the middle initial or name is the third unit. If it is not possible to determine the surname in a name, consider the name written last as the surname.

Study the indexing order of the following names. The *underscored* letters determine the correct alphabetic order of the names.

Examples of Rule 1A

Filing Segment	Index Order of Units in Names		
NAME	KEY UNIT	UNIT 2	UNIT 3
L. Reid	REID	L	
Lisa Reid	REID	LISA	
Michael Reidman	REIDMAN	MICHAEL	
Michael W. Reidman	REIDMAN	MICHAEL	W
Alexandra Reidmeir	REIDMEIR	ALEXANDRA	

B. Business Names Index business names as they are written using letterheads or trademarks as guides. Each word in a business name is a separate filing unit. If a business name contains a personal name, index the name in the order it is written. For example, **Leon** is the key unit in the business name *Leon Brown Construction.*

Study the indexing order of the following names. The *underscored* letters determine the correct alphabetic order of the names.

Examples of Rule 1B

Filing Segment	Index Order of Units in Names			
NAME	KEY UNIT	UNIT 2	UNIT 3	UNIT 4
Forster Joyce Tours	FORSTER	JOYCE	TOURS	
Fort Tryon Meat Market	FORT	TRYON	MEAT	MARKET
Forte Music Center	FORTE	MUSIC	CENTER	
Mid City Hardware	MID	CITY	HARDWARE	

Examples of Rule 1B (continued)

Filing Segment NAME	Index Order of Units in Names			
	KEY UNIT	UNIT 2	UNIT 3	UNIT 4
Midas Muffler Shop	MIDAS	MUFFLER	SHOP	
Nancy Grey Realty	NANCY	GREY	REALTY	
Nancy Taylor Career Courses	NANCY	TAYLOR	CAREER	COURSES
Naomi Forte Airport	NAOMI	FORTE	AIRPORT	
New Plan Realty	NEW	PLAN	REALTY	
New York Art Glass	NEW	YORK	ART	GLASS
North Star Taxi Service	NORTH	STAR	TAXI	SERVICE

RULE 2: Minor Words and Symbols in Business Names

Articles, prepositions, conjunctions, and symbols in business names are separate filing units. Index all words in the name in the order that they are written except for the word *The*. When the word *The* is the first word in a filing segment, consider it as the last filing unit. Symbols (&, ¢, #, $, etc.) are separate indexing units also. Spell them out in full when indexing (AND, CENT or CENTS, NUMBER or POUND, DOLLAR or DOLLARS, etc.).

How are symbols indexed?

Study the indexing order of the following names.

Examples of Rule 2

Filing Segment NAME	Index Order of Units in Names			
	KEY UNIT	UNIT 2	UNIT 3	UNIT 4
The In Town Motel	IN	TOWN	MOTEL	THE
Inside & Outside Painters	INSIDE	AND	OUTSIDE	PAINTERS
The Inside Lounge	INSIDE	LOUNGE	THE	
Wilkes Bakery	WILKES	BAKERY		
Wilkes $ Saver	WILKES	DOLLAR	SAVER	

RULE 3: Punctuation and Possessives

What punctuation is disregarded when indexing?

Disregard all punctuation when indexing personal and business names. Commas, periods, hyphens, apostrophes, dashes, exclamation points, question marks, quotation marks, and slash marks (/)—all of these are ignored. Close up the letters or words and index the name as one unit.

Study the indexing order of the following names.

Examples of Rule 3

Filing Segment NAME	Index Order of Units in Names KEY UNIT	UNIT 2	UNIT 3	UNIT 4
Ellison-Jones Lumber	ELLISONJONES	LUMBER		
Ell's & Rod's Diner	ELL<u>S</u>	AND	RODS	DINER
Robert T. Ells	ELLS	<u>R</u>OBERT	T	
Emery/Baxter Video Systems	E<u>M</u>ERYBAXTER	VIDEO	SYSTEMS	
Outdoor Life Book Club	<u>O</u>UTDOOR	LIFE	BOOK	CLUB
Out-Look Point Cafe	OUT<u>L</u>OOK	POINT	CAFE	
Out-of-Town Productions	OUT<u>O</u>FTOWN	PRODUCTIONS		
Sinclair, West, & Dodd	<u>S</u>INCLAIR	WEST	AND	DODD
Michael Sinclair-Smith	SINCLAIR<u>S</u>MITH	MICHAEL		

Review 1

On a separate sheet of paper, write the following names in indexing order in correct alphabetic order. Underscore the letter that determines the correct order. Check your answers with your teacher.

1. George R. Banks
2. Banks' Portable Coaches
3. Alicia Benavides Travel Agency
4. Bank of America
5. M. Banks
6. Bank-o-Rama
7. The Bank-Town Credit Union
8. Banks & Banks Plumbing
9. Bankers Trust Company
10. Bank's Window Repairs

RULE 4: Single Letters and Abbreviations

A. Personal Names Initials in personal names (E. Towne) are separate filing units. Abbreviated personal names (Wm., Jos., Thos.) and shortened names (Debbie, Liz, Bill) are separate filing units and indexed as they are written. Do not spell out abbreviations or try to outguess shortened names. Cher may or *may not* be short for Cheryl!

B. Business Names When single letters are part of a business or an organization name, index the letters as they are written. If a space separates the letters, each letter is a separate unit; letters written without spaces are one unit. M K G Company is four units, but MKG Company is two units.

When are single letters one filing unit?

Abbreviated names using the first letters of words in the *complete* business or organization name are one unit, regardless of the spacing or punctuation. For example, abbreviated names such as IBM, GE, and Y W C A) are one filing unit. Acronyms, which are names made up of initial letters of words, (M. A. D. D., ARMA, G E I C O) are one unit.

Abbreviated words (Mfg., Corp., Inc., etc.) are one unit and indexed as written. Radio and television station call letters are always one unit as well. The call letters in *WEZO* Radio and *W X X I* Television are considered one unit regardless of spacing.

Study the indexing order of the following names.

Examples of Rule 4

Filing Segment Name	Index Order of Units in Names				
	Key Unit	**Unit 2**	**Unit 3**	**Unit 4**	**Unit 5**
A & A Carton Co.	A	AND	A	CARTON	CO
A B A Pizzeria †	A	B	A	PIZZERIA	
Billie Aaron	AARON	BILLIE			
W. Aaron	AARON	W			
Wm. Aaron	AARON	WM			
A-Art Alarm Systems	AART	ALARM	SYSTEMS		
K R B, Inc.†	K	R	B	INC	
KB Associates, Inc.	KB	ASSOCIATES	INC		
K-B Associates Income Tax Svc.	KB	ASSOCIATES	INCOME	TAX	SVC
K B S C Television	KBSC	TELEVISION			
S E S Enterprises †	S	E	S	ENTERPRISES	
S. A. D. D.	SADD				
S C M ††	SCM				

† Letters are part of the name (four filing units).
†† Letters are complete name (one filing unit).

RULE 5: Titles and Suffixes

A. Personal Names Index all titles LAST when they are used with a *full* personal name (surname plus at least a first name or initial). Courtesy titles (Mr., Mrs., Ms.), professional titles (Dr., Prof., Senator, Mayor), and religious titles (Father, Brother, Sr., Rev.) are used to determine correct alphabetic order *only when personal names are identical.*

When a name contains a professional suffix (CRM, M.D., Ph.D.) or a seniority suffix (I, II, Jr., Sr.), consider the suffix a filing unit after indexing the full name. Place numeric suffixes (II, III) before alphabetic suffixes (Jr., Sr.).

When a name contains both a title and a suffix, the title is still the last unit. Study the coding of the following name, which contains two suffixes and a title.

6   2   3   4   5
Mr./Lawrence/W./Akira,/Jr.,/CRM

When are titles key units?

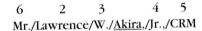

Titles followed by either a given name or a surname only are indexed and filed as written. Father Manuel, Mr. Fox, and Queen Elizabeth—the key units in these names are Father, Mr, and Queen, respectively.

Study the indexing order of the following names.

Examples of Rule 5A

Filing Segment NAME	Index Order of Units in Names KEY UNIT	UNIT 2	UNIT 3	UNIT 4
R. Michael Bernstein	BERNSTEIN	R	MICHAEL	
R. Michael Bernstein II	BERNSTEIN	R	MICHAEL	II
R. Michael Bernstein III	BERNSTEIN	R	MICHAEL	III
R. Michael Bernstein, Jr.	BERNSTEIN	R	MICHAEL	JR
R. Michael Bernstein, Sr.	BERNSTEIN	R	MICHAEL	SR
Brother John	BROTHER	JOHN		
Brother John M. Cain	CAIN	JOHN	M	BROTHER
Dr. John M. Cain	CAIN	JOHN	M	DR
Miss Cindi Davis	DAVIS	CINDI	MISS†	
Mrs. Cindi A. Davis	DAVIS	CINDI	A	MRS
Mrs. Cindi Davis-Cooper	DAVISCOOPER	CINDI	MRS	
Dr. Akita's Pharmacy	DR	AKITAS	PHARMACY	
Prince Charles	PRINCE	CHARLES		
Sister Maria	SISTER	MARIA		

† *Titles and suffixes are not used for indexing except when needed to distinguish between two or more identical names. Titles are included in Business Records Control to show the correct indexing order if a title is needed to determine order. Miss is Unit 3 in the name, but it is not needed because the name is not an identical name. Therefore, Davis/Cindi/nothing (Miss) comes before Davis/Cindi/A.*

B. Business Names All titles in business names are indexed as written. See Rule 1B.

Study the indexing order of the following names.

Examples of Rule 5B

Filing Segment NAME	Index Order of Units in Names KEY UNIT	UNIT 2	UNIT 3	UNIT 4
Dr. Brown's Beverages	DR	BROWNS	BEVERAGES	
Dr. Doolittle Clinic	DR	DOOLITTLE	CLINIC	
Miss Sarah Jane Bakery	MISS	SARAH	JANE	BAKERY
Mister Romero's Imports	MISTER	ROMEROS	IMPORTS	
Mr. Anthony's	MR	ANTHONYS		
Mrs. Bell's Donuts	MRS	BELLS	DONUTS	
Professor's Book Co.	PROFESSORS	BOOK	CO	

Review 2

On a separate sheet of paper, write the following names in indexing order in correct alphabetic order. Underscore the letter that determines the correct order. Check your answers with your teacher.

1. A & W Video Rentals
2. Dr. Ben's Health Spa
3. Patrick Bennett, Sr.
4. W S N Y Radio
5. Bennett-Marks, Inc.
6. W E N C O
7. Ms. Susan Johnson, CRM
8. AT&T
9. Dr. Susan Johnson
10. Ann Walker & Joel Biez Motor Co.
11. Patrick Bennett II
12. Mrs. Gwyn Bennett-Jones

Alphabetic Card Filing

An **alphabetic card filing system** consists of cards filed in alphabetic order in storage containers such as those shown in Figure 2-1 on page 27.

Alphabetic card filing is one of the simplest filing systems. It has many uses in both business and personal filing situations. Much of the information, or data, once stored on cards is now easily stored on computer because card files convert so easily to computer files. Your early filing tasks will be in card filing and, if your computer hardware and software allow, computer filing as well.

Examining Alphabetic Card Filing Systems

Who uses card files?

Almost everyone has used an alphabetic card file and has a need for one. Card files are used to organize recipes and holiday mailing lists in the home. Some libraries use a card index for book location. Businesses use card files for names, addresses, and telephone numbers of employees, customers, and prospective customers. Card files are used for maintaining supplies and equipment inventories and for keeping membership lists for social and business organizations.

A study of alphabetic card filing includes an understanding of cards, guides, tabs, and captions. The following paragraphs discuss these subjects, as well as the organization of an alphabetic card filing system.

Cards

Cards, by their very nature, are suitable for a variety of uses in record systems. They are available in a variety of sizes, colors, and designs. Common sizes are 5" x 3", 6" x 4", 8" x 5", and 14" x 12". The amount of information to be filed determines the size selection. Cards are available lined, unlined, or lined on one side and unlined on the other. Generally the lined cards are used for writing on the card; unlined cards are used for printed cards. (See Figure 2-2.)

Other card characteristics make cards an easy and efficient means of storing and retrieving information. You will remember these card features because they spell the word *CARDS*: Cards are *c*ompact, easily *a*rranged and *r*earranged, *d*urable, and *s*elf-supporting. Cards make it possible to store a lot of information in a small space; the common desktop wheel file illustrates this feature. The ease of adding and removing cards keeps a card file current. Cards hold up well in situations where the records are handled frequently. Cards are self-supporting in a tray or vertical file drawer. Cards store neatly in a horizontal position as well, with one card overlapping the other like those stored in a visible card cabinet or binder. Cards are often stored on rotary wheel and rotary carrousel files. Figure 2-1 shows examples of card storage equipment.

Guides

A **guide** is a file divider with a projecting metal or plastic tab used to separate and identify a section of the files and to facilitate reference. The guides are usually made of material heavier than that of the cards so that they will withstand heavy use. (See Figure 2-3.)

Figure 2-1 Card Record Storage Equipment

Vertical Card File Cabinet
Source: © Jim Whitmer Photography

Visible Card File Cabinet
Source: Kardex Systems, Inc.

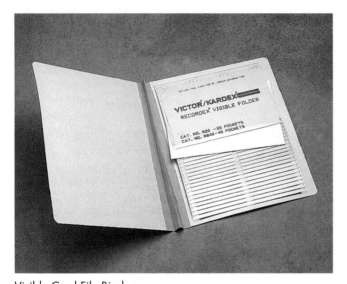

Visible Card File Binder
Source: Photography by Erik Von Fischer/Photonics

Rotary Carrousel File
Source: Photo Courtesy of DATUM FILING SYSTEMS, INC.

Tabs

A **tab** is a projection beyond the top of the main body of the guide upon which an identifying label is attached. Tabs are easily visible when the file is scanned. They are described by their cut and position.

The **tab cut** is the width that the tab occupies in relation to the total width of the guide. A one-third tab cut occupies one-third the total width of the guide. Likewise, a one-fifth tab cut occupies one-fifth the width of the guide.

Figure 2-2 File Card

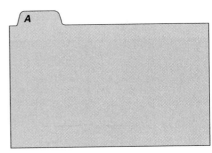

Figure 2-3 Card Guide

The **tab position** is the location of the tab on the guide. Tabs are available in different positions. Positions are determined from left to right. In Figure 2-4, the one-third-cut tab guides are staggered in three different positions: The A guide is in first position; the B guide, second position; and the C guide, third position. In Figure 2-5, the tabs are shown in first position only. If there are enough cards in the file to separate the guides, this straight-line arrangement of guides is preferred.

Tabs are made of the same substance as the guide or made of plastic or metal with a plastic "window" through which information on the tabs is easily read.

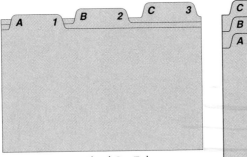

Figure 2-4 One-Third-Cut Tab Guides in Staggered Arrangement

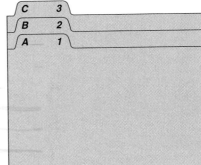

Figure 2-5 One-Third-Cut Tab Guides in Straight-Line Arrangement

Captions

A **caption** is the content-identifying information on labels—anything written, typed, or printed on the tab or tab label. The label *A* in Figure 2-3 is a caption. Figures 2-4 and 2-5 show the caption *A 1* on the tab of the first guide. Numbers are sometimes included in the captions to help place the guides correctly in a file drawer.

Organization

Cards are placed in a file so that the names are arranged in alphabetic order from front to back. Figure 2-6 shows a drawer from a name card

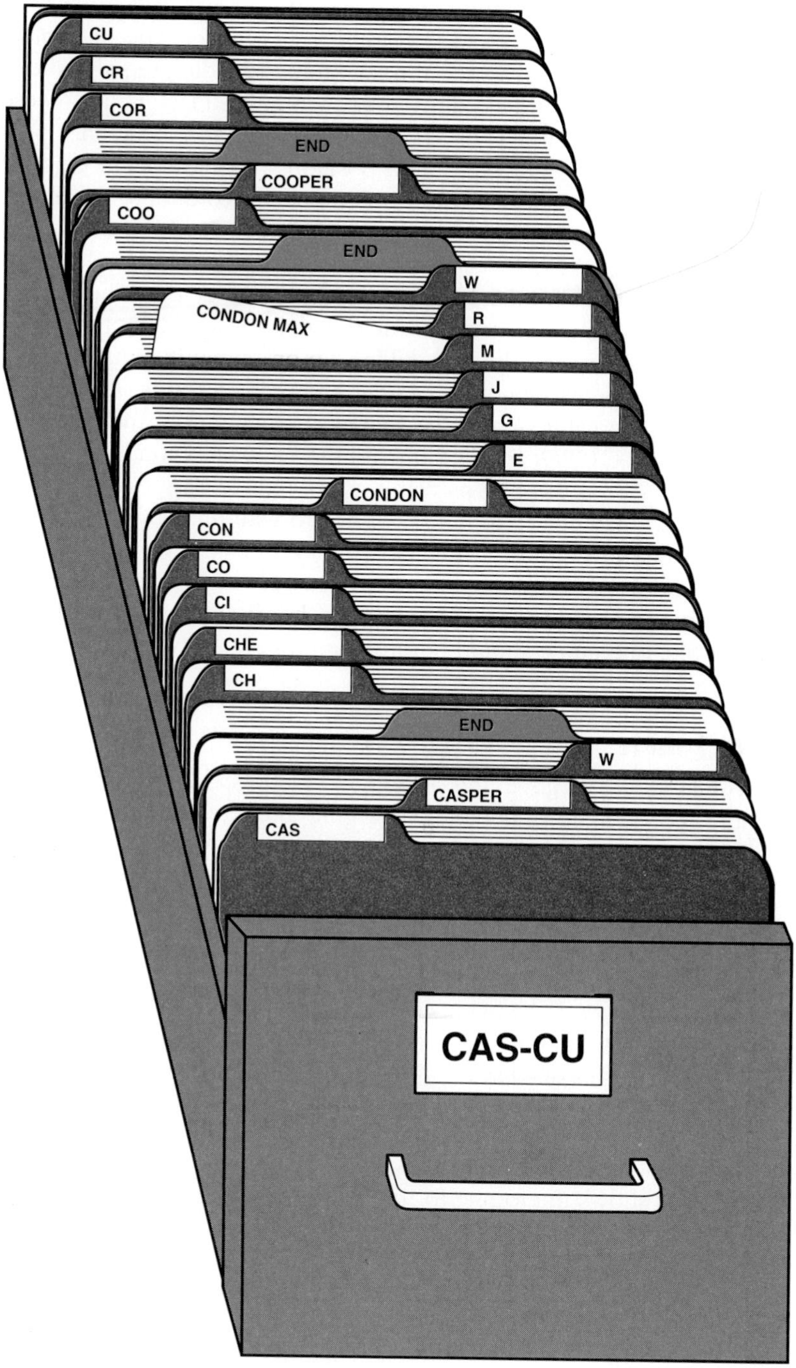

Figure 2-6
Name Card File

CU
CR
COR
END
COOPER
COO
END
W
R
CONDON MAX
M
J
G
E
CONDON
CON
CO
CI
CHE
CH
END
W
CASPER
CAS

CAS-CU

file. Notice the liberal use of guides in studying the illustration. This file is an example of a large, active name card file. This straight-line filing system makes use of one-third-cut guides in three positions.

Figure 2-6 shows the *primary guides* in a straight line in first position indicating the principal alphabetic divisions of the drawer. The *secondary guides* in second position are special name guides dividing the alphabetic divisions into subdivisions according to frequently used last names. These subdivisions end with an END or STOP guide in the same position.

Third-level (tertiary) guides in third position are special letter guides dividing a single surname section into subsections according to the initial letters of the first names. Notice the alphabetic guides E, G, J, M, R, and W after the surname *CONDON*.

Cards are filed behind the appropriate identifying guides. The captions on two consecutive guides indicate the alphabetic range of the names to be filed between the two guides. For example, in Figure 2-6, *CAS* is the first guide caption and *CASPER*, the second. Cards bearing names from *CAS* to *CASPER* are filed behind the first guide, and cards with the key unit *CASPER* are filed behind the *CASPER* secondary guide. The special *CASPER* section stops with the END guide. The *CAS* section continues with a name such as *CASTRO*. A card with the name *CINTRON* is filed between the *CI* and *CO* guides.

In an active card file, one guide should be provided for about every 20 cards. Smaller files do not require such an extensive guide plan. For a less active file, one guide should be provided for about every half-inch or inch of cards.

Drawer Labels

A **drawer label** is a handwritten or printed label placed on the outside of a file drawer to identify its contents. In Figure 2-6, the drawer label caption is *CAS-CU*. Cards in this drawer range from those with key units beginning with *CAS* to those cards with key units beginning with *CU*.

What is a drawer label?

Preparing Index Cards

Cards are prepared on either a typewriter or a computer. Computer-generated cards are printed on continuous-feed card stock. Regardless of how the cards are prepared, the format is the same: The card includes (1) the filing segment keyed in indexed order, (2) the filing segment keyed in *as-written* form, and (3) the address.

Figure 2-2 shows the format for preparing name and address index cards. This format is neat and easy to read. The filing segment is keyed in indexed order on the third line from the top edge of the card and two spaces from the left edge in all capitals, no punctuation. The name is keyed again a double-space below in upper- and lowercase. Remember, when *The* is the first word in a name, key it at the end of the filing segment and consider it last when indexing.

If the card is to be filed according to a numeric system, the name is given a code number. The code number is then keyed in the upper right corner of the file card (See Figure 2-2.)

Preparing Cross-References

A cross-reference card may be needed to find some personal and business names in the file. A **cross-reference** is an additional file entry indexed under one or more related headings or names. When filers look for a record in places other than the specific card location, the cross-reference card refers them to the original record. The following situations describe uses of a cross-reference.

What is a cross-reference?

Unusual Names

With names like Henry Scott and Mai Soong, a filer may not know which is the surname. Sometimes an unusual spelling of a name, such as Smythe, may make retrieval difficult. If filers look under Smith, the cross-reference refers them to the original record: SEE SMYTHE. A cross-reference is prepared for Mai Soong as shown in Figure 2-7.

```
SOONG MAI

Mai Soong
153 Flores Street
San Mateo, CA 94402-1033
```

Original Card

```
MAI SOONG

SEE SOONG MAI
```

Cross-Reference Card

Figure 2-7
Original and
Cross-Reference Cards
for an Unusual Name

Alternate Personal Names

When a person is known by more than one name, a cross-reference may be needed. Such names include a person doing business as (d.b.a.) an alternate name. In some offices, a cross-reference may be necessary when an alternate name is known for a hyphenated woman's name. For example, when Della Cruz marries Carl Duncan, she may use Della Cruz-Duncan, Mrs. Carl Duncan, Mrs. Della Duncan, or simply keep her maiden name. The name on the original file entry is the name the person prefers. Prepare cross-references for alternate names when they create retrieval problems.

Cross-references for Mrs. Della Cruz-Duncan are shown in Figure 2-8.

No cross-reference is needed for Michael Sinclair-Smith. The surname Sinclair-Smith has always been Sinclair-Smith, and no one is likely to look under the name Smith. Peter Yamaguchi does business as (d.b.a.) Peter Guchi. A cross-reference for **Peter Guchi** under his actual name, Peter Yamaguchi, is shown in Figure 2-9.

The name Leo Hennesey & Sons Livestock, Inc., is sometimes referred to as Hennesey's. A cross-reference may be needed for Leo Hennesey & Sons Livestock, Inc., under the alternate name Hennesey's, as shown in Figure 2-10.

Figure 2-8
Original and
Cross-Reference Cards
for the Name of a
Married Woman

```
CRUZDUNCAN DELLA MRS

Mrs. Della Cruz-Duncan
Box 317
Alexandria, PA 16611-0317
```

Original Card

```
DUNCAN DELLA CRUZ MRS

SEE CRUZDUNCAN DELLA MRS
```
```
DUNCAN DELLA MRS

SEE CRUZDUNCAN DELLA MRS
```
```
DUNCAN CARL MRS

SEE CRUZDUNCAN DELLA MRS
```
```
CRUZ DELLA MS

SEE CRUZDUNCAN DELLA MRS
```

Possible Cross-Reference Cards

Figure 2-9
Original and
Cross-Reference Cards
for a Person Doing
Business Under a
Different Name

cross referenced name

```
GUCHI PETER

Peter Guchi
800 Dresser Tower
Houston, TX 77000-0000
```

Original Card

Actual name

```
YAMAGUCHI PETER

SEE GUCHI PETER
```

Cross-Reference Card

Figure 2-10
Original and
Cross-Reference Cards
for a Company Referred
to by an Alternate
Name

```
LEO HENNESEY AND SONS LIVESTOCK INC

Leo Hennesey & Sons Livestock, Inc.
Portsville Pike
Tulsa, OK 74110-9034
```

Original Card

```
HENNESEYS

SEE LEO HENNESEY AND SONS
LIVESTOCK INC
```

Cross-Reference Card

Compound and Hyphenated Business Names

A compound business name is a name made up of more than one surname. Compound names create retrieval problems when the filer remem-
bers only one of the names.

See Figure 2-11 for a cross-reference for Fisher & Porter Co.

```
FISHER AND PORTER CO

Fisher & Porter Co.
796 66th Ave.
Oakland, CA 94621-3714
```

Original Card

```
PORTER AND FISHER CO

SEE FISHER AND PORTER CO
```

Cross-Reference Card

Figure 2-11
Original and
Cross-Reference Cards
for a Compound
Business Name

A cross-reference for Woodson-Holmes Enterprises is shown in Figure 2-12.

Cross-references for compound names are prepared by rotating the names on the cross-references until every name is a key unit.

Figure 2-13 shows a cross-reference prepared for Rivera, Vadilla, and Melville, Attorneys at Law.

```
WOODSONHOLMES ENTERPRISES INC

Woodson-Holmes Enterprises, Inc.
4114 Knox Avenue
Chicago, IL 60641-1902
```

Original Card

```
HOLMESWOODSON ENTERPRISES INC

SEE WOODSONHOLMES ENTERPRISES INC
```

Cross-Reference Card

Figure 2-12
Original and
Cross-Reference Cards
for a Hyphenated
Business Name

```
RIVERA VADILLA AND MELVILLE ATTORNEYS AT
LAW

Rivera, Vadilla, and Melville,
Attorneys at Law
311 W. Chestnut St.
Louisville, KY 40202-1809
```

Original Card

```
VADILLA MELVILLE AND RIVERA ATTORNEYS AT
LAW

SEE RIVERA VADILLA AND MELVILLE
ATTORNEYS AT LAW


MELVILLE RIVERA AND VADILLA ATTORNEYS AT
LAW

SEE RIVERA VADILLA AND MELVILLE
ATTORNEYS AT LAW
```

Cross-Reference Cards

Figure 2-13
Original and
Cross-Reference Cards
for a Compound
Business Name

Abbreviated Names and Acronyms

When abbreviated names (IBM) and acronyms (S.A.D.D.) are used for filing, a cross-reference may be needed. A cross-reference for AFT under the spelled-out name American Federation of Teachers is shown in Figure 2-14.

```
AFT


AFT
555 New Jersey Avenue
Washington, DC 20001-0000
```

```
AMERICAN FEDERATION OF TEACHERS

SEE AFT
```

Original Card   Cross-Reference Card

Preparing unnecessary cross-references is time- and space-consuming. However, omitting necessary cross-reference reduces file efficiency. Use good judgment when deciding whether or not to prepare a cross-reference for a particular record.

Summary

Alphabetic indexing rules are an important first step in learning to file personal and business names. Office workers will misfile records unless they know alphabetic indexing rules and consistently apply them when filing.

An alphabetic card filing system is a simple filing system with many uses. The size and durability of cards make them suitable for storing a variety of information in a variety of storage containers. They are stored vertically in drawers, flat in visible file cabinets or binders, or on rotary wheel or carrousel files. Guides are used in a card file to divide and subdivide the alphabetic sections of the file and make filing and retrieval tasks fast and efficient.

Sometimes names that are referred to in more than one way require a cross-reference. Generally, cross-references may be needed for some unusual and obscure names, alternate names, compound names, and hyphenated names. Good judgment dictates whether or not locating a name will be confusing and a cross-reference should be prepared.

Terminology Review

alphabetic card filing system	(p. 25)
alphabetic indexing rules	(p. 17)
alphabetizing	(p. 19)
caption	(p. 28)
coding	(p. 18)
cross-reference	(p. 31)
drawer label	(p. 30)
filing segment	(p. 18)
guide	(p. 26)
indexing	(p. 18)
indexing order	(p. 19)
indexing rules	(p. 17)
key unit	(p. 18)
tab	(p. 27)
tab cut	(p. 27)
tab position	(p. 28)

Questions For Discussion

1. What are indexing rules? Why are they necessary? (Obj. 1)
2. Describe the three steps in the indexing process. (Obj. 2)
3. Write your name in indexing order. What did you write first, second, third? (Obj. 2)
4. How are filing segments coded? Write your full name and code it. (Obj. 2)
5. List the characteristics of cards that make them so useful as a record storage medium. (Obj. 3)
6. Why are variable card sizes an advantage of card filing systems? (Obj. 3, 4)
7. What is a guide? a tab? a caption? (Obj. 4)
8. Explain tab cut and tab position. (Obj. 4)
9. Describe the guide plan (cut and position of guides) for a typical card file. (Obj. 5)
10. What is a cross-reference, and why is it sometimes a necessary part of a filing system? (Obj. 6)

▶ Applications

Use a separate sheet of paper to write your answers to the following applications:

1. What is the *key unit* in each of the following names? What is the *second unit* in the same name? (Obj. 2)

   a. John C. Samuels
   b. L. Ann Conrad
   c. George Mendosa Corporation
   d. Bianco and Bosak Memorials
   e. The Sunbelt Resorts
   f. Point-of-View Paints
   g. Mr. Alexander's
   h. At Home Window Repair
   i. D & L Feeds, Inc.
   j. Wm. Saga Carpeting

2. Indicate whether the alphabetic order of the two names in each of the following pairs is correct or incorrect. (Obj. 2)

   a. Jane D. Woods
      Jane Woods Fashions
   b. KSTP-FM Radio
      K & W Vendors, Inc.
   c. Wilma J. Hands
      Wm. J. Hands
   d. AAIM Group, Inc.
      A R M A
   e. Ms. Sims' Music Shop
      Dr. C. Sims
   f. Point of View Landscaping
      The Point Restaurant
   g. Jos. Saxe
      Joseph A. Sax
   h. Charles A. Barker, Sr.
      Charles A. Barker III
   i. $ Saver Weekly
      Dollar Rent A Car
   j. Anthony Sinclair-Smith
      Sinclair & Sinclair Public
      Accountants

3. On a separate sheet of paper, write the following filing segments in indexing order on the left side of the page to represent the original card entry. Write the cross-reference on the right side of the page. For those names that in your judgment do not require a cross-reference card, write "No cross-reference needed." (Obj. 6)

   a. Genaro Leon
   b. IBM, Inc.
   c. Lopez & Blanding Pool Co.
   d. Tom Smyth
   e. B & J Bowling
   f. GE
   g. Sing Yee
   h. Jane Adams
   i. Taylor-Parker Co., Inc.
   j. Mrs. Gwyn Wellington-Jones

Practice Set Application

At this time, complete Job 1, *Alphabetic Indexing of Personal Names*, in OFFICE FILING PROCEDURES, Eighth Edition. Instructions and supplies for this job are included in the practice set.

Chapter Three

Alphabetic Indexing Special Names

Learning Objectives

After completing Chapter 3, you will be able to do the following:

1. Index and arrange in alphabetic order names containing articles and particles.

2. Index and arrange in alphabetic order identical names.

3. Index and arrange in alphabetic order business names containing numbers.

4. Index and arrange in alphabetic order names of organizations and institutions.

5. Index and arrange in alphabetic order government names.

6. Arrange subject titles in correct order in an alphabetic name file.

Alphabetic Indexing Rules Concluded

The indexing order of the more common types of individual and business names was presented in Chapter 2. The alphabetic indexing rules in Chapter 2 included the indexing order of units in personal and business names; names containing minor words, punctuation, possessives, single letters, and abbreviations; and names containing titles and suffixes.

Chapter 3 concludes your study of alphabetic indexing rules. Chapter 3 rules include (1) names containing articles and particles, (2) identical names, (3) business names containing numbers, (4) names of organizations and institutions, and (5) government names. Chapter 3 also illustrates the practical use of subject titles as key units. You will learn that some records are better organized first by a subject title, rather than by name.

RULE 6: Prefixes—Articles and Particles

What are articles and particles?

Combine an article or particle in a personal or business name with the part of the name following it to form one filing unit. The indexing order is not affected by spaces or punctuation between a prefix and the rest of the name. Disregard the spaces and punctuation when indexing names containing articles and particles.

Examples of articles and particles are these: a la, D', Da, De, Del, De la, Della, Den, Des, Di, Dos, Du, El, Fitz, Il, L', La, Las, Le, Les, Lo, Los, M', Mac, Mc, O', Per, Saint, Sainz, San, Santa, Santo, St., Ste., Te, Ten, Ter, Van, Van de, Van der, Von, Von der.

Examples of Rule 6

Filing Segment NAME	Index Order of Units in Names KEY UNIT	UNIT 2	UNIT 3	UNIT 4
Professor Maria D'Amico	DAMICO	MARIA	PROFESSOR	
Damico Match Company	DAMICO	MATCH	COMPANY	
Delaberto Nursery	DELABERTO	NURSERY		
De La Camp Sports Wear	DELACAMP	SPORTS	WEAR	
LaSalle Interior Designers	LASALLE	INTERIOR	DESIGNERS	
La Salle Robotics, Inc.	LASALLE	ROBOTICS	INC	
Francis J. Saint John	SAINTJOHN	FRANCIS	J	
San Francisco Cab Company	SANFRANCISCO	CAB	COMPANY	
St. James Hospital Supplies	STJAMES	HOSPITAL	SUPPLIES	

Filing Segment NAME	Index Order of Units in Names KEY UNIT	UNIT 2	UNIT 3	UNIT 4
Van den Berg Computer Supplies	VANDENBERG	COMPUTER	SUPPLIES	
Gerald Q. Van Den Berg, Ph.D.	VANDENBERG	GERALD	Q	PHD
Vanden Berg Moving & Storage	VANDENBERG	MOVING	AND	STORAGE

RULE 7: Numbers in Business Names

Arrange alphabetically any numbers *spelled out* in business names (Seven Hills Productions). Arrange Arabic numerals (3, 4, 5) in business names in ascending order BEFORE ALL ALPHABETIC LETTERS OR WORDS. The names 7 Eleven Food Store and 20th Century Fox Film Corp. come before the name John Adams in the file.

When numbers appear in other than the key unit in a name (Pier 36 Cafe), arrange the name alphabetically but immediately before a similar name without a number. For example, the name B4 Photographers comes before the name Balloon-A-Grams of New York.

All Arabic numerals (2, 3, 4) come before all Roman numerals (I, II, III). Star 4 Productions is followed by the name Star III Enterprises and Star Cinema Supplies Corp.

Arrange names with inclusive numbers (13-30 Corp.) by the first digit(s) only (13). If a hyphenated number is NOT inclusive (20-20, 30-14) disregard the hyphen and consider the number one filing unit (2020, 3014).

Ignore the letter endings when arranging digit numbers that contain *st, d,* and *th* (21st, 2d, 4th). Consider only the digits (21, 2, 4). Be sure to place the numbers in ascending order (2, 4, 21).

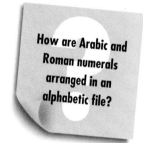

How are Arabic and Roman numerals arranged in an alphabetic file?

Filing Segment NAME	Index Order of Units in Names				
	KEY UNIT	UNIT 2	UNIT 3	UNIT 4	UNIT 5
2 Broadway Shop, Inc.	2	BROADWAY	SHOP	INC	
2M Gulf Service Center	2M	GULF	SERVICE	CENTER	
11th and 23d Auto Shop	11	AND	23	AUTO	SHOP
24-Hour Gold	24HOUR	GOLD			
25 East Owners Corp.	25	EAST	OWNERS	CORP	
A 2 Z Flea Market	A	2	Z	FLEA	MARKET
A to Z Luggage, Co.	A	TO	Z	LUGGAGE	CO
A-to-Z Traders, Inc.,	ATOZ	TRADERS	INC		
Atwood and Morrill Co.	ATWOOD	AND	MORRILL	CO	
Eleventh Photo Gallery	ELEVENTH	PHOTO	GALLERY		
Pier 39, Inc.	PIER	39	INC		
Pier IV Restaurant	PIER	IV	RESTAURANT		
Two Flags Butcher Supplies	TWO	FLAGS	BUTCHER	SUPPLIES	
Two Park Avenue Barber Shop	TWO	PARK	AVENUE	BARBER	SHOP

In order to achieve a correct ascending numeric sort on the computer, right-align all numbers. The computer sorts by reading left to right. The numbers 7, 30, and 100 are read and sorted incorrectly in this order: 100, 30, 7. However, when you front-load the digits with zeros so that the numbers are right-aligned (007, 030, 100), the computer reads left to right and sorts the numbers correctly in this order: 007, 030, 100.

RULE 8: Organizations and Institutions

How are organization and institution names indexed?

Index and file all organizations and institutions according to the names written on their letterheads. "The" used as the first word in a name is considered the last filing unit. Organizations and institutions include any of the following:

banks and other
  financial institutions
clubs
colleges
hospitals

hotels
lodges
magazines
motels
museums

newspapers
religious institutions
schools
unions
universities

Examples of Rule 8

Filing Segment NAME	Index Order of Units in Names				
	KEY UNIT	UNIT 2	UNIT 3	UNIT 4	UNIT 5
Bank of Houston	BANK	OF	HOUSTON		
Church of St. Thomas More	CHURCH	OF	STTHOMAS	MORE	
Democrat & Chronicle	DEMOCRAT	AND	CHRONICLE		
Ebony	EBONY				
Education Digest	EDUCATION	DIGEST			
El Dorado Motel	ELDORADO	MOTEL			
First National Bank of Morris	FIRST	NATIONAL	BANK	OF	MORRIS
Hudson County Community College	HUDSON	COUNTY	COMMUNITY	COLLEGE	
The Lakewood Inn	LAKEWOOD	INN	THE		
National Management Association	NATIONAL	MANAGEMENT	ASSOCIATION		
The Riverside Church	RIVERSIDE	CHURCH	THE		
San Diego Evening Tribune	SANDIEGO	EVENING	TRIBUNE		

Review

On a separate sheet of paper, write each of the following names in indexing order. Alphabetize the names; then write the names in correct filing order. Underscore the letter that determines the order. Check your answers with your teacher.

1. El Sol Tailor's Shop, Inc.

2. 8th Avenue Deli & Flowers

3. 7 Hour Photo

4. San Carlos Hotel

5. Framingham State College

6. Eleventh Avenue Camera Store

7. 7-11 Store

8. Sanana Designs, Ltd.

9. 711 Plumbing Corp.

10. Association of Management Consulting Firms

11. Ft. Lauderdale News

12. Bank of Raleigh

RULE 9: Identical Names

What determines the correct alphabetic order of identical names?

When personal names and names of businesses, institutions, and organizations are identical (including titles as explained in Rule 5), addresses determine the correct filing order. Although not considered to be indexing units, addresses are a secondary means of distinguishing between identical names. Compare addresses in this order:

1. City names.

2. State or province names when city names are identical.

3. Street names, including *Avenue, Boulevard, Drive,* and *Street,* when the city and state names are identical.
   a. File street names that begin with digits (18th Street) in ascending numeric order before alphabetic street names.
   b. File street names that include compass directions as written (East Main Street). File numbers appearing after compass directions before alphabetic names: East 8th Street comes before East Avenue.

4. House or building numbers when the city, state, and street names are identical.
   a. File house or building numbers written as figures (802 Nott Street) in ascending numeric order before alphabetic building names (Coachlight Towers).
   b. When a street address *and* a building name are both included in an address, use the street address and disregard the building name.
   c. ZIP codes are not considered in determining filing order.

Identical names occur frequently; therefore, a consistent method for indexing such names is needed. Sometimes family members of different generations live at the same address; in these cases, seniority titles determine the correct order of the names. Seniority designations are part of the name; therefore, consider them before considering addresses. Study the examples of identical names that follow. Because the names are identical, only the key units of the names are shown. Study the units in the address that determine the correct filing order. The underscored letter or number determines the correct filing order of the names.

Examples of Rule 9

Filing Segment NAME	KEY UNIT	CITY	STATE	STREET
Ana Gonzales 3400 W. Big Beaver Street Burlington, OK 73722-2411	GONZALES	BURLINGTON	OK	3400 W BIG BEAVER STREET
Ana Gonzales 21 Becker Avenue Calypso, NC 28325-8472	GONZALES	CALYPSO	NC	21 BECKER AVENUE

Index Order of Units in Names

Filing Segment NAME	Index Order of Units in Names			
	KEY UNIT	CITY	STATE	STREET
Yoko Hayashi 143 W. 81st Street Troy, MI 48084-3001	H̲AYASHI	TROY	MI	143 W 81ST STREET
Yoko Hayashi 301 Broadway Troy, NY 12180-2770	HAYASHI	TROY	N̲Y	301 BROADWAY
Frank Jones 46 Greenwood Avenue Billings, MT 59101-1101	J̲ONES	BILLINGS	MT	46 GREENWOOD AVENUE
Frank Jones 2 Lark Street Billings, MT 59101-1101	JONES	BILLINGS	MT	2 L̲ARK STREET
Frank Jones 88 Lark Street Billings, MT 59101-1101	JONES	BILLINGS	MT	8̲8 LARK STREET
Frank Jones Terrace Heights* 40 State Street Billings, MT 59101-3847	JONES	BILLINGS	MT	40 S̲TATE STREET

When a street address and building name are included in an address, disregard the building name.

Rule 10: Government Names

You must be able to recognize a government name in order to correctly index it. A government name is any department, bureau, office, or the like, that is supported by taxes.

Index all government names first by the names of the governmental units:

Level	Example of Governmental Unit
Federal	United States Government
State	California State of
City	Spokane City of
County	Livingston County of
Village	Alfred Village of

What is considered first when indexing government names?

Next, index the distinctive name of the department, bureau, office, or board you are filing. The words "office of," "Department of," "Bureau of," etc., are separate filing units when they are part of the official name.

Federal Government Names

Index federal government names first by the name of the governmental unit—UNITED STATES GOVERNMENT. Then index by the *most distinctive* part of the name of the department, bureau, office, etc. For example, *Agriculture* is the distinctive part of the name Department of Agriculture. The United States Department of Agriculture is indexed in this way:

UNITED STATES GOVERNMENT
AGRICULTURE DEPARTMENT OF

By indexing the name of the governmental unit first—UNITED STATES GOVERNMENT—you file all United States Government departments, agencies, bureaus, etc., in one location.

State and Local Government Names

Index state and local government names first by the name of the governmental unit. Use "STATE OF," "COUNTY OF," "CITY OF," and "VILLAGE OF" when indexing state and local government names. For example, NEW YORK STATE OF will come before such names as NEW YORK STATE PIPE COMPANY. In this way all New York State government names are filed in one location.

Foreign Government Names

Index foreign government names first by their distinctive or official English names—CHINA, ITALY, JAPAN, etc. Then index by the balance of the formal name, if needed, and in the official name. For example, CHINA REPUBLIC OF will come before CHINA TEA HOUSE. Branches, departments, and divisions follow in order by their distinctive names.

States, colonies, provinces, cities, and other divisions of foreign governments are followed by their distinctive or official government names as spelled in English—SOUTH KOREA/SEOUL CITY OF. The trend toward global economics has increased correspondence with foreign government offices. The only way to store and retrieve documents efficiently from these offices is to index in only one language—English. File foreign business and government names under their English names and prepare cross-references for their foreign equivalents when necessary. Figures 3-1 and 3-2 are examples of cross-references of foreign business and government names.

Figure 3-1
Original and Cross-Reference Cards for a Foreign Business Name

ALUMINUM CORPORATION OF BELGIUM THE	LALUMINUM BEIGE SOCIETE ANONYME
The Aluminum Corporation of Belgium Brussels, Belgium	SEE ALUMINUM CORPORATION OF BELGIUM THE

Original Card   Cross-Reference Card

```
URUGUAY REPUBLIC OF
PUBLIC EDUCATION SECRETARY OF

Secretary of Public Education
Montevideo, Uruguay
```

Original Card

```
REPUBLICA ORIENTAL DEL URUGUAY
SECRETARIO DE EDUCATION PUBLICA

SEE URUGUAY REPUBLIC OF
PUBLIC EDUCATION SECRETARY OF
```

Cross-Reference Card

Figure 3-2
Original and Cross-Reference Cards for a Foreign Government Name

Note

The *United States Government Manual* and the *Congressional Directory*, published annually, report a current list of United States government agencies and offices. *Countries, Dependencies, Areas of Special Sovereignty, and Their Principal Administrative Divisions*, published by the U. S. Department of Commerce, National Bureau of Standards, provides a list of geographic and political entities of the world and associated standard codes. The *State Information Book* by Susan Lukowski provides an up-to-date list of state departments and their addresses. *The World Almanac and Book of Facts*, updated annually, includes facts and statistics on many foreign nations and gives the English spellings of many foreign names.

Examples of Rule 10

Filing Segment NAME	Index Order of Units in Name INDEXED FORM OF NAME
The Alfred Sub Shop	ALFRED SUB SHOP THE
Water Department Village of Alfred	ALFRED VILLAGE OF WATER DEPARTMENT
Department of Taxation Kingdom of Belgium (Belgium*)	BELGIUM KINGDOM OF TAXATION DEPARTMENT OF
Department of Health State of California	CALIFORNIA STATE OF HEALTH DEPARTMENT OF
Department of Transportation Franklin County	FRANKLIN COUNTY OF TRANSPORTATION DEPARTMENT OF
Department of Education City of New York	NEW YORK CITY OF EDUCATION DEPARTMENT OF
Department of Parks & Recreation City of New York	NEW YORK CITY OF PARKS AND RECREATION DEPARTMENT OF
New York City Press, Inc.	NEW YORK CITY PRESS INC
New York Times, Inc.	NEW YORK TIMES INC
Department of Sanitation City of San Diego	SANDIEGO CITY OF SANITATION DEPARTMENT OF
San Diego Gas & Electric Co.	SANDIEGO GAS AND ELECTRIC CO
Equal Employment Opportunity Commission United States Government	UNITED STATES GOVERNMENT EQUAL EMPLOYMENT OPPORTUNITY COMMISSION
Water Resources Council United States Government	UNITED STATES GOVERNMENT WATER RESOURCES COUNCIL
United States Lines, Inc.	UNITED STATES LINES INC

*Either the short form Belgium or the long form Kingdom of Belgium is acceptable. Be consistent in the use of the form you prefer.

Review

On a separate sheet of paper, write each of the following names in indexing order. Alphabetize the names; then write the names in correct filing order. Underscore the letter that determines the order. Check your answers with your teacher.

1. Alex Johnson
2979 Avenue D
Denver, CO 80207-2144

2. Interior Ministry
Republic of Pakistan

3. University of Wyoming
Box 3434, University Station
Laramie, WY 82071-3434

4. Alex Johnson
22 West Main St.
Denver, CO 80207-2134

5. Wyoming Resources Corp.
Claydesta Tower East
Midland, TX 79705-2112

6. U. S. Steel Corp
130 Lincoln Avenue
Vandergrift, PA 15690-1210

7. Office of the Aging
Wyoming County
Courthouse Square
Tunkhannock, PA 18657-0024

8. Ministry of Finance
Republic of Pakistan

9. U. S. Department of Defense
The Pentagon
Washington, DC 20301-0999

10. Alex Johnson
2020 Avenue D
Denver, CO 89027-4121

11. John Ritter
Hwy 59
Albany, TX 76430-1099

12. John Ritter, Jr.
50 Rockline Rd.
Albany, NY 12237-2121

Subjects as Primary Titles

The use of subject titles as key units is sometimes preferable when filing some names. A subject index determines the specific subject titles to be used. The index is authorized by someone in the organization who is responsible for making records management decisions. The subject title then becomes the first part of the filing segment. Personal or business names are used for subsequent indexing.

In name card files, indexing some names by a particular subject first may be more useful than indexing by name. For example, the Yellow

Why are subject titles sometimes key units in an alphabetic name file?

Pages of your telephone directory list names first by subject or service and then by name. Examples of subject titles found in name card files include FLORISTS, INSURANCE AGENCIES, RESTAURANTS, and TAXIS. Sometimes you can't remember the name of a restaurant. Sometimes the services (Florists or Taxis) are more important to you than the particular names.

As you study the examples of subjects as titles, note the following:

1. The subject title is used as the first unit(s) before the name.

2. The subject titles are interfiled alphabetically with other names in the name file.

3. The names in each subject category are arranged in alphabetic order.

Examples of Indexed Names and Names When Subjects Are Used as Key Units

Filing Segment NAME	Index Order of Units in Names KEY UNIT	UNIT 2	UNIT 3	UNIT 4	UNIT 5
Jeremy Anderson	ANDERSON	JEREMY			
Marjorie Flanders	FLANDERS	MARJORIE			
Florists Florists Transworld Delivery	FLORISTS	FLORISTS	TRANSWORLD	DELIVERY	
Florists Flowers By Paul	FLORISTS	FLOWERS	BY	PAUL	
Florists Kertin Florist	FLORISTS	KERTIN	FLORIST		
Insurance Agencies Aetna Insurance Co.	INSURANCE	AGENCIES	AETNA	INSURANCE	CO
Insurance Agencies Nationwide Insurance	INSURANCE	AGENCIES	NATIONWIDE	INSURANCE	
Nancy Kelly	KELLY	NANCY			
David Lansberry	LANSBERRY	DAVID			
Restaurants The Castle	RESTAURANTS	CASTLE	THE		
Restaurants Kilborn Inn	RESTAURANTS	KILBORN	INN		
Restaurants Lazaro's	RESTAURANTS	LAZAROS			

Summary

You have studied the five remaining alphabetic indexing rules in this chapter. Remember to combine articles and particles with the names they modify. Use the city, state, and street names to determine order of identical names. When comparing filing units, place all Arabic numerals before Roman numerals and place all numeric filing units before alphabetic filing units.

When the subject or service is more important than the name you're filing, index the name first by the subject or service. You may not always remember the name of a taxi company or a florist when you need one. If you file first by subject, the taxis that give the best service and your favorite florists and restaurants are grouped in one location.

Government names are easy to index. First, identify the name of the governmental unit, and then index by the most distinctive part of the name in the department, bureau, or office you are filing.

Chapter 3 concludes only the study of alphabetic indexing rules. The application of the rules is just beginning. With some practice, you will be able to index correctly all personal, business, and government names. Know the rules well because you will continue to apply them to all the filing systems presented later in the textbook.

Questions For Discussion

1. What are articles and particles in names and how are they indexed? (Obj. 1)
2. What filing units determine the alphabetic order of identical names? In what order are the names considered? (Obj. 2)
3. How are numbers (digits) indexed in business names? (Obj. 3)
4. How are names of organizations and institutions indexed? (Obj. 4)
5. In what order are filing units considered when indexing government names? (Obj. 5)
6. How are subject titles filed with other names in an alphabetic name file? (Obj. 6)

Applications

> Use a separate sheet of paper to complete the following applications.

1. Use two columns. Write the key unit of each name in column 1. Write the second filing unit of each name in column 2. (Obj. 1)

a. Delsomma Restaurant
b. Karen Del Spina
c. San Francisco Pharmacy
d. Marie De Lorenzo
e. David St. James

f. Emily De La Cruz
g. Elco Solvents Corp.
h. Dexter Sainz John
i. Santa Lucia Restaurant
j. El Condor Travel & Tours, Inc.

2. Write the following names in indexing order. Arrange the names in correct alphabetic order. Underscore the letter or number that determines the correct order of the names. (Obj. 2)

a. Wm. Bush
4040 E. Vernon Ave.
Burbank, CA 91504-3429

b. Wende Bush
101 Stanley Blvd.
Damascus, MD 20872-4100

c. Foo Yung
146 Harrison Ave.
Dallas, OR 97338-6161

d. Wm. Bush
3274 Vernon Ave.
Burbank, CA 91504-3428

e. Foo Yung
2100 Oakridge Drive
Dallas, NC 28034-6219

f. Consuelo Dominguez
77 N. Main St.
Du Bois, PA 15801-0023

g. Wm. Bush
2101 Empire Ave.
Burbank, CA 91504-1010

h. Consuelo Dominguez
407 Chestnut St.
Charleston, WV 25301-2121

i. Wende Bush
10 St. Charles St.
Damascus, MD 20872-4100

j. Willie Bush
95 St. Charles St.
Dallas, TX 75399-3751

3. Index and code the following names. Alphabetize the names; then report your answer by writing the names in correct filing order. Underscore the letter or number that determines the correct order. (Obj. 3)

a. 9 to 5 Zipper Sales
b. West 24th Street Antiques
c. Ten Downing St. Cleaners
d. 13-19 White Street Co.
e. West Main Lumber Co.

f. West 135 Street Apartments
g. 1st Place Restaurant
h. West 4 Street Bookstore
i. 20th Century Draperies, Inc.
j. First Run Fabrics, Inc.

4. Determine the correct alphabetic order of the names in each group of three names. Show the order by writing the numbers of each name (1, 2, 3) in the order you have arranged the names. (Obj. 1, 3, 4)

a. (1) Society for Adolescent Psychiatry; (2) A-1 Cleaners; (3) A to Z Playschool

b. (1) The Bank of Beverly Hills; (2) Assn. of Comedy Artists; (3) 8 Ball Billiard Parlor

c. (1) <u>Mack</u> 5 Enterprises; (2) <u>Mack</u> Truck Sales & Service; (3) <u>Mack</u> IV, Inc.

d. (1) <u>College</u> of <u>Santa Fe</u>; (2) College of <u>St. Rose</u>; (3) Ms. Gloria <u>Santana</u>

e. (1) <u>14-18</u> Riverside Repairs; (2) <u>1st</u> Place Pet Shop; (3) <u>First</u> State Bank

f. (1) <u>Association</u> Day Care Center; (2) <u>American</u> Management Associates; (3) <u>Society</u> for Animal Rights, Inc.

g. (1) <u>Van Patten</u> Hotel; (2) <u>Snowed</u> Inn; (3) <u>Vanderlind</u> Motel

h. (1) <u>Pier 2</u> Marina; (2) <u>2</u> by 4 Lumber Co.; (3) <u>Pier Royale</u> Cafe

i. (1) <u>Gt.</u> Neck Optometry; (2) <u>Grossman</u> Sales, Inc.; (3) Assn. of General <u>Merchandising</u> Chains

5. Write the following names in indexing order. If a name or address is incomplete, add what is necessary to index the name correctly. Arrange the names in correct alphabetic order. Show your answers by writing the names in correct filing order. Underscore the letter that determines the correct order. (Obj. 2, 5)

a. Department of Transportation
Village of Dansville
Dansville, NY 14437-2044

b. Crime Victims Compensation Board
State of Oklahoma
Oklahoma City, OK 73105-2121

c. Department of Agriculture
State of Oklahoma
Oklahoma City, OK 73105-8823

d. Commission of Cable Television
State of New York
270 Broadway
New York, NY 10122-3241

e. Ms. Minna Johnson
92 Riverside Plaza
Conrad, IA 50621-1277

f. Office of the Aging
Steuben County
Bath, NY 14810-7233

g. Ms. Minna Johnson
28 Fredonia Street
Conrad, MT 59425-0115

h. U.S. Department of Justice
Tenth St. & Constitution Ave. NW
Washington, DC 20530-3663

(Continued on page 52)

    i. Ms. Minna Johnson
       22 Fredonia Street
       Conrad, MT 59425-0112

    j. U.S. Bureau of Labor Statistics
       441 G Street NW
       Washington, DC 20212-0441

6. Index and code the following names. Use the subject title RESTAURANTS as the key unit for all restaurants. Arrange the names in correct alphabetic order. Report your answers by writing the names in correct filing order.(Obj. 3, 4, 6)

    a. Geraldine T. Ronstadt
    b. The Vineyard Restaurant
    c. Phil's Country Kitchen   _Restaurant_
    d. U S News & World Report
    e. USAir
    f. Peg's and Don's Eatery _Rest_
    g. Us Magazine
    h. Willow Tree Lounge & Restaurant
    i. 6-6 Diner
    j. Martin Rather

Practice Set Application

At this time, complete Job 2, *Alphabetic Indexing of Personal, Business, and Government Names,* and Job 3, *Comprehensive Card Filing Practice,* in OFFICE FILING PROCEDURES, Eighth Edition. Instructions and supplies for these jobs are included in the practice set.

Chapter Four

Alphabetic Correspondence Filing

Learning Objectives

After completing Chapter 4, you will be able to do the following:

1. Define the alphabetic correspondence filing methods.

2. Identify and describe the storage equipment commonly used for correspondence filing.

3. List the supplies necessary to establish the alphabetic correspondence name file.

4. Describe the placement of drawer, guide, and folder label captions.

5. Describe the arrangement and use of guides and folders in the alphabetic correspondence name file.

6. List the procedures for filing correspondence that has been released for filing.

7. Prepare, sort, and file correspondence for alphabetic correspondence filing.

Defining The Alphabetic Correspondence File

What are three alphabetic correspondence filing methods?

The **alphabetic correspondence file** is a collection of letters, memorandums, and related documents, received or written, arranged in alphabetic order. Correspondence in alphabetic correspondence filing systems is filed *alphabetically* by three methods: geographic location, subject, or name. How the correspondence is most likely to be requested determines the filing method.

Geographic Method

A business often operates branch offices, stores, or manufacturing plants in different locations in a city. Business activity may expand to different states or to countries around the world. Worldwide market potential will increase as more and more countries adopt free-enterprise economies. Management decisions for business activities taking place in multiple locations often require arranging correspondence and other records by geographic localities. **Geographic filing** is the method of storing and retrieving records alphabetically first by location and then by individual, organization, or project.

Subject Method

A commonly used filing method arranges correspondence by subject. For example, all correspondence related to EMPLOYMENT may be kept together. Office tasks may require that all information dealing with a particular function or subject be grouped under that subject. Certainly when looking for job applicants, you would not want to—nor would you be able to—remember the name of every applicant that had applied for employment with your organization. In such cases, the content, or SUBJECT, of the correspondence is more important than the particular name. **Subject filing** is a method for classifying, coding, and filing records first by subject and then by individual, organization, or project.

Name Method

Correspondence is most frequently arranged by name. The **alphabetic correspondence name file** is a collection of letters and memorandums received or written and arranged in alphabetic order by name. Although the alphabetic correspondence name file classifies correspondence primarily by name, an occasional subject title may be interfiled with the names as well. For example, arranging all employment letters *first* by the subject title EMPLOYMENT can be very useful when retrieving letters of application.

You have already indexed, coded, sorted, and filed personal and business names in Chapters 2 and 3. You will use these same skills to file correspondence. Filing paper records remains an important skill in today's offices, since about 95 percent of office records are *hard copy* records. **Hard copy** is the paper copy of a record. Some offices, such as legal and medical offices, may require or prefer hard copy records. These hard copy records must be systematically filed for retrieval as needed.

Correspondence can be photographed and stored on film. Documents can be scanned and stored on disks. One 12-inch disk stores as many records as eighty file cabinets. However, offices rarely use electronic storage for correspondence. Therefore, you will study the most frequent correspondence filing systems in the modern office: alphabetic filing using a file-drawer or open-shelf storage. You will examine (1) the equipment commonly used to file correspondence, (2) the supplies needed to establish the filing system, and (3) the procedures followed to prepare and file the paper records.

What is the most frequently used correspondence filing system?

Examining Correspondence Filing Equipment

The common types of manual filing equipment include (1) *top-access,* (2) *side-access,* and (3) *top- or side-access* storage equipment.

What are three common types of manual filing equipment?

Top-Access Equipment

Top-access file storage is file equipment that contains records stored vertically on edge and dropped into or lifted up and out for storage and retrieval. The vertical file cabinet shown in Figure 4-1 is a type of vertical/top-access storage equipment. Today, the **vertical file** is the most familiar, and most used, storage equipment for business correspondence. You've seen them in your school. Vertical files have pull-out drawers that hold business papers in a front-to-back vertical arrangement. File access is vertical (from the top). The drawers are equipped with compressors. A **compressor** (or follower) is a movable support placed behind guides and folders to allow contraction or expansion of the drawer contents and to hold records in a vertical position.

Vertical file cabinets are available in a variety of colors and in one- to six-drawer units. If too many drawers are opened at one time, the file cabinet can topple over—watch out for those old models! Newer models allow only one drawer to be opened at one time. The cabinets are made of wood or metal and may be water- and fire-resistant as well.

What is a compressor?

Figure 4-1
Vertical File
Source: *Tennsco Corp.*

Side-Access Equipment

Side-access file storage is file equipment that stores records vertically with access from the side. The **shelf file** is a side-access file consisting of horizontal open shelves, similar to open bookshelves. (See Figure 4-2.) Folders are placed upright on the shelves in a side-by-side arrangement and accessed from the side. Sliding wire or metal supports keep the folders upright. Notice the use of color labels on the folders in the illustration. Chapter 8 shows color-coded filing systems and explains how the color blocks produced by these labels help to detect misfiled records.

Figure 4-2
Shelf File
Source: *PRO/file Systems*

Open-shelf files are recommended by records professionals because of these advantages: (1) they require less aisle space because file drawers are eliminated, (2) they provide maximum use of wall space with floor-to-ceiling storage capacity, and (3) they provide handy, open, side access to folders. However, when single documents are retrieved from folders, shelf filing is inefficient. Unlike retrieving vertically from a top-access file, the entire folder must be removed from the shelf file to retrieve a single document. Floor-to-ceiling shelves maximize office storage space, but unless you're seven feet tall, retrieving from such lofty heights can be dangerous. It is wise to reserve the elevated shelves for your less active records.

What are the advantages of shelf files?

Top- or Side-Access Equipment

The lateral file drawers shown in Figure 4-3 combine the features of both the vertical file and the shelf file. The **lateral file** cabinet provides the same top-access drawer filing as the vertical file cabinet. However, folders can be placed in an upright, side-by-side arrangement as in the shelf file.

Figure 4-3
Lateral File Drawers
Source: Kardex Systems

How are lateral drawer files similar to shelf files? to vertical files?

Lateral files resemble shelf filing inside a file drawer. Because the lateral file cabinet drawer requires less pull-out space than the vertical file cabinet drawer, less aisle space is required. Some lateral file drawers not only pull out, but the drawer fronts pull down as well. In these designs, side access is possible. Because they require less aisle space and may provide either top access or side access, lateral files are widely used for records storage.

Examining Correspondence Filing Supplies

What supplies are needed to establish the correspondence file?

The supplies needed to establish the alphabetic correspondence file include (1) *Guides* to mark the alphabetic sections of the filing system, (2) *Folders* to hold the papers, and (3) *Labels* to identify drawer, shelf, and folder contents. In Chapter 2 you studied guides, tabs, labels, and captions used in card filing. These terms are reviewed here as they apply to correspondence filing.

Guides

Why are guides necessary?

A guide is a divider, with a projecting metal or plastic tab, used to identify a section of the files and to facilitate reference. Guides are made of durable pressboard material to sustain heavy use and to help support the folders in the file. Tabs are available on either the top or the side of the guide. A top-tab guide is used for top-access filing; a side-tab guide is used for side-access filing. (See Figure 4-4.)

Figure 4-4
Top-Tab Guide and Side-Tab Guide
Source: *Photography by Eric Von Fischer/Photonics and Kardex Systems, Inc.*

In addition to alphabetic guides, special name or special subject guides may be needed. Special name guides point either to common surnames or to frequently used correspondents' names (BAKER, SMITH, or AVON AUDIO INC). Special subject guides point to the location of correspondence filed together under a special subject title (ADVERTISING RATES, APPLICATIONS, or TAXES).

What are special guides?

Folders

Papers are never filed loosely between the guides. Papers are placed in folders that protect them and keep them upright and accessible. A **folder** is a sheet of heavy paper, usually manila, or vinyl, scored and folded in half to hold papers. A tab on the back fold projects to the side or top approximately one-half inch for identification of folder contents. The **score marks** (fold lines) at the bottom of the "V" fold can be refolded in an expanded "U" shape. This expansion allows adding more papers to the folder.

Plastic folders come in a variety of colors. Although more expensive than manila folders, plastic folders are more durable during excessive handling and can be used again and again.

Placement of guides and folders in file drawers or on shelves makes guide and folder tabs easily visible. The more visible the guides and folders, the faster the record retrieval. Manufacturers of guides and folders make provisions for this visibility by cutting the tabs of both guides and folders in alternate sizes and locations along the top or side edges. Like the guides, file folders are available in different tab cuts (widths) and positions (location).

What are score marks?

Tab Cut

The folder tab cut is the width of the tab relative to the width of the folder. Figure 4-5 shows the standard folder cuts—fifth-, third-, half-, and full-cut folders. The fraction refers to the portion of the total folder width that is used for the folder tab. A half-cut folder tab, for example, occupies one-half the total width of the folder. A full-cut, or straight-cut folder tab occupies the full width of the folder.

Tab Position

The location of a tab on a guide or folder is its position. The tab position is the location of the tab on the guide or folder. Alternate tab positions allow guides and folders to be arranged in a number of ways in the vertical or lateral file. Tabs are at the top for top-access files. Tabs are located on the side of guides and folders for side-access files. Figure 4-6 shows a one-third cut manila folder with the tab in third position.

What is a tab cut? a tab position?

Figure 4-5
Standard Cuts
of Folders

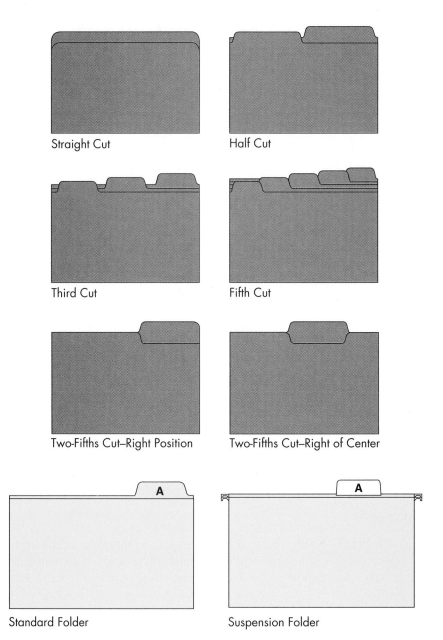

Straight Cut

Half Cut

Third Cut

Fifth Cut

Two-Fifths Cut–Right Position

Two-Fifths Cut–Right of Center

Figure 4-6
Manila Folder
(third-cut, third
position) and
Suspension
Folder

A

A

Standard Folder

Suspension Folder

Suspension (Hanging) Folders

Suspension folders have two metal or plastic rods extending beyond the top front and back flaps of the folder. The ends of the rods rest on parallel rails in the file drawer. The rails provide a carrier for the folders. The advantage of hanging folders over traditional folders is that no compressors are needed in the drawers to hold records upright. Overcrowded traditional folders tend to sag in the file. Suspension folders reduce folder sag. Figure 4-6 shows both the traditional manila folder and the suspension folder.

Labels

Drawer, shelf, guide, and folder labels provide important identifying information for the correspondence file. The following paragraphs describe label preparation.

Drawer Label

The drawer label identifies the drawer contents. Always label file drawers. It is too time-consuming to open drawer after drawer looking for a particular section of the alphabetic file. The drawer label is constructed of card stock torn from perforated sheets and slipped into holders on the outside of drawers. The label caption is centered on the label and typewritten or computer-printed in all capitals without punctuation. The drawer label caption for the alphabetic correspondence file can be either an open or a closed caption. Open captions show the beginning of the alphabetic range contained in the drawer. The closed caption shows the beginning and ending alphabetic range of correspondence in the drawer. Figure 4-7 shows open and closed captions for file drawer labels.

Why label the file drawer?

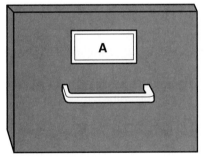

Open Caption

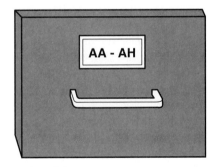

Closed Caption

Figure 4-7
Open Caption and Closed Caption

Shelf Label

Individual shelf labels are inserted into metal holders on the front or end edges of the shelf file. A perforated sheet of labels is generally used. Center the information in capitals with no punctuation. The use of large print, if available, is preferable for easy readability.

Where is the shelf label located?

Guide Label

Guide labels should fit the size of the tab and accommodate the reference information typed or printed on them. Perforated sheets are available for preparing guide labels. Type the caption two spaces from the left edge of the label, two spaces from the top edge, in all capitals, with no punctuation. Then tear the label from the perforated sheet and insert it into the plastic or metal tab. The top-tab guide label is prepared to be read horizontally; the side-tab guide label is prepared either horizontally or vertically.

Sets of alphabetic guides are available with preprinted captions or with preprinted inserts. Alphabetic guides mark and separate the major divisions of an alphabetic filing system (A-AC, AD-AG). The number of guides in a set will vary from a set of 23 guides to a set of 160 guides, depending on the size of the file. The more folders in the file, the more alphabetic subdivisions necessary. Approximately 20 guides are used in a single file drawer.

Folder Labels

A folder label identifies the contents of a folder. It is both difficult and inefficient to type directly on the folder tab. Folder labels are available in sizes to fit the size of the folder tab. Labels are placed on the front of the tab or wrapped around the tab. Side-tab folder labels that wrap around the tab are visible from both sides of the folder. You can see the caption coming or going! The labels are either gummed or pressure-sensitive. The pressure-sensitive labels on sheets or folded strips are the simplest to use.

Folder labels are prepared on the typewriter or printed on the computer, using the label feature available on most database and word processing software programs. Key the caption as follows: Two spaces from the left edge of the label and as close to the top as possible, key the alphabetic letter(s) that correspond to those on the guide label behind which the folder will be filed. Then five spaces to the right of the alphabetic letter(s), key the name in indexing order—all caps, no punctuation. If additional lines are needed, place them directly under the first letter of the name.

Information on wrap-around side-tab labels is keyed immediately above the color bar separator as well as below the color bar separator so that information is readable from both sides. Figure 4-8 shows the correct format for the top-tab and side-tab folder label captions in the alphabetic correspondence name file. Hanging folder labels are inserted into a plastic tab that fits in slots on the front or back flap of the folder.

What is the format for the individual folder label?

Figure 4-8
Top-Tab Folder Label and Side-Tab Folder Label

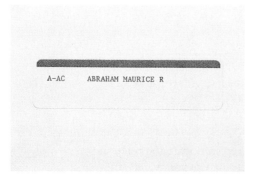

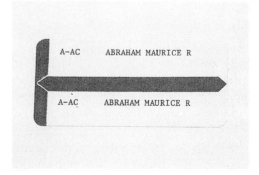

Preparing new labels on the computer is time-consuming. For this reason, a label-making machine, called a *labeler,* is sometimes used. The labeler is equipped with a keyboard, display, and self-adhesive labels. Key in the information, and out comes the completed label.

Review

1. Explain the differences among the alphabetic correspondence filing methods—geographic, subject, and name.

2. Give a reason why you might select the shelf file over the vertical file.

3. Explain the difference between open and closed captions.

Arranging Guides and Folders

Now that you know about correspondence filing equipment and supplies, you are ready to see how they all work together to establish the alphabetic correspondence name file. Although positions of guides and folders may vary from one filing system to another, the preferred guide and folder plan in the correspondence file is a *straight-line* arrangement.

Straight-Line Filing

In **straight-line filing**, the guide tabs and folder tabs occupy single horizontal positions that are readable in a straight line from the front to the back of the file. Straight-line filing is preferred because (1) the eye scans in a straight line and (2) folders are added and deleted with no disruption to the file arrangement.

For many years file guides and file folders were commonly arranged in a staggered pattern in vertical storage equipment because it was thought to provide for easier reading of captions. In a staggered arrangement, the guide and folder tabs are arranged in different horizontal positions creating a zigzag arrangement. Study the third-cut folders in Figure 4-5. If all three-position folders were used in the file, the folders would create a staggered arrangement. The staggered arrangement of folders requires zigzag eye movements when scanning the file. When folders are added or removed, the once neat horizontal arrangement of folders eventually becomes a jumbled mess. Today, records users know that straight-line arrangement of guides and folders results in more efficient records storage and retrieval. Refer to the straight-line arrangement of the guides and folders in Figure 4-9 as you study the description of guides and folders that follows.

Why is straight-line filing preferred?

Figure 4-9
Alphabetic Name File

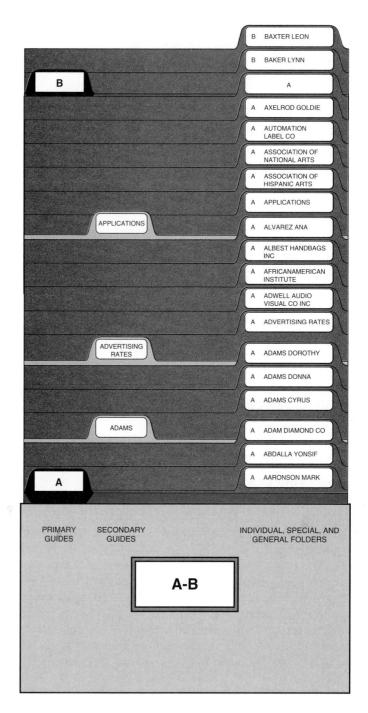

| | PRIMARY GUIDES | SECONDARY GUIDES | INDIVIDUAL, SPECIAL, AND GENERAL FOLDERS |

A-B

Guide Arrangement

Alphabetic guides are the major file divisions and are considered the **primary guides** in the alphabetic correspondence name file. They are fifth-cut guides placed in the first position (moving left to right) and precede all the other material in the section of the file they identify. Special name guides and special subject guides are **secondary guides** interfiled alphabetically. They are a subdivision of the primary alphabetic guide they follow. They are fifth-cut guides placed in the next position to the right of the primary guides.

Folder Arrangement

Individual folders, special subject folders, and general folders are third-cut folders with the tab in third position. All folders are filed with tabs and labels in a straight line at the right of the file drawer. The Association of Records Managers and Administrators (ARMA) recommends in its publication *Filing Procedures Guideline* that third-cut folders be used. Third-cut folders are used in Figure 4-9. However, these guidelines also suggest that tab size must accommodate the caption length. Longer names may require the use of half-cut folders.

Guide tabs and folder tabs are arranged in specific locations in top-access or side-access vertical files. Reading from left to right in a top-access file, primary guide tabs are at the left side of the drawer; secondary guide tabs are in a line to the right of the primary guide tabs; and folder tabs are in the far right position in the drawer. For side-access vertical files, the same sequence follows except the tabs are read top to bottom. Primary guide tabs are at the top; secondary guide tabs are below primary guide tabs; and folder tabs, below the secondary tabs. Figure 4-9 illustrates the primary guide, secondary guide, and folder tab arrangement in a vertical top-access file drawer.

How many tab positions are used in Figure 4-9?

General Folders

The tab on each general folder bears the same alphabetic caption as the primary guide behind which the general folder is filed. These folders are given the name **general** (or miscellaneous) **folders** because they hold papers from all persons or companies with insufficient correspondence to require the use of an individual folder. For example, in Figure 4-9 the A general folder holds all papers from infrequent correspondents with names beginning with the letter A (Aaron Tire Company, John Abrams, and Academy of Political Science, etc.).

General folders close each alphabetic section. If there is no individual folder for a correspondent, then place the document in the general folder at the *end* of the alphabetic section.

Individual Folders

Individual folders contain records of an individual correspondent. Prepare individual folders for persons or companies when correspondence and other documents relating to them increase in volume. Generally when

When should individual folders be prepared?

five pieces of correspondence relate to the same person or organization, an individual folder is prepared. Sometimes the anticipated activity of a particular company or client will prompt the initial preparation of an individual folder. The use of individual folders speeds up the retrieval of active correspondence and also helps to relieve the often overcrowded general folder.

Special Subject Folders

Special subject folders contain correspondence related to one specific subject. Place the folder directly after the special guide marking its location. Interfile the special subject guide alphabetically with the names already on file. File correspondence in the special subject folder alphabetically by correspondents' names.

Receiving and Filing Correspondence

How correspondence is originally filed determines the value of a filing system as an information resource. If the file continues to be a valuable resource, then procedures for preparing correspondence and placing it into the files must be followed systematically and consistently by *all* file users.

Receiving the Correspondence

When correspondence is first received, it is time-stamped and distributed. When the correspondence has been read or responded to in some way, it is released for filing.

Time Stamp

In many companies a mail room clerk opens the mail and marks each letter with a dated rubber stamp or a time-stamp machine. The **time stamp** records the date, and sometimes the time, of the receipt of each piece of mail. Look for the time-stamp *mark*, also referred to as the *time stamp*, in the coded letter in Figure 4-10.

After mail is time-stamped, it is sorted according to recipients' names or departments and delivered to them. After a letter has been read and answered, both the original letter and a copy of the reply are released to the records department for filing.

Release Mark

What is a release mark?

The **release mark** is an agreed-upon mark placed on a record showing that the record is ready for storage. The mark is made on the letter by a secretary or by the person who originally received the letter. The initials of either person are written in the upper left part of the original letter. A copy of an answering letter does not need a release mark.

Figure 4-10
Coded Letter with
Cross-Reference
Notation

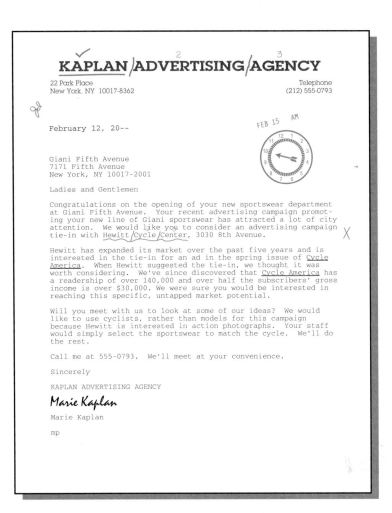

KAPLAN /ADVERTISING /AGENCY

22 Park Place
New York, NY 10017-8362

Telephone
(212) 555-0793

February 12, 20--

FEB 15 AM

Giani Fifth Avenue
7171 Fifth Avenue
New York, NY 10017-2001

Ladies and Gentlemen

Congratulations on the opening of your new sportswear department
at Giani Fifth Avenue. Your recent advertising campaign promot-
ing your new line of Giani sportswear has attracted a lot of city
attention. We would like you to consider an advertising campaign
tie-in with Hewitt /Cycle /Center, 3030 8th Avenue.

Hewitt has expanded its market over the past five years and is
interested in the tie-in for an ad in the spring issue of Cycle
America. When Hewitt suggested the tie-in, we thought it was
worth considering. We've since discovered that Cycle America has
a readership of over 140,000 and over half the subscribers' gross
income is over $30,000. We were sure you would be interested in
reaching this specific, untapped market potential.

Will you meet with us to look at some of our ideas? We would
like to use cyclists, rather than models for this campaign
because Hewitt is interested in action photographs. Your staff
would simply select the sportswear to match the cycle. We'll do
the rest.

Call me at 555-0793. We'll meet at your convenience.

Sincerely

KAPLAN ADVERTISING AGENCY

Marie Kaplan

Marie Kaplan

mp

Filing Correspondence

Filing correspondence is not so much a question of "Where shall I file it?"
but rather "How will I or my co-workers most likely ask for it?" Always
file correspondence with the retrieval process in mind—file *to find!* Refer
to Figure 4-10, the coded letter, as you study the procedures that follow.

Inspecting

When the records department receives material for filing, a filer inspects it.
Inspecting is checking to see that a record has been released in the proper manner for filing. Letters that have not yet been read or acted upon
should not be filed.

What is inspecting?

Indexing

Indexing is determining the filing segment of each record. The filing segment is the name by which a piece of correspondence is filed. Sometimes

---

it appears that more than one name in a letter can be used as the filing segment. In this case, you must decide which name to use as the filing segment for filing purposes.

In general, correspondence is filed under the most important name on the document—usually the customer, client, or patient. Here are some helpful guidelines when selecting the filing segment:

1. Use either the *name of the company written in the letterhead* of a business letter or the *name in the signature block* of a personal business letter.

2. Use the *company name* that appears in the letter address of an outgoing letter for the filing segment; if no company name appears in the letter address, then use the *name of the individual* in the letter address as the filing segment.

3. If a *subject* or a *name* written *in the body of a letter* is considered to be of greater importance to filing and finding, use that subject or that name as the filing segment. Write the filing segment on the top right side of the letter. For example, a letter *from* a credit bureau *about* one of your customers would be filed in the customer's folder, not under the name of the credit bureau.

4. When *special sections,* such as *special subjects* or *names,* are part of a filing system, use them as filing segments. Write the filing segment in exact form on the top right side of letters or other materials being coded for filing in special sections. For example, if there is a special section in the filing system for APPLICATIONS, code the letter by writing APPLICATIONS at the top of the letter.

Once the filing segment is selected, code the filing unit to show the proper filing order of the filing units. Coding is the physical process of marking or highlighting the filing units to indicate the order in which they are considered when filed. When you write a note to someone, you may occasionally underline the most important part in order to be sure that the person "gets the message." Do the same to code papers for filing: Underline the most important filing unit in the filing segment. This underlined unit is the *key* (first) *unit* by which the name will be filed. Separate the filing units with diagonal lines. Then number each of the remaining units according to the alphabetic indexing rules learned in Chapters 2 and 3. Each filing unit is given a number that shows its place in the indexing order of the name in relation to other names in the filing system. For example, when the name South-Western Publishing Co. is selected as the filing segment, it is coded in this way:

The underlined word, *South-Western,* is the **key unit**—the first unit by which the name will be filed. *Publishing* is the second unit. *Co.* is the third filing unit in this name.

Precoding

Sometimes a secretary or the person to whom a letter is addressed in the organization will code a document at the time it is released for filing. In this instance the document has been **precoded**. The filing segment has already been checked or underlined. Such a check mark is shown in the letter in Figure 4-10.

Preparing Cross-References

Sometimes the filing segment of a letter may have an alternate name under which the correspondence may be requested. A cross-reference makes it easier to locate such a letter. A cross-reference is a file entry that attracts attention to one or more related headings. When there is a probability that a letter may be called for by a name other than the one selected as the filing segment, prepare a cross-reference in this way:

What is a cross-reference?

1. Draw a wavy line under the cross-reference name if it appears in the letter, or write the cross-reference name in the margin of the letter.

2. Mark the name to cross-reference with an "X" in the margin either opposite the name with a wavy underscore or next to the name written in the margin as the cross-reference. (See Figure 4-10.)

3. Prepare a *cross-reference sheet* and file it under the name selected as the cross reference. The cross-reference sheet is the same size as the documents in the file, but it is usually in a color other than white. The name is coded on the cross-reference sheet as shown in Figure 4-11.

An example of the need for a cross-reference is a company name composed of two personal names. Either of these names might be used when someone requests records from the files. For example, in the company name Larson & Richards, the correspondence is filed under *Larson*. If someone looks for the record under the name *Richards,* a cross-reference sheet filed under the name *Richards* refers a filer to the name *Larson & Richards*. In Figure 4-11, a cross-reference was prepared for Hewitt Cycle Center because Giani Fifth Avenue may be doing business with them as well as with Kaplan Advertising Agency. The cross-reference shows the relationship of the names.

Sorting

After inspecting, indexing, coding, and preparing necessary cross-references, sort the records to be filed. **Sorting** is the process of placing papers in alphabetic order before they are taken to the files and placed in folders.

Sorting serves two purposes. First, sorting saves time. If materials were not sorted, you would have to move back and forth from one cabinet or shelf section to another in a random manner. This random movement wastes time, and since "time is money," money is wasted. Second, sorting makes it easier to find an unfiled record. If records are needed before they are filed, they can be found more easily if they are held in a sorted order rather than in random order.

Figure 4-11
Cross-Reference Sheet

CROSS-REFERENCE SHEET

Name or Subject
Hewitt/Cycle/Center

Date of Record
Feb. 12, 20--

Regarding
Tie-in with Giani

See

Name or Subject
Kaplan Advertising Agency

Date Filed _Feb. 18, 20--_ By _K.L._

Papers may be sorted by using specialized equipment such as sorting trays. Sorters are composed of a series of alphabetically labeled guides that are held together in either a vertical or horizontal position. (See Figure 4-12.)

Figure 4-12
Sorting Equipment
Source: *Esselte Pendaflex*
Corporation

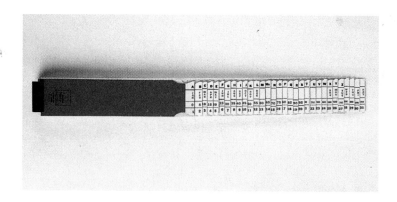

If special sorting equipment is not available, sort papers into alphabetic units in the following manner:

1. Divide materials into alphabetic stacks according to the first letters of the key units in the filing segments. For example, use five alphabetic stacks: A-D, E-H, I-M, N-S, T-Z.

2. Sort each of the five stacks into single alphabetic units. For example, sort the A-D stack into separate stacks for A, B, C, and D.

3. Finally, alphabetize individual names in each alphabetic section.

Steps 1 and 2 are known as *rough sorting*. Step 3 is *fine sorting*.

Filing

Place all correspondence in folders with the letterhead or the letter address at the left side of the folder and with the writing facing forward. In *individual folders*, arrange letters according to the date of writing. Place the most recent letter *in front*.

In *general folders*, and in single *special subject folders*, arrange the filing segments in alphabetic order. Then within each group of letters from and to the same person or company, arrange correspondence according to the date written. Place the letter with the most recent date in front of all others with the same name. For example, in a general folder captioned DE, file letters as follows (reading from the front of the folder to the back):

How is correspondence filed in general folders?

	Order of Letters	Correspondents' Names	Dates on Letters
(Back)	6	Delmar Corporation	August 2, 20—
	5	Delmar Corporation	August 20, 20—
	4	Delmar Corporation	September 2, 20—
	3	Irene Delgado	July 18, 20—
	2	Kimberly D'Eletto	September 26, 20—
(Front)	1	Kimberly D'Eletto	October 5, 20—

Review

1. Explain straight-line filing.

2. How does the arrangement of correspondence in the individual folder differ from the arrangement of correspondence in the general folder?

3. Code the following name: Dr. William J. Burns, Jr.

Summary

Correspondence may be filed alphabetically by geographic location, by subject, or by name. The common types of equipment for storing correspondence are top-access and side-access file containers. The vertical file is a commonly used top-access file; the shelf file is a commonly used side-access file. Guides, folders, and labels are needed to establish the correspondence file. The placement of the captions on guide and folder tabs must be consistent to create a neat and efficient file. Straight-line filing is the preferred arrangement of guides and folders in the file.

When correspondence is received, it is time-stamped and distributed. After correspondence is released, the filing procedures include the following: (1) inspecting, (2) indexing, (3) coding, (4) preparing cross-references as necessary, (5) sorting, and (6) filing.

Terminology Review

alphabetic correspondence file	(p. 54)
alphabetic correspondence name file	(p. 54)
compressor (or follower)	(p. 55)
folder	(p. 59)
general (miscellaneous) folder	(p. 65)
geographic filing	(p. 54)
hard copy	(p. 55)
individual folders	(p. 65)
inspecting	(p. 67)
key unit	(p. 68)
lateral file	(p. 57)
precoded	(p. 69)
primary guides	(p. 64)
release mark	(p. 66)
score marks	(p. 59)
secondary guides	(p. 65)
shelf file	(p. 56)
side-access file storage	(p. 56)
sorting	(p. 69)
special subject folders	(p. 66)
straight-line filing	(p. 63)
subject filing	(p. 54)
suspension folders	(p. 60)
time stamp	(p. 66)
top-access file storage	(p. 55)
vertical file	(p. 55)

Questions for Discussion

1. Name and define the three alphabetic correspondence filing methods. (Obj. 1)
2. Name two types of equipment commonly used to store and protect business papers. Give an example of each type. (Obj. 2)
3. List the supplies necessary to set up an alphabetic correspondence file. (Obj. 3)
4. Describe the placement of the captions on drawer and shelf labels, guide labels, and folder labels. (Obj. 4)
5. Describe the straight-line guide and folder arrangement in the alphabetic correspondence name file. (Obj. 5)
6. Explain the use of primary guides in the alphabetic correspondence name file. (Obj. 5)
7. Explain the use of general folders in the alphabetic correspondence name file. (Obj. 5)
8. Why are special sections useful in an alphabetic correspondence name file? (Obj. 5)
9. List the six steps for filing correspondence that has been released for filing. (Obj. 6)
10. What is a precoded letter? (Obj. 6)

▶ Applications

Place the dated correspondence listed below in correct filing order in special subject, special name, and general alphabetic folders. The folders bear the captions A, B, COLLEGES AND UNIVERSITIES, C, D, E, FOSTER, and F. On a separate sheet of paper, list the numbers of each name (1-15) in correct filing order. (Obj. 7)

Name of Correspondent	Date of Correspondence
1. Maurice DeBear	9/12/—
2. Aaron Berg	9/12/—
3. Alfred State College	9/19/—
4. D & E Feed Co.	9/20/—
5. Foster Wheeler, Inc.	10/4/—
6. Bennington College	10/5/—
7. Alfred University	10/8/—
8. Coliseum Books, Inc.	10/8/—
9. Jan Friedman	11/12/—
10. Lena Foster	11/13/—
11. Award Travel Agency	11/13/—
12. Alfred State College	11/13/—
13. Charles Collano	11/15/—
14. Edith De Castro	11/15/—
15. Jan Friedman	12/11/—

Practice Set Application

At this time, complete Job 4, *Alphabetic Correspondence Filing*, in OFFICE FILING PROCEDURES, Eighth Edition. Instructions and supplies for this job are included in the practice set.

Chapter Five

Computer Database Rules and Procedures

Learning Objectives

After completing Chapter 5, you will be able to do the following:

1. Define computer database terms.

2. Identify information needed on a database design sheet.

3. Describe how ASCII affects computer sorting.

4. Define **input** and **output.**

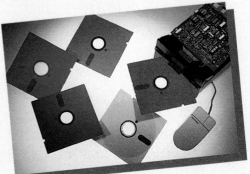

5. List rules for entering records into a computer.

6. Explain the use of leading zeros.

7. Explain how the computer sorts numbers in addresses.

8. Describe how to achieve correct order for identical names with titles using a computer.

9. Define **backup** and explain why backups are necessary.

10. List five ways to handle disks carefully.

11. List information needed on a disk label.

12. Describe how color accenting on disk labels is useful.

Computer Databases

Computers play an important role in our daily lives. Naturally, they play an important role in records control. Computers can rapidly sort records and arrange names in alphabetic order. They are excellent tools for sorting, manipulating, entering, or retrieving almost any kind of information. They are indispensable for maintaining mailing lists.

    When information about records is stored in the computer, records users may save themselves lengthy manual searches through large filing systems to retrieve information. An alphabetic index stored in the computer can also be used to direct the user to the location of the actual paper record. In Chapter 5, you will learn basic information about computer databases and how to care for your computer and disks. In addition, you will learn how to apply the alphabetic indexing rules presented in Chapters 2 and 3 to computer records.

How does the computer assist records control?

Database Structure

Records are stored in a computer in a database. A **database** is a storage area for data. It is made up of files; files are made up of records; records are made up of data fields. A **field** is one piece of data in a record. A first name, middle name, and last name would each be a field (units in manual filing) in a database. A **computer record** is one complete entry—the total collection of fields—concerning one person, subject, or other item. A **file** is a collection of related records treated as a unit, such as a customer list. Study the terms listed in Figure 5-1. You will use many of these terms when you work with a computer database.

    A computer database file contains the records for *all* correspondents, subjects, numbers, or locations in the filing system, not just records for

What is a database?

What is a file?

Figure 5-1 Database Terms

Data	The facts and figures that make up the raw material processed by the computer.
Data entry	The process of entering data into a computer. Data may be keyed, faxed, or scanned into the computer, or entered by voice or audio devices.
Data processing	The manipulation of data to produce information.
Extension	Additional characters beyond a database filename separated by a period. Usually three additional letters are allowed.
Field name	The title given to a unit of data in a record. Each field must have a name that clearly identifies its contents. Usually the field name cannot be longer than 8 to 11 characters, including spaces.
Field length	The maximum number of characters that will occupy a field.
Filename	The distinctive name for the database. Usually, the name cannot be longer than 8 characters.
Key field	The field that uniquely identifies any record in the database. For example, an employee number, a social security number, or a name is unique for each record.

Fields must be identified by the type of data that will occupy each field. Types of fields used in most databases are character, date, numeric, logical, and text.

Character field	A type of field that combines alphabetic, numeric, and/or symbol characters to form words.
Date field	A type of field used for measuring time. Usually, dates must be keyed as MM/DD/YY— 02/14/05. A date field will not accept letters.
Numeric field	A type of field used for performing mathematical operations.
Logical field	A type of field in which, usually, only one character is keyed: *Y* for *yes*, *N* for *no*, *T* for *true*, or *F* for *false*.
Text field	A type of field used for larger amounts of information—sentences and/or paragraphs. Sometimes called a *memo field*.

one correspondent. The database filename should indicate the contents of the file. For example, a database filename such as SUBJFILE might contain records stored by their subjects. ALPHANDX might be the filename for an alphabetic index.

Using the computer saves filing time and space because all records can be accessed from one location. The computer can tell you the number of records in the filing system. It can retrieve selected information from those records and print it in a report.

Review

1. Why use a database for records control?
2. List five types of computer fields.

Database Planning and Design

A computer database needs to be planned and designed completely on paper before any data is keyed into the computer. Thorough planning allows database users to achieve the maximum benefits and results from the database. When the database is well-planned and designed, numerous changes in the structure won't be needed in the future.

Why should you plan and design your database on paper?

    The starting point of the database design is to determine the database structure. Remember, the database structure consists of fields, records, and files.

    When designing a database that meets current and future needs, ask and answer a number of basic questions. How will the database be used? What types of data will be included in the database? What kinds of reports will be needed from the database? Using a standard form for planning and designing the database helps to organize the data to achieve the desired results.

Database Design Sheet

A database design sheet should be completed before the database is created in the computer. The design sheet should contain blank spaces for writing important information such as the database filename, a description of the database that identifies its purpose, the date the database was created, and the field names. Additional information, such as a description of the information that will be keyed into each field, the field length (maximum number of characters), the type of field (character, numeric, etc.), and an indication whether the field is indexed or sorted or not, might be included. The longest name or words in each field must be counted, including blank spaces, to determine the field length or width. If field names or lengths change, fields are added or deleted, or if field descriptions change, *make the changes on the database design sheet* as well as in the computer database. The database design sheet serves as the plan and the history of the database and can be referenced quickly. Study the completed database design sheet in Figure 5-2. Although this database has only a few fields, the design sheet can accommodate much more complex database designs.

ASCII Codes

All computers have an internal coding system that decides how data will be treated. The **American Standard Code for Information Interchange (ASCII)** is the internal coding system used by most computers. The acronym *ASCII* is pronounced "ask ee." All characters keyed into a computer are interpreted as a code number. ASCII assigns numeric values to common characters: the space, punctuation marks, symbols and

---

Figure 5-2 Database Design Sheet

DATABASE DESIGN SHEET

Database name (filename) <u>MEMBERS</u> **Date** <u>Current</u>
Database description <u>Microcomputer Club Members</u>

	Field Name	Field Description	Field Type	Field Length	Sort/Index
*1.	LASTNAME	Member last name	C	28	Y
2.	FRSTNAME	First name/initial	C	12	Y
3.	MIDINIT	Middle initial	C	1	Y
4.	BLDGNO	Bldg./house number	C	6	Y
5.	STREET	Street name or number and direction or PO Box No.	C	30	Y
6.	CITY	City Name	C	24	Y
7.	ST	Two-ltr. state abbrev.	C	2	Y
8.	ZIP	Member's Zip Code + 4	C	10	N
9.	PHONENO	Area code and number (501/555-8700)	C	12	N
10.	EQUIP	Equipment owned by member	T	60	N

* Key field

What determines how a computer sorts?

special characters, numbers, and letters. These numeric values affect the sequence of sorting, from lowest to highest numbers, in the following order:

1. space (lowest numeric value)
2. symbols, special characters, and punctuation marks
3. numbers 0-9
4. uppercase letters A-Z
5. lowercase letters a-z (highest numeric value)

A space is sorted before any other character. For example, Day is sorted before Dayton and John Smith is sorted before John A. Smith. ASCII applies the *nothing before something* principle you learned in alphabetic indexing Rule 1.

Because some software programs have a different ordering system than ASCII, you need to check the internal coding system of your computer before designing and creating a database. Computer users must understand how their computer sorts spaces, symbols, numbers, and letters before keying any data into the computer. A sample list of names may be keyed and sorted to determine how alphabetic or numeric order is achieved in your computer.

Review

1. Why is a design sheet helpful in creating a database?

2. What is ASCII?

Alphabetic Indexing Rules And Databases

Consistency in applying the indexing rules in electronic records systems is just as necessary as it is in manual records systems. The rules must be applied in the same way by all records system users. When changes are made in rules to accommodate the way a computer sorts, document the changes, and make everyone aware of the changes so they can use the new rules consistently.

Input is the data entered into a computer. Input is also the act of entering data into a computer. Data may be keyed, faxed, or scanned into the computer. Voice and other audio devices also may be used to input data into the computer. Deciding how you want the data to come out of the computer helps determine how to input the data. **Output** is the result obtained from the computer operation. The output may be printed on the computer screen or on paper. Output printed on paper is called a *printout* or a *hard-copy report*.

How is data input into the computer?

Correct output in printed reports requires consistency of input. The following general rules apply for inputting records into a database. (Check your computer software programs for specific instructions that apply to those programs.)

1. Key all data in uppercase (CAPITAL) letters because the computer reads uppercase letters before lowercase letters.

2. Omit all punctuation marks. The computer sorts punctuation marks before letters.

3. Spell out minor words and symbols in business names. The computer will sort symbols before alphabetic characters or words.

4. Key Roman numerals as Arabic numerals (2, 3, 5, 10, etc.). The computer reads Roman numerals as capital letters. Therefore, ASCII numeric values of those letters (II, III, V) will determine the order of Roman numerals.

5. Insert leading zeros before Arabic numbers of unequal length that will be sorted. A **leading zero** is one that is added to the front of numbers so that all numbers align on the right and are the same length. If the longest number in the field that will be sorted has four digits, then zeros are added to the left of smaller numbers so that all numbers have four digits (0004, 0011, 0342, 7895).

Databases used for records management usually use only text fields, which print all letters and numbers flush left. Adding leading zeroes to the left of numbers causes the numbers to align on the right and sort correctly. Databases used for math computations use numeric fields, which automatically align at the right so leading zeroes are not necessary.

Indexing and coding of filing segments are essential procedures in any filing system. Inconsistency in applying the rules for computer input results in misfiled records. For a computer database, application of Alphabetic Indexing Rules 5, 7, and 9 requires special attention.

Why are rules necessary for inputting records into a database?

RULE 5: Titles and Suffixes

Remember that according to Indexing Rule 5, numeric titles should be arranged before alphabetic titles. Because the computer reads Roman numerals as capital letters, seniority titles such as II and III must be keyed as Arabic numerals—2 and 3. Note the way that alphabetic and numeric titles are sorted in the following example. *CPA* is sorted before *II* and *III* because the computer reads the Roman numerals as capital *i* (I). However, when the Roman numerals are changed to Arabic numbers (*2* and *3*), these titles sort before *CPA*. *JR* and *SR* are arranged in alphabetic order with other alphabetic titles and suffixes.

RECORD#	KEY UNIT	UNIT 2	UNIT 3	UNIT 4
1	SERGIO	VICTOR	J	2
2	SERGIO	VICTOR	J	3
3	SERGIO	VICTOR	J	CPA
4	SERGIO	VICTOR	J	II
5	SERGIO	VICTOR	J	III
6	SERGIO	VICTOR	J	JR
7	SERGIO	VICTOR	J	MR
8	SERGIO	VICTOR	J	PHD
9	SERGIO	VICTOR	J	SENATOR
10	SERGIO	VICTOR	J	SR

Rule 7: Numbers in Business Names

Leading zeros must be used to ensure that the computer will sort numbers in business names correctly. In the list of names in Example 1 below, numbers 10, 300, and 4 are out of order because the computer reads from the left. However, when leading zeros are added, as in Example 2, the numbers sort in correct numeric order.

Why are leading zeroes added to numbers that are to be sorted?

Example 1

KEY UNIT	UNIT 2	UNIT 3	UNIT 4
10	AVENUE	BAKERY	
300	QUALITY	SERVICE	STORE
4	AND	UNDER	DAYCARE

Example 2

KEY UNIT	UNIT 2	UNIT 3	UNIT 4
004	AND	UNDER	DAYCARE
010	AVENUE	BAKERY	
300	QUALITY	SERVICE	STORE

Rule 9: Identical Names

As you learned in Chapter 3, when names, including titles, are identical, order is determined by addresses. Addresses are considered in this order: city, state, street name, house/building number. In order to comply with Rule 9, separate database fields sometimes may be needed for the city, state, street, and building or house number.

When street names are in the same field as the house/building numbers, the house/building numbers will sort first because the computer reads from the left. Leading zeros may be needed before numbered street names that do not contain the same number of digits (008 Street, 056 Street, 118 Avenue) so they will be in correct numeric order.

Additionally, leading zeros may be needed before house and building numbers, especially when more than one house or building number are on the same street. In Example 1 that follows, leading zeros are not used to equalize the length of the house/building numbers. City and state names are identical and don't need to be sorted; therefore, the ADDRESS field is sorted. Note that the computer has read the house and building numbers from the left, and the street names are not in alphabetic order. The numbered street (18 Street) also is not arranged before the alphabetic street names of Sunrise and Sunset.

Example 1

ADDRESS	CITY	ST
1200 SUNRISE	BOULDER	CO
34 SUNRISE	BOULDER	CO
54 18 STREET	BOULDER	CO
904 SUNSET	BOULDER	CO

To arrange the addresses correctly, a separate field is needed for the house/building number. Example 2 shows the correct arrangement when the STREET field and the BLDGNO fields are sorted.

Example 2

BLDGNO	STREET	CITY	ST
0054	18 STREET	BOULDER	CO
0034	SUNRISE	BOULDER	CO
1200	SUNRISE	BOULDER	CO
0904	SUNSET	BOULDER	CO

Review

1. What are leading zeros?
2. Why are separate fields needed for street names and house/building numbers?

Computer Usage

Using a computer requires taking responsibility for the records stored on the computer's internal hard disk and on external disks. Part of this responsibility is proper maintenance of the computer. Backing up your computer records, taking care of your computer disks, and disk labeling are important procedures for ensuring that your electronic records will be available when you need them.

Backup Methods and Procedures

A **backup** is an additional copy of a database or an individual data file. Large multi-user computer systems have software that automatically backs up at the end of each day. A single computer user, however, has other choices for backing up records.

A backup copy should be made of all application software disks before the software is loaded onto the hard disk. Therefore, backing up the software from the hard disk is a waste of time and disks. Software can be reloaded from the original disks if needed. However, backups of the data are critical.

Data files should be "backed up" each time additions, deletions, or changes of any kind are made. A backup copy of files used daily is often called a *working disk*. Some situations may require a backup only once a month. Some backup software will back up only those files in which changes were made since the last backup.

Store the backups in another location. Storing the backup disks on the desk beside the computer won't help if the computer workstation is destroyed or damaged by fire, flood, or another major disaster. Chapter 13 contains a detailed discussion of disaster prevention and recovery of records after a disaster.

Disk Maintenance

Disks are delicate and susceptible to damage from many sources. Therefore, it is vital that disks be handled and stored with care. Ways to care for your disks properly are listed in Figure 5-3.

Figure 5-3 Disk Care and Maintenance

DISK CARE AND MAINTENANCE

1. Avoid extreme temperatures and direct sunlight. Disks operate efficiently between 50 and 120 degrees. Allow disks to reach room temperature before use.

2. Keep disks away from magnetic fields. Keep telephones and color TVs away from disks or disk drives.

3. Discard a disk that has been contaminated with any liquid or solvent fumes. Fingernail polish remover can affect the surface of a disk and should not be used near disks or computers.

4. Keep disk drives and disks dust free; use a plastic cover over the computer. Store disks vertically in a dust-proof container.

5. Use write-protect tabs to prevent overwriting critical data.

6. Make backup copies.

7. Keep smoke and liquids away from the computer.

8. Do not use a damaged disk.

9. Do not write directly on a disk. Instead, write on disk labels before you affix them to the disks.

Source: *Information Dimensions, Inc.*

Disk Labeling

Prepare disk labels before they are affixed to the disk, as you learned from Figure 5-3. Key label captions on the computer or a typewriter. Use only a felt-tip pen to write additional information on the label after it is affixed to the disk.

Captions on disk labels correspond to the filing system. Key information in all capitals, two spaces from the left edge. Disk labels should contain the filename, dates of records on the disk, software name, file code (if used), and type of equipment on which the information was created. The dates on the labels assist the records retention program as you will learn in Chapter 7. Color accenting is recommended for separating types of disks. Use disk labels that have color bars across the top or color dots. For example, label backup or working software program disks (software) in Color 1; label working data disks in Color 2. Disk binders may also separate disks by color. Use a different color binder for each set of records, with the disk label color matching the binder color.

Guides used in disk storage containers have tabs with label captions that correspond to the filing and coding system used. Guide labels also may separate disks by type of software, such as word processing, spreadsheet, and database. Color-accented guides should be inserted in front of each set of disks. Color labels of standard size and hue ensure consistency of color coding. Key information on guide labels two spaces from the left edge. Use standardized terms on all labels. Color-accented disk labels are shown in Figure 5-4. Additional information regarding color accenting is presented in Chapter 8.

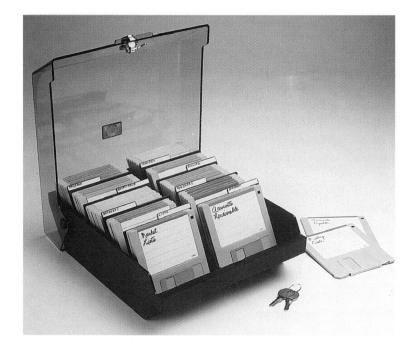

Figure 5-4
Color-Accented
Disk Labels
Source: Fellowes
Manufacturing Company

Summary

Computers can assist filers in searching through records stored in a database much more rapidly than they can search through a large number of file folders. All records can be accessed from one location—the computer workstation. A database is a set of interrelated records that are organized by fields, records, and files. A computer database file contains records (a collection of fields) for *all* correspondents, subjects, numbers, or locations in the filing system. Thorough planning and design of the database is essential before creating the database in the computer.

The American Standard Code for Information Interchange (ASCII) is the internal coding system used by most computers. Understanding how your computer sorts capital and lowercase letters, numbers, symbols, and spaces will help in designing a database and using the computer for sorting records. By first determining what the result should be—the output—the records manager can determine how to input the records. Keying all data in uppercase letters, spelling out minor words and symbols, omitting punctuation, keying Roman numerals as Arabic numerals, and using leading zeros are important rules for achieving a correct computer sort.

Using computers for storing records requires acceptance of the responsibility for maintaining the records and equipment. Creating backups of records is one of the best ways to prevent the loss of data. Preventing damage resulting from dust, heat, static, smoke, and liquids is essential.

Proper labeling is as important for efficient filing and retrieval of electronic records as for paper records. Color accenting on labels and guides may be used to separate disks by software programs and by types of disks used with each program (program, working, or backup).

Terminology Review

Questions for Discussion

1. Define *database*, *field*, *computer record*, and *file*. (Obj. 1)
2. What information needs to be included on a database design sheet? (Obj. 2)
3. Describe the ASCII numeric values from lowest to highest. How do these values affect the computer sorting of names? (Obj. 3)
4. Define *input* and *output*. (Obj. 4)
5. List five rules for entering records into a computer. (Obj. 5)
6. Why are leading zeros keyed before numbers? (Obj. 6)
7. What happens when a street address field that contains house and building numbers is sorted? How do separate address fields help to achieve the correct order of addresses? (Obj. 7)
8. Explain how to obtain correct numeric order of identical names with seniority titles, such as II and III, when using the computer. (Obj. 8)
9. What is a backup and why are backups needed? (Obj. 9)
10. List five ways to handle disks carefully. (Obj. 10)
11. What information should be on a disk label? (Obj. 11)
12. Why is color accenting on disk labels helpful? (Obj. 12)

Applications

▶ **1.** Write the ten names with titles listed below in indexing order on a separate sheet of paper. Index and code the names. Indicate their alphabetic order by numbering the names 1-10. (Obj. 8)

Mark A. Crosswhite, Jr.	Miss Micaela Valdivia
Mrs. Micaela Valdivia	Mark A. Crosswhite, Sr.
Mark A. Crosswhite, Attorney	Mark A. Crosswhite II
Mark A. Crosswhite, CPA	Ms. Micaela Valdivia
Mark A. Crosswhite, JD	Mark A. Crosswhite III

2. Write the ten names and addresses listed below in indexing order on a separate sheet of paper. Index and code the names and addresses. Indicate the correct alphabetic order of the names by numbering them from 1-10. (Obj. 8)

Anchors Away Tour Co. 3456 Harbor Drive St. Paul, MN 55155-4561	Anchors Away Tour Co. 1920 Harbor Drive St. Paul, MN 55155-2010
Anchors Away Tour Co. 15 East Longview Street St. Paul, MN 55155-1015	First Savings Bank 5600 18th Avenue St. Paul, MN 55155-5600
Anchors Away Tour Co. 1200 N. First Street St. Paul, MN 55155-1200	4th Street Art Gallery 74 N. Fourth Street St. Paul, MN 55155-1020
Travel Life Magazine PO Box 52088 New York, NY 10035-2088	Anchors Away Tour Co. 1120 Avenue of the Americas New York, NY 10036-1120
TechSystems, Inc. 67200 Avion Parkway Chesapeake, VA 23320-7200	Coach 'N Four Motel 900 Airport Drive Chesapeake, VA 23320-4892

Practice Set Applications

At this time, complete Job 5, *Alphabetic Name Database*, Job 6, *Database Project I*, and Job 7, *Database Project II* in OFFICE FILING PROCEDURES, Eighth Edition. Instructions and supplies for these jobs are included in the practice set.

Computer Applications

1. On a separate sheet of paper, create a database design sheet, using Figure 5-2 as an example. Use the ten names you indexed and coded in Application 1 on page 87 to complete the design sheet. Use the following information for the database.

Date: Current
Database filename: CUSTLIST
Database description: Customer List
Fields: NAME, TITLE
Field lengths: Count the longest name or words in each field. Be sure to count blank spaces.

Sort/index the NAME and TITLE fields.

2. If a computer is available for your use, create the CUSTLIST database in your computer. Key the names listed in Application 1 on page 87 in indexing order into the NAME field. Key the title for each name in the TITLE field. Proofread carefully. If you are using the template, open filename **CH5AP2.DBF**. Index or sort the NAME and TITLE fields in that order.

3. Create and print a report of the CUSTLIST (CH5AP2.DBF) database.

Title your report: CUSTOMER LIST.
Print the NAME and TITLE fields in order.
Use these column headings: Name, Title.

Check to see that all titles have sorted correctly. Make necessary corrections if the titles are not in correct order. Print a report to give to your teacher for checking.

4. On a separate sheet of paper, create and complete a database design sheet, using Figure 5-2 as an example. Use the ten names and addresses listed in Application 2 on page 87 and the following information to create the database.

Date: Current
Database filename: ALPHANDX
Database description: Alphabetic Index of Records Database
Fields: NAME, ADDRESS1 (building number), ADDRESS2 (street name or PO Box), CITY, ST (state name), ZIP (ZIP + 4)
Field lengths: Count the longest name or words in each field. Count the blank spaces too.

Sort/index NAME, CITY, ADDRESS2, and ADDRESS1 fields.

5. If computers are available for your use, create the ALPHANDX database on a computer. Key the names and proofread carefully. If you are using the template, open the **CH5AP5.DBF** file. Index or sort the NAME, CITY, ADDRESS2, and ADDRESS1 fields in that order.

6. Create and print a report of the ALPHANDX (CH5AP5.DBF) database. Title your report: ALPHABETIC INDEX OF RECORDS DATABASE. Print the NAME, ADDRESS1, ADDRESS2, and CITY fields in that order. Use these column headings: Name, Number, Street, and City. If you are using the template, retrieve report filename **ALPHNDX.FRM,** and print it. Be sure that the names and addresses are sorted correctly. If they are not, make any corrections necessary to achieve correct order. Give your final report to your teacher for checking.

Part 3

Records Maintenance Procedures

Chapter Six

File Maintenance and Control

Learning Objectives

After completing Chapter 6, you will be able to do the following:

1. List practices for good file maintenance.

2. Describe four types of records charge-out methods.

3. List procedures for canceling charge-outs for borrowed records.

4. List two factors determining charge-out time limits.

5. Describe three follow-up methods for records not returned by their due date.

6. Describe a method for records charge-out that eliminates the need for follow-up.

7. List procedures for handling requests to reserve records for a future charge-out date.

8. Compare electronic and manual charge-out and follow-up systems.

9. Describe the use of bar codes for records charge-out and follow-up.

Checklist For Good File Maintenance

In Chapter 4 you learned to establish the alphabetic name correspondence file. You learned (1) to prepare labels, (2) to arrange the guides and folders in the file, and (3) to insert correspondence into folders. Once a file is organized, the next important task is to maintain and control it. Through constant use, a filing system can deteriorate unless someone maintains the file and controls the movement of records in and out of the system. Chapter 6 explains both manual and electronic maintenance and control procedures to ensure that the file, once established, continues to be an efficient and useful source of information.

Here is a checklist that will help you to maintain filing system efficiency. These guidelines can be used to improve an old system as well. Office filing problems may result from ignoring one or more of the following guidelines:

How can you maintain file efficiency?

1. Plan and follow your records control routines carefully. Begin by scheduling a definite time each day for filing tasks.

2. Index, code, and process papers according to specific rules and routines.

3. Code all papers to be filed. This ensures that they will be returned to the correct folder when they are borrowed.

4. Identify one person to direct filing and records control operations.

5. Allow only trained personnel to work with the filing system.

6. Keep a records management manual (guide) available and up to date.

7. Be watchful of overcrowded files. Give attention to the following:
   a. Provide room for expansion in all file drawers and on all file shelves.
   b. Screen out unneeded records during scanning and coding. Don't file unneeded records.
   c. Continue to scan material already in the file. Remove inactive records. Such a "weeding out" requires knowing which folders and/or papers are used for reference and which are not. One way to recognize file inactivity is to make a tally mark on the top edge of a paper or a folder each time it is requested. A lack of tally marks indicates a "dead" folder or letter.
   d. Check file folder capacity frequently. Divide active, overcrowded folders by date, placing the more current dates in front.
   e. Transfer records from active files to inactive or storage files according to a carefully developed transfer program (Chapter 7).
   f. Dispose of records according to the established records retention and distribution schedule (Chapter 7).

8. Select equipment and supplies only after a careful study of the need and probable uses (Chapter 12).

9. Maintain order and neatness in all phases of filing by doing the following:
   a. Type and place captions on guide and folder tabs in a uniform style.
   b. Replace worn folders.
   c. Return folders to the file in neat alignment with folders already in the file. Use compressors in file drawers and supports on shelves to keep folders upright.
   d. Mend torn sheets and straighten "dog ears."
   e. Remove pins and clips from papers before filing.
   f. Keep tops of filing cabinets or shelves clear of all materials.
10. Check general folders regularly and prepare individual folders for active correspondents.
11. Add special subject, geographic, and date sections as needed to make the system more efficient.
12. Do not keep extra copies of materials in the files. Photocopy control is an important part of file maintenance. When copies are needed for distribution, make only the exact number of copies.
13. Follow a plan for charging out and tracing borrowed records.

Manual Charge-Out and Follow-Up of Records

What steps does a complete charge-out and follow-up system include?

Records departments exist to lend records to those who need them. The process must be swift but controlled. Lending must be strictly controlled because some who borrow materials forget to return them. Left unchecked, the results of unreturned file materials are lost papers, frustrated borrowers, and unhappy records personnel. Records may be charged out and followed up by using either a manual- or computer-controlled system.

A complete system for controlling borrowed papers includes procedures for the following steps: (1) requesting records and folders, (2) charging out records and folders, (3) canceling charge-out for returned records, (4) following up on borrowed records, and (5) reserving records.

Requesting Records and Folders

What information is entered on the requisition form?

A request for records may be made over the telephone, in person, or in writing. A **requisition form** is a written request for a record or for information from a record. Generally prepared in duplicate, a requisition form requires entry of specific information about the record or information requested, including (1) the record name or code, (2) the date of the record, (3) the name of the borrower and office, (4) the check-out date of the record, and (5) the due date for return of the record. A sample requisition form is shown in Figure 6-1.

FILE NAME, NUMBER, OR SUBJECT	DONALDSON RICHARD		
CHARGED TO: Amber Weinstein		**DEPT:** Purchasing	**DATE CHARGED** March 19, 20--
COMPLETE FOLDER REMOVED: ☐ **RECORDS REMOVED (DESCRIBE):**			**FOLLOW-UP DATE** April 3, 20--
Letter from Richard Donaldson dated Feb. 4, 20--			

Figure 6-1
Requisition Form

Charging Out Records and Folders

Information requested from the file may be a single paper, an entire folder, a series of papers, or several folders. All records requests require a charge-out system of some kind. A **charge-out** is recorded information that accounts for records that are removed from the files. Methods commonly used to show charged-out records include (1) the OUT guide, (2) the requisition sheet, (3) the OUT folder, and (4) the carrier folder.

Why is a charge-out method necessary?

OUT-Guide Method

An **OUT guide** is a marker placed in the file to show that a folder or records have been borrowed. The two main styles of OUT guides are OUT guides with a pocket and OUT guides with printed lines.

OUT Guide with Pocket

The OUT guide with a pocket is a guide, generally made of vinyl for durability and reuse, with a pocket in the upper right corner to hold a requisition form. (See Figure 6-2.) Follow these procedures when using an OUT guide with a pocket:

1. Place a copy of the requisition form in the pocket.
2. Place the OUT guide in the exact location of the folder, letter, or other records removed from the file. The guide substitutes for the borrowed records.
3. Place a duplicate copy of the requisition form in a follow-up file. The follow-up file is explained later in this chapter.

OUT Guide with Printed Lines

The OUT guide with printed lines (also called an OUT card) is a manila guide with an OUT tab. Information filled in on preprinted lines on the

Figure 6-2
Vinyl OUT Guide
with Pocket
Source: *TAB Products*
Company

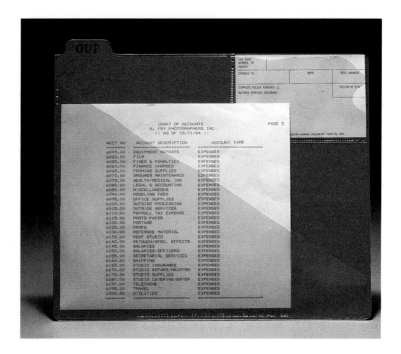

How is the OUT guide used to charge out borrowed records?

guide includes (1) the name of the borrower, (2) a reference to the borrowed materials, and (3) the charge-out date for the records. (See Figure 6-3.) Follow these procedures when using an OUT guide with printed lines:

1. Copy the information from the requisition form to the ruled form of the OUT guide.

2. Replace the folder or papers removed from the file with the OUT guide, which shows who borrowed the records and the charge-out date.

3. Place the requisition form in the follow-up file.

Figures 6-4 and 6-5 show the use of OUT guides in a side-access file and a top-access file. Notice that the prominence of these OUT guides makes it easy to find the correct location when borrowed records are returned to the file.

Requisition Sheet Method

The **requisition sheet** is a request for records that also serves as a marker placed in a folder for charged-out papers. Follow these procedures when using a requisition sheet similar to the one shown in Figure 6-6 on page 98:

1. Prepare two copies of the requisition sheet.

2. Place one copy in the file folder from which you have removed papers; this copy serves as an OUT indicator.

3. File the second copy in the department follow-up file.

Figure 6-3
OUT Guide with Printed Lines

TAKEN BY	NUMBER, SUBDIVISION OR NAME	DATE	TAKEN BY	NUMBER, SUBDIVISION OR NAME	DATE	TAKEN BY	NUMBER, SUBDIVISION OR NAME	DATE

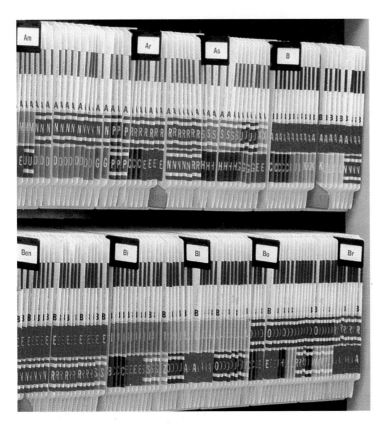

Figure 6-4
OUT Guide in Side-Access File
Source: *The Smead Manufacturing Company*

Figure 6-5
OUT Guide in Top-Access File
Source: *Jeter Systems Corporation*

OUT

To Records Dept.
REQUEST FOR PAPERS
Date Records Wanted __6/21/--__

Description of Records
Date __1/18/--__
Name __M R Conrad__

Address __Phoenix, AZ__

Subject __Matter concerning Bancroft & Serrano__
Requested by __Rose Toshiba__
Department __Administration__

For Records Dept. Use
Return Date __6/25/--__

Figure 6-6
Requisition Sheet

The requisition sheet, generally the size of a sheet of paper, is not a visible marker when scanning the file. Although it identifies papers removed from a folder, the requisition sheet is inappropriate for marking locations of charged-out *folders*.

OUT Folder Method

An **OUT folder** may be used to substitute for a folder that has been removed from the records area. OUT folders, often a distinctive color for quick identification, are of two types: (1) a folder with a clear plastic pocket attached to the inside back flap for insertion of a requisition form (see Figure 6-7) and (2) a folder with a ruled form printed on the front (see Figure 6-8).

When using the pocket-type OUT folder to charge out records, follow these procedures:

1. Prepare the requisition form in duplicate.

2. Place one copy of the form in the clear plastic pocket of the OUT folder and substitute the OUT folder for the original folder.

3. Place the second copy in the follow-up file.

> How does a requisition sheet serve both as a request for records and as an OUT indicator?

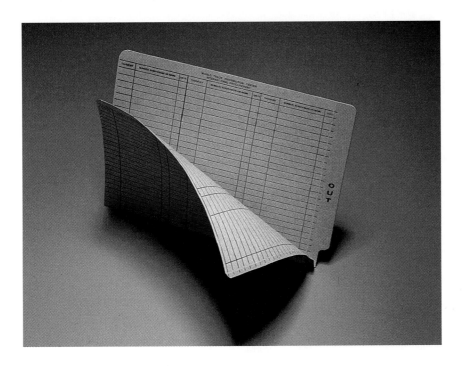

Figure 6-7
OUT Folder with Pocket

OUT

Name or Subject	Date Wanted
Johnson Pearl	*10/26/--*
Re	Date of Letter
Employment	*10/5/--*
Taken by	Date taken
Mark Brown	*10/26/--*
Signed	Dept.
M.B.	*Personnel*
REQUISITION	
	Return Date *11/2/--*

Figure 6-8
OUT Folder with
Printed Lines
Source: *TAB Products Co.*

When using the OUT folder with printed lines to charge out records, follow these procedures:

1. Copy the information from the requisition form to the printed ruled form on the outer face of the OUT folder.

2. Place the OUT folder in the original folder's location in the file.

3. Place the requisition form in a follow-up file.

Regardless of its type, the OUT folder substitutes for the borrowed folder. Until the original folder returns, all materials received for filing are temporarily held in this OUT folder.

Carrier Folder Method

For requests for entire folder contents, consider transferring the folder contents to a carrier folder. A **carrier folder**, made of heavy manila stock and distinctive color, "carries" folder contents to the borrower. Using carrier folders has several advantages over removing and sending regular file folders to borrowers:

How is the carrier folder different from the OUT folder?

1. Carrier folders are more durable than the standard file folders and can withstand the extra handling.

2. Carrier folders, available in distinctive colors, display phrases such as "Return to Files." These distinguishing characteristics help remind borrowers to return the folders to the records department.

3. Original folders remain in place to accept incoming papers. Filing goes on as usual.

When using a carrier folder, remember to use an OUT guide or requisition sheet in the original folder in place of the borrowed records.

Review

1. How does the use of requisition forms differ when charging out records with (1) the OUT guide with printed lines and (2) the OUT guide with a pocket?

2. Compare the use of an OUT folder and a carrier folder.

Canceling Charge-Out for Returned Records

Charge-outs against a borrower are canceled when papers are returned to the files. The method used in the charge-out system determines how to cancel charge outs.

OUT Guides and Folders with Pocket

Why are requisition forms saved when records are returned?

When using OUT guides and folders with pockets, cancel the charge-outs in this manner:

1. Remove the requisition form from the pocket of the OUT guide or OUT folder and destroy the form.

2. Remove the requisition form from the follow-up file and *save* this form. The saved requisition forms help determine which records should remain in the files when transferring inactive records to storage.

3. Upon return of the original folders to the file, transfer, in proper order, all accumulated materials to them.

4. Save the OUT guides and OUT folders for reuse.

OUT Guides and OUT Folders with Printed Lines

When using OUT guides and OUT folders with printed lines, cancel the charges in this manner:

1. Cross out the charge written on the OUT guide or folder when papers are returned.

2. Remove the copy of the requisition form held in the follow-up file to cancel the charge against the borrower. As usual, save the requisition form to document file activity.

3. Save the OUT guides and OUT folders for reuse.

Requisition Sheets

When using requisition sheets, cancel the charges in this manner:

1. Remove the requisition sheet from the file folder and destroy it.

2. Remove the copy of the requisition sheet from the follow-up file and save it. The saved requisition sheet copies help determine which records should remain in the files when transferring inactive records to storage. They are useful, as well, to report to management the activity of the filing system, for example, the percentage of the filed records being accessed daily.

Following Up on Borrowed Records

When you borrow a book from the library, you arrange to keep the book for a certain number of days. You return it on the due date unless you request an extension of time. The library keeps an accurate record of all books borrowed and starts a tracking procedure (a follow-up) if the book is not returned on time. The records department uses a similar procedure. A **follow-up** is a check on the return of borrowed records within a reasonable or specified time. Follow up helps ensure the return of borrowed records.

Why is it necessary to follow up on borrowed records?

Time Limits for Borrowed Records

You achieve control over the return of file materials by establishing time limits for the return of borrowed records. The length of time that records may remain out of the files area varies with the user's needs and company policy—from a few hours to several months.

Time limits vary from one firm to another because of the differences in the value of records or the demand from other borrowers for the same records. Some records held in files are very valuable or they are needed often by other members of the organization. Company rules usually determine that these records may not be borrowed for a period of time greater than one day. Other less valuable records may be borrowed for periods of a week, ten days, or two weeks. In general, it is better to allow relatively short periods of time for the return of records (for example, five working days). The shorter the time permitted, the better the chance of a timely return of borrowed records. Remember, however, that the purpose of filing is to respond to the information needs of your organization. Extend time limits for returning borrowed records when it is evident that the borrower still needs them. Extend the time by writing a new due date on the original requisition or by preparing a new requisition and noting a change of date on all OUT forms held in the main file.

Manual Follow-Up Methods

What are commonly used follow-up methods?

If all borrowed records were returned on time, there would be no need for following up on, or tracking, overdue papers. However, all records do not return on time. Use telephone calls or written reminders to request the return of overdue records. To check for overdue records, use one of three basic methods: (1) scanning the files, (2) maintaining a charge-out log, or (3) using a follow-up file.

Scanning the Files

A simple way to check the due dates of borrowed materials is to scan the files for OUT guides and folders and check the due dates. This method works for a relatively small and inactive filing system. For example, when the filing area consists of approximately five cabinets or sections and when about two percent of the total records are filed or retrieved from the system daily, the scanning method may be appropriate for identifying past-due charge-outs.

Maintaining a Charge-Out Log

The charge-out log, shown in Figure 6-9, is a simple follow-up method for records departments with 6 to 15 cabinets or shelf sections. A **charge-out log** keeps a running record of borrowed file materials. Upon receipt or preparation of records requisitions, post the data from these requisitions to the charge-out log. The charge-out log requires information about each borrowed record: (1) record description, (2) borrower's name, (3) charge-out date, (4) due date for return, (5) date actually returned, (6) date for sending overdue notice, if necessary, and (7) a new extended date, if necessary. Upon return of borrowed materials, record the return date on the charge-out log.

Using a Follow-Up File

The follow-up file is a means of checking on borrowed records to ensure that they are returned by a specified time. In a large records department, a follow-up file is a convenient method for tracking papers that are overdue; it is also helpful in completing on time a variety of time-related office tasks.

CHARGE-OUT LOG

Name on Borrowed Record	Date of Record	Name of Person or Department Borrowing Record	Date Borrowed	Date Due	Date Returned	Date Overdue Notice Sent	Extended Date
Desoto Auto Repair	3-1	Bill Hartman	3-6	3-11	3-11		
Applications Word Processing Lute, Renee	2-24	Michelle Nienkemper	3-7	3-12	3-8		
Mom's Restaurant	1-4	E. Kinworthy	3-8			3-14	3-16
St. Charles' Graphics	2-20	James Daniel	3-10	3-15			

Figure 6-9
Charge-Out Log

You will recall that requisition forms and OUT slips are prepared in duplicate. One copy of the form goes into the main file. The other goes into a follow-up file behind the due date for the record. Study the follow-up file shown in Figure 6-10.

The follow-up file consists of 12 monthly primary guides and one set of 31 secondary guides captioned for days in the month. File requisition copies behind the due date. After checking and processing the requisitions held behind the date guide each day, move the date guide for that day to the next-month section. Thus, the daily guides keep advancing. Unless a large volume of OUT forms must be handled, a single set of daily guides is generally sufficient.

The follow-up file is sometimes called a *tickler file* because it "tickles" the mind to remember to follow up! To use any follow-up file effectively, be sure to enter all future events that you want to remember *and* check the file every day to see what needs to be done that day.

Eliminating Follow-Up
No matter how carefully you follow charge-out and follow-up procedures, important papers may be misplaced in transit or accidentally destroyed. Use of the office copier to send copies of records to the borrower rather than the original guards against such calamities. With this method, remove the requested record from the folder only long enough to be copied. Refile the original and send the copy to the borrower with instructions to destroy it after use. This copying method is practical for requests for a single letter or a few related papers.

Why is the follow-up file sometimes called a "tickler file"?

When is no follow-up necessary?

Figure 6-10
Follow-Up File

Reserving Records

The records department may receive advance requests for records needed at a future date. One way to ensure the delivery of the requested records when they are needed is to place a requisition form behind the appropriate date in the follow-up file. Placing an OUT guide or requisition sheet in the main file showing the date the records are needed is a good idea also. This additional step keeps others from borrowing the records during reserved times.

Use a similar procedure for requests made for records already checked out. Prepare in duplicate a requisition form with a notation to send the materials to the next person upon return of the records. Place one copy of the requisition behind the due date in the follow-up file; attach the second copy to an OUT guide placed in the main file.

Review

1. Name three manual follow-up methods.
2. Explain when a follow-up method is not needed.
3. Explain the use of an OUT guide or a requisition sheet when reserving records for use at a future date.

Electronic Charge-Out and Follow-Up of Records

The computer has changed performance procedures for many office tasks. It should be no surprise then that the charge-out and follow-up for controlling borrowed records can be "computerized" as well. By using a computer keyboard or a barcode scanner, information normally recorded on requisitions can be keyed or scanned into the computer instead.

Using the Computer for Charge-Out and Follow-Up Systems

Computer software programs can identify and track any record from creation or receipt to transfer to inactive storage or destruction. These computer programs will track unlimited numbers of records and produce a variety of useful reports such as file inventories, file activity, records retention periods, and records destruction dates. The computer even generates notices to those with overdue records.

Using Barcode Charge-Out and Follow-Up Systems

Since the first barcodes appeared in supermarkets in the early 1950s, barcoding has taken over the gathering of data in virtually every industry in the world. Barcoding is a fast and accurate means of gathering and transmitting data to a computer. No small wonder that barcoding has found its way into the business office to eliminate the tedious, error-prone manual tasks of file tracking. **File tracking** is a method of knowing where charged-out records are when you need them. In general, a complete barcoding system includes four components: (1) the barcodes, (2) a barcode reader, (3) a recharger/downloader, and (4) a personal computer and software.

What are the four components of a barcode tracking system?

Barcodes

TAB Products Co. provides preprinted barcodes in self-adhesive label form. Each barcode is unique but does not contain any specific document information. Identifying information unique to each record must be entered into the computer. Then the record is assigned to a particular preprinted barcode label to be affixed to the record. A barcode label is shown in Figure 6-11. A barcode must be assigned to all users of the system as well. If preprinted barcode labels are not used, then labels must be prepared. Barcode labels can be prepared on a computer using an available barcode labeler program or on a stand-alone, portable barcode label printer.

Figure 6-11
Barcode Label
Source: *TAB Products Co.*

Barcode Scanners

Barcode scanners, or readers, are the barcode data collection devices. Portable, hand-held, and battery-powered, the barcode scanner passes over the barcodes, storing up to 3,000 scans before downloading into the computer and recharging is necessary. Figure 6-12 shows the FILE TRACKER datawand, a portable barcode reader.

Recharger/Downloader

The recharger/downloader device transfers the data from the portable, hand-held scanner to the computer. When the scanner is connected to the recharger/downloader, the data stored in the scanner is downloaded (transmitted) to the computer and the power batteries in the scanner are recharged.

Figure 6-12
FILE TRACKER
Datawand and
Recharger/Downloader
Source: *TAB Products Co.*

Personal Computer and Software

The computer and the software convert the scanned data into useful information. For example, upon request for a folder or paper, the record barcode and the borrower's barcode are scanned. When scanner data are downloaded to the computer, a variety of useful information may be computer-generated. With just a few keystrokes, FILE TRACKER displays who has the record, how long the record has been charged out, and when the record is due back. The FILE TRACKER not only locates files, but it also provides other critical records management information such as: (1) how often a file is used, (2) when a file was last used, (3) when a file should be destroyed, and (4) how many files exist for a particular person or company. In addition, reports can be generated showing "past due" notices, missing files, and total files activity.

Summary

File maintenance and control are important responsibilities in any filing system. Worn-out folders should be replaced; overcrowded folders should be weeded out and/or divided.

Charge-out procedures track borrowed records, and a follow-up system controls their return. A manual system of charge-out and follow-up requires requisitions and some form of OUT indicators. A follow-up file is also necessary unless the filing system is relatively small and inactive.

Setting up an electronic charge-out and follow-up system for records control requires more time and money than a manual system. In addition to providing file location information, electronic systems can generate "past due" notices and report on total files activity. Electronic document management systems provide faster and more accurate records control and are cost-effective for large, active filing systems.

✔ Terminology Review

carrier folder	(p. 100)
charge-out	(p. 95)
charge-out log	(p. 102)
file tracking	(p. 105)
follow-up	(p. 101)
OUT folder	(p. 98)
OUT guide	(p. 95)
requisition form	(p. 94)
requisition sheet	(p. 96)

Questions for Discussion

1. List five practices that help to ensure good file maintenance. (Obj. 1)

2. What are the five steps that make up a complete charge-out and follow-up system for controlling the use of filed records? (Obj. 2)

3. What information is needed on the requisition form? (Obj. 3)

4. Explain the use of the requisition form in a manual charge-out and follow-up system. (Obj. 2)

5. What are the four methods commonly used for charging out borrowed records? (Obj. 2)

6. Explain how the uses of the OUT guide and the OUT folder are alike and how they are different. (Obj. 2)

7. What are two advantages of using a carrier folder? (Obj. 2)

8. How are the charges canceled when borrowed materials are returned to the files? Assume you are using the OUT guide with a pocket method. (Obj. 3)

9. What factors determine the length of time records should be charged out? (Obj. 4)

10. Name the three methods for following up on, or tracking, papers not returned to the file when expected. (Obj. 5)

11. How does the follow-up file help to follow up on records borrowed from the files? (Obj. 5)

12. Is it possible to release records from the files without a charge-out or follow-up plan? Why or why not? (Obj. 6)

13. Why is it necessary to reserve records for later use? How is this done? (Obj. 7)

14. List the four components of a barcode charge-out and follow-up system. What is the function of each component? (Obj. 9)

15. What advantages does an electronic charge-out and follow-up system have over a manual one? (Obj. 8)

Practice Set Application

At this time, complete Job 8, *Requisition and Charge-Out Procedures*, in OFFICE FILING PROCEDURES, Eighth Edition. Instructions and supplies for this job are included in the practice set.

Chapter Seven

Retention, Transfer, and Disposition Procedures

Learning Objectives

After completing Chapter 7, you will be able to do the following:

1. Define **records retention.**

2. Define a **records inventory** and list information to collect during a records inventory.

3. Define **vital, important, useful,** and **nonessential** records.

4. Define **active, inactive,** and **long-term** records.

5. Describe active, inactive, and long-term records storage.

6. Define **archives**.

7. Define and use a **records retention and destruction schedule.**

8. Define **records transfer** and describe records transfer methods.

9. List supplies and equipment used for transferring records.

10. Describe an index used in an inactive records center.

11. Describe three control files used in an inactive records center.

Records Retention

As you learned from Chapter 1, some records have value to an organization longer than others. In a busy office, records can accumulate to an overwhelming volume. For example, an architectural firm of twenty architects who are each working on five design projects may create or receive from 100 to over 1,000 records each day. Imagine the filing that is required daily just to keep up! Without records control, records gradually take over valuable work space. Part of records control is a records retention policy. **Records retention** is the established policy and procedure for determining what records to keep, where to keep them, and how long to keep them.

In Chapters 2 through 6, you have been working with records in the maintenance phase of the records cycle—filing and retrieving. The disposition phase (transferring, retaining, or destroying) of the records cycle is discussed in Chapter 7. Manual transfer procedures are the focus of Chapter 7. With the use of barcodes, as discussed in Chapter 6, all folders, boxes, and other transfer containers can be tracked throughout the disposition phase. A fully automated records system often reduces the number of lost records.

Department managers and records department staff establish records retention policies that are based on legal and practical guidelines. The legal department or counsel and upper management must approve the recommended policies. A *records inventory and analysis* should be conducted to obtain information needed to prepare a records retention and destruction schedule.

How do records retention policies help control records?

Records Inventory and Analysis

A **records inventory** is a survey conducted to find the types and volume of filed records, their location, and frequency of use. An inventory is the first step in preparing an accurate records retention and destruction schedule. The records inventory also provides information about the company's records so that the appropriate filing method (alphabetic, numeric, geographic, or subject) can be selected. Information collected during the inventory usually includes the following:

What procedure is used to identify all records in an organization?

Location of records by department or office.

Name of records series.

Dates of records series.

Location by building, floor, and room, if needed.

Type of equipment used—cabinets, shelves, or vaults.

Number of cabinets, shelves, and other storage containers.

Rate of reference—daily, weekly, monthly, or annually—and why.

Records media—paper, microfilm, electronic, or optical.

Size of the records—letter, legal, tab/checks, EDP, or other.

Housing—folders, binders, cassettes, etc.

Value—vital, important, useful, or nonessential.

Retention requirements.

A form for recording the necessary records data will make collection run smoothly. The sample inventory form in Figure 7-1 is completed by each department. Records are identified on this form by series. A **records series** is a group of related records that normally are used and filed as a unit to determine the records retention period. For example, in an accounting department, the accounts payable records for January 1 through December 31, 2006, are a records series.

Figure 7-1 Records Inventory Worksheet

RECORDS INVENTORY WORKSHEET — INVENTORIED BY: *Andrew Matheson* — EXTENSION: *424* — DATE: *6/25/00*

DEPT. NO.	DEPT. NAME	SERIES NO.	RECORDS SERIES NAME
305	*Legal*	*1900*	*Litigation*

DATES FROM	DATES TO	SEQ.	FILE ORDER & LIMITS BY	RANGE	LOCATION BLDG.	LOCATION FLOOR	LOCATION ROOM	EQUIPMENT TYPE	EQUIPMENT QUANTITY	CUBIC FEET	REFERENCE WKLY.	REFERENCE MO/CU.FT.	ACTION
1/1 95	*12/31 95*		*case no.*		*2*	*2*	*206*	*Cab*	*4*		—		
1/1 96	*12/31 96*		*case no.*		*2*	*2*	*206*	*Cab*	*2*		—	—	
1/1 97	*12/31 97*		*case no.*		*2*	*2*	*206*	*Cab*	*3*		—	—	
1/1 98	*12/31 98*		*case no.*		*2*	*2*	*206*	*Cab*	*4*		—	—	
1/1 99	*12/31 99*		*case no.*		*2*	*2*	*206*	*Cab*	*4*			✓	
1/1 00	*6/1 00*		*case no.*		*2*	*2*	*203*	*Cab*	*2*		✓		

SERIES SPAN

YEAR STARTED	YEAR ENDED
1995	*2000*

MICROFILM APPLICATION

ELIGIBLE AFTER	SYSTEM
1 yr after case closed	*Microfiche*

ACTION

TRANSFERRED	DESTROYED
CU.FT.	CU.FT.

SAVINGS

EQUIPMENT	SPACE

DESCRIPTION & USE: *Case files for litigation in these cases are closed.*

FORMS

RETENTION REQUIREMENTS

OPERATING	OFFICE *5*	TOTAL *20*
LEGAL	TOTAL *20*	SOURCE *state statute*
TAX	*7*	
AUDIT	*7*	

MEDIUM: ☒ PAPER; ☐ MICROFILM (☐ ROLL, ☐ JACKET, ☐ FICHE, ☐ COM, ☐ APERTURE); ☒ MAGNETIC MEDIA (☐ CARD, ☐ TAPE, ☒ DISK); ☐ ______

USE: ☐ INTRA.DEPT.; ☐ INTER. DEPT.

SIZE: ☒ LETTER 8 1/2 X 11; ☒ LEGAL 8 1/2 X 14; ☐ TAB/CHECK 3 X 7 1/2; ☐ EDP 14 X 17; ☐ ______

HOUSING: ☒ FOLDERS; ☐ BINDERS (☐ RING, ☐ POST); ☐ LOOSE; ☐ ______

TYPE: ☐ TRANSACTION; ☐ SUBJECT (☐ FILE PLAN); ☐ REPORTS; ☐ GRAPHIC (PLAN, MAP, ETC.); ☒ *case files*

SERIES CLOSED: ☐ ANNUALLY; ☐ EXPIRATION; ☒ *when case is closed*

AUDIT: ☐ TAX; ☒ INTERNAL

COPY: ☒ RECORD; ☐ DUPLICATE; ☐ INFORMATION

SERIES SUMMARIZED

VALUE: ☐ VITAL; ☐ HISTORICAL; ☐ MICROFILMED WHEN? ______

RECOMMENDED POLICY

OFFICE	STORAGE	TOTAL
1	*5*	*20*

POLICY REVIEW

	SIGNED	DATE
OPERATING	*A.K. Simmons*	*7-15-00*
LEGAL	*Lee Moore*	*7-21-00*
TAX	*Anne De Vore*	*8-3-00*
AUDIT	*Jana Trent*	*8-10-00*
RECORDS MGMT.	*Carlos Diaz*	*8-25-00*

APPROVED POLICY

OFFICE	STORAGE	TOTAL
1	*5*	*20*

After the records inventory has been completed, analysis of the inventory information takes place. This analysis determines the value of records from creation through active, inactive, and final destruction phases. Records analysis provides the basis for establishing the retention periods and destruction procedures. To determine which records to keep or destroy, you need to know their value and purpose. The purposes of records—*administrative, fiscal, legal,* and *historical*—are defined and described in Chapter 1. The value of records follows.

Why are records kept and used?

The Value of Records

Records are one of the most important assets of an organization because they provide the memory of what happened in the past—the history. Each record in an organization is evaluated and classified as vital, important, useful, or nonessential to the organization. Each category refers to the information value and to the length of time that a record should be retained (kept).

Vital records are the recorded information that is essential for the continuation or reconstruction of an organization after a disaster. These records establish the legal and financial position of the organization and are irreplaceable. Articles of incorporation, patents, formulas, accounts receivable records, inventory lists, contracts, and other legal papers are examples of vital records. Vital records generally are stored in the active records area in fireproof safes or vaults. Access, however, is restricted to a selected list of users.

Why are vital records stored in fireproof safes or vaults?

Important records relate to the daily operations and are necessary for continuation of an organization. Examples of important records are accounts payable records, tax records, sales records, payroll records, and some correspondence records. These records may be replaced but at considerable cost and inconvenience. Important records are stored in safes and vaults in active or inactive storage areas.

Useful records are of limited, but helpful, reference value. They may have entered the system with limited reference value or their value may have decreased over time. Useful records may be replaced at some inconvenience, but their loss would not seriously impair daily operations. Bank statements and general correspondence, such as letters and memos, may be destroyed after their value has declined. These records are stored in file cabinets or on shelves in inactive storage areas until the time for their destruction.

Are important records replaceable?

Which useful records may be destroyed?

Nonessential records may never have had any value or have no present value to the organization. They should be destroyed after use. Routine memos, announcements and bulletins to employees, and telephone messages that have been answered are nonessential records. Electronic mail (e-mail) messages that have been received and responded to should be purged from the computer system too. Nonessential e-mail messages take up disk space. Nonessential records should never be kept. If, however, someone cannot let go of routine pieces of paper, a special

What records are nonessential?

file folder may serve as temporary storage. Periodic reviews of this folder usually will result in the destruction of some nonessential records.

Records that have become nonessential over time should be sent to an inactive records area and destroyed according to the records retention and destruction schedule. Control and maintenance of the records transfer and retention policies will prevent long-term storage of nonessential records.

1 Review

1. Why are records retention policies necessary?

2. How are records values determined?

Records Accessibility

Records are maintained, transferred, stored, and destroyed according to the information they provide to the organization. Records that are referred to most frequently are maintained differently from those records that require infrequent or no reference. *Active, inactive,* and *long-term* are terms used to describe records activity.

An **active record** is used regularly: three or more times a month. Because of their frequent usage, active records are stored in easily accessible locations as shown in Figure 7-2. Accessibility to the user is essential for active records. If file cabinets or shelves are used, active records are stored in the most accessible drawers or on the most accessible shelves.

An **inactive record** is used less than 15 times a year. Because inactive records are accessed less often than active records, they occupy the least accessible drawers and shelves—the upper and lower drawers and shelves, for example. Inactive records are often stored in another location where floor space is less costly. They may also be packed in storage boxes or cases and sent to a storage center. (See Figure 7-3.) The company may own the storage center, or it may rent space in a commercial records center. A commercial records center may be a large warehouse or it may be an underground facility. Wherever the records are stored, boxes are stacked eight or more high, and aisles can be narrow—about 30 inches across.

A **long-term record** is inactive but continues to have value to the organization. Long-term records may be kept for legal or historical purposes and are stored indefinitely or for a specified period of time. Long-term storage often is referred to as archival storage or *archives.* **Archives** is a permanent storage place for records. *Archival* is a term used to identify the life expectancy of records. *Life expectancy* or *archival* may apply to the medium or the data stored on the medium. Depending on the value of the records, long-term records may be stored in boxes or in vaults, but archives are stored separately from other inactive records.

How often are active records used?

How often are inactive records used?

Retention and Destruction Schedule

The decision to store or destroy records is based on a records retention and destruction schedule. A **records retention and destruction schedule** is an established timetable for maintaining records, transferring inactive records to storage, and destroying records with short-term value. Legal requirements, state and federal government requirements, as well as company retention requirements form the basis for the number of months or years to retain certain records.

What is the basis for storing or destroying records?

A records retention program reduces storage costs and increases retrieval efficiency. Destruction or transfer of unneeded records to less costly storage reduces costs. Time spent searching through a massive accumulation of old records is also costly. Transferring and destroying records at regularly scheduled intervals eliminates clutter and shortens retrieval time.

Guidelines for establishing a records retention program and developing a records retention and destruction schedule are available from several sources. The U.S. Government publishes the *Guide to Records Retention Requirements,* which may be obtained from the Superintendent of Documents, U.S. Government Printing Office. Each state also has retention guidelines for certain records. Donald S. Skupsky's well-researched and detailed book, *Recordkeeping Requirements,* is available from Information Requirements Clearinghouse, 3801 East Florida Avenue, Suite 400, Denver, CO 80210.

Records retention and destruction timetables are based on the *information* contained in the records and not on the media itself. Retention and destruction schedules include electronic, optical, and microrecords along with paper records.

A portion of a records retention and destruction schedule is shown in Figure 7-4. Records are identified on this schedule by the information contained in the records. Active records are retained in the originating office until they are transferred to the records center. Note that some records, such as general correspondence and telephone messages, are never transferred to an inactive records center. Some records are retained permanently (P), some for 30 days (30D), and some just for the actual time (ACT) that they are needed. Catalogs, for example, usually are not considered records for most organizations and are needed only for a short time. Study the schedule carefully.

Figure 7-4 Records Retention and Destruction Schedule

RECORDS RETENTION AND DESTRUCTION SCHEDULE

| Office of Record | Record Name | Retention Periods | | |
		Yrs. in Office	Yrs. in Center	Total Years
Accounting	Accounts Payable	03	03	06
Accounting	Accounts Receivable	03	03	06
Accounting	General Journals	03	03	06
Accounting	Payroll Records	03	03	06
Administration	Deeds	03	P	P
Administration	General Correspondence	01	—	01
Administration	Maintenance Records	01	—	01
Administration	Telephone Messages	30D	—	30D
Finance	Audit Reports	03	—	03
Finance	Bank Deposits	03	03	06
Finance	Budgets	01	—	01
Human Resources	Attendance Records	01	—	01
Human Resources	Retirement Benefits	03	P	P
Legal	General Contracts	03	17	20
Legal	Product Warranties	03	17	20
Public Relations	Advertising	01	—	01
Purchasing	Catalogs	ACT	—	ACT
Purchasing	Purchase Orders	03	03	06
Sales	Orders	01	—	01
Shipping	Bills of Lading	01	—	01

ACT—Actual time used

D—Days

P—Permanent

Source: Adapted from Donald S. Skupsky, Recordkeeping Requirements, Information Requirements Clearinghouse, Denver, Colo., 1988, pp. 101–110.

Records Transfer

Records transfer is the process of moving inactive records from the office to inactive or archive storage areas. In records departments, active files occupy the most accessible drawers and shelves. As new records are received, folders become crowded, and some records become less useful. Consequently, less active records are moved out, or transferred, to allow efficient access to the more active records.

Regular transfer of records reduces volume and storage equipment costs. Many businesses don't have records retention and destruction schedules and don't transfer and destroy records regularly. Consequently, the volume of records becomes overwhelming, filing and retrieval are slowed, and unnecessary purchases of additional equipment often are made.

Perpetual transfer and periodic transfer are two commonly used methods of transferring records. The volume and use of the active records determines which method to use. Records identified as inactive during the records inventory and analysis are transferred immediately. After the inventory, records in the active system identified as inactive are transferred on a periodic or perpetual basis, according to the records retention and destruction schedule.

Why are records transferred?

Perpetual Transfer

The **perpetual transfer method** is a *continuous* process of moving records from active to inactive storage areas. In offices where work is completed in units, such as in an architectural firm, a medical office, or a legal office, all records relating to a completed job or case can be transferred at the same time. After the job or case is completed, use of the records drops immediately, and these records are moved to inactive storage. The perpetual transfer method is not recommended for frequently accessed correspondence or other records.

Periodic Transfer

The **periodic transfer method** is a procedure for moving records at stated intervals from active to inactive storage areas. Many organizations

---

transfer records at the end of their fiscal year. Entire folders of records are transferred to inactive storage. New folders are prepared for new active records that will accumulate until the next transfer period. However, the guides are not transferred; therefore, new ones aren't needed. In the inactive storage area, the general folders serve as guides because their captions are the same as the guides.

Regularly transferring records at the end of one period of time, usually once or twice a year, is commonly done. When using the **one-period transfer method**, *one entire period of records,* such as six months or one year, are transferred at one time. Entire folders of records may or may not be transferred. Each office reviews its records and transfers its inactive records at the same time. Records to be transferred will carry dates that fall within the period of time being transferred, such as January 1 through June 30, 2005, or January 1 to December 31, 2006. If records for January through June are transferred at the end of June, records for July through December must be transferred during a second scheduled transfer.

A move to inactive storage of records that were received just prior to the transfer and that may still be active is inconvenient and a disadvantage of this method. Records may be retrieved from both active and inactive storage if the requested records cover more than one time period. For example, a folder for the Tabuchi Camera Company was transferred in July of last year. More records accumulated from July to December, and a new folder was established in the active records area. To access all records for the Tabuchi Camera Company, the user would retrieve the folders from both active and inactive records areas.

Review

1. Why are records transferred from active to inactive storage?

2. What determines which transfer method to use?

Transfer Procedures

What are the five steps in the transfer process?

The transfer process involves five steps: (1) determining when records are to be transferred, (2) determining what records are to be transferred, (3) preparing records for transfer, (4) arranging the transfer, and (5) receiving records in the storage area. Organizational policy usually determines when records are transferred. The records retention and destruction schedule determines which records to transfer. Each department and office must follow the policy and identify which of its records will be transferred, according to the schedule.

When a decision to transfer records has been made, transmittal forms are completed, the records are boxed, and the storage center is notified. Adequate equipment and storage space must be available in the inactive storage area before the records are transferred. When the records manager is assured that equipment and space are available and that the records center staff is ready to receive the records, the transfer process may begin.

A records transmittal form, similar to the one shown in Figure 7-5, is prepared for each box to be transferred. Information about a series of records contained in several boxes may be recorded on a multi-copy form, completed by the transmitting department. This department retains one copy, and two copies accompany the box. The box is logged in at the inactive records center, and the storage location (aisle and shelf) is recorded on the transfer form. A copy of the form is returned to the sending department and retained for reference when records in the box are requested.

Note that records retention and destruction information is supplied on the form in Figure 7-5 according to the established retention and destruction schedule. The form in this example requires a records disposal authorization number (Column 4). The department records retention and destruction schedule identifies departmental records by number, which is recorded in Column 5. The records management department will record the location of the records in the records center (Column 7), the retention period (Column 8), the disposal year (Column 9), and a check mark or date when the records are disposed of (Column 10).

Figure 7-5 Records Transmittal Form

BOX NUMBER		DESCRIPTION OF RECORDS (exact description of contents of each box)	REC DISP AUTH NO	DEPT SCHED ITEM NO	YEAR OF RECORD		LOCATION IN RECORDS CTR.	RET PER	DISP YEAR	DISP
CURRENT YEAR	SEQUENTIAL NUMBER				BEG	END				
20--	1530	Accounts payable invoices & ledgers	106	ACC100	00	01				
20--	1531	Depreciation schedules, mortgage	106	ACC200	00	01				
		payments, property records								
20--	1532	Payroll accounting records	106	ACC300	00	01				

TRANSMITTAL OF RECORDS TO RECORDS CENTER

Page 1 of 1

DEPARTMENT Administration
OFFICE Accounting
ADDRESS Farrar Bldg., Rm 102

Please type or print.

SHADED AREAS FOR RECORDS MGMT. USE ONLY

11. DATE TRANSFERRED 1/10/- -
SIGNATURE OF PERSON RELEASING RECORDS C. R. Gregson
TELEPHONE X3264
RECEIVED IN RECORDS CENTER BY: Al Marcos
DATE 1/10/- -

FORM 10 (REV. 92) DISTRIBUTION: WHITE & YELLOW – RECORDS CENTER; PINK – FILE COPY

Transfer Supplies and Equipment

The active records center and the inactive storage center use the same components and controls for locating and releasing stored records. Such control requires that storage locations be identified, that boxes be labeled, and that the records be controlled and maintained from one central location or desk. An index of records in the storage center, records request forms, charge-out and follow-up procedures, and destruction procedures are necessary for controlling inactive records.

In large storage areas or records centers, the aisles, shelf sections, and boxes have assigned location numbers. These numbers are written on box labels as well as on records control forms or cards held at the control desk. For example, a box location might be: Aisle 4, Section 12, Box 325.

Transfer Boxes and Labels

Transfer boxes used for inactive storage usually have lift-off or lift-up tops. Removable tops allow quick access for filing and retrieving records. Legal records often are stored in boxes with fold-down tops. A fastener holds the top in place and prevents dust from entering the box.

Some transfer boxes are designed with label information on one end. Contents and location information are marked directly on the box. Labels identifying the contents and providing location information also may be affixed to the box. Whatever kind of labeling is used, complete content and location information is needed in order to file accurately and to retrieve quickly any requested information. Two of the boxes shown on the left in Figure 7-6 have lift-off tops. The small box has a fold-over top and a label printed on one end. The box on the right is a legal box and has a fold-over top.

Figure 7-6 Transfer Boxes
Source: *Fellowes Manufacturing Company*

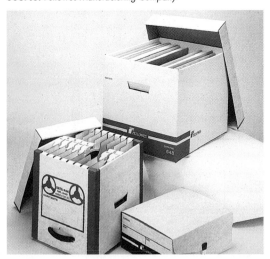

Guides and Folders

Guides used in active files are not transferred to inactive storage with the transferred records. General folders, which have the same labels as guides, can serve as guides for locating folders in inactive storage.

Plastic folders, if used, stay in the active files. They are more expensive than manila folders, and such an expense isn't warranted for transfer to inactive files. Manila folders need to be prepared to replace plastic folders in the transfer file.

Organizations that transfer large volumes of records often transfer hanging folders along with the records. They do so because removing the files from the hanging folders takes more time and therefore increases labor costs. Employee time and wage cost savings exceed the cost of replacing the hanging folders. Employee costs are often the highest costs of filing and retrieving records.

Equipment

Inactive storage centers use less expensive storage equipment, usually steel shelving. The shelving may reach to the ceiling, as in a warehouse. Remember that *air space is less expensive than floor space.* Rolling ladders or high-rise order pickers (motorized lifts) may be used to raise records center staff to the highest shelves to store and retrieve boxes.

What is a high-rise order picker?

Review

1. Why is a transmittal form used when records are transferred to storage?
2. What differences exist among active records supplies and equipment and inactive records supplies and equipment?

Control Files in Storage Center Operations

Four types of control files are required for maintaining order in inactive storage operations: (1) an inactive records index for locating and retrieving stored records, (2) a charge-out and follow-up file, (3) a destruction date file, and (4) a destruction file. Each of these files is discussed in this section.

Inactive Records Index

The **inactive records index** is an index of all records in the inactive storage center. Sometimes called the *master control file,* it is maintained at a central location or desk. The index contains the same information as the

Why is an index needed for inactive records?

records transmittal form shown in Figure 7-5 on page 119. Contents of storage boxes, locations, dates of the records, retention periods, and disposal information are part of the index. Records centers that use transmittal forms such as the one shown in Figure 7-5 record all information on that form. Specially designed multi-copy index cards may be completed by records center personnel. One copy is affixed to the box, one copy is stored in the index, another copy is stored in the destruction data file (discussed below). However, the index usually is maintained in a computer.

If a card system is used for the index, the cards are filed alphabetically by departments. Primary guides show department names such as ACCOUNTING, ADMINISTRATION, HUMAN RESOURCES, and MANUFACTURING. Secondary guides show the types of records stored in the center and may be labeled CORRESPONDENCE, PURCHASE ORDERS, ACCOUNTS RECEIVABLES, and so on. Secondary guides also may include any records series dates.

Requests for records from the records center may be received by the center on special request forms or taken over the telephone. A telephone request requires that records center personnel complete the proper request form.

When the Accounting Department requests the accounts receivable records for July 1 through December 31, 2004, the filer scans the index. The index card is located behind the ACCOUNTING primary guide and the ACCOUNTS RECEIVABLE (dates) secondary guide. Location information from this card is written on a routing slip and placed in the transfer box. The box is opened, and the requested records are removed and sent to the requester. One copy of the multi-copy request form is placed in the box on an OUT guide to show that records have been removed. One copy of the request form is attached to the borrowed records. The final copy is placed in the charge-out and follow-up file.

Charge-Out and Follow-Up File

Charge-out and follow-up procedures are necessary in inactive records centers as well as in active records areas. The **charge-out and follow-up file** is a tickler file that contains request forms filed by dates that records are due back in the inactive records center. Written reminders, telephone calls, or e-mail messages are used to notify users that records should be returned to the center.

Destruction Date File

The **destruction date file** is a tickler file containing copies of index cards or forms completed when records are received in the inactive records center. Destruction schedules for various types of records are determined before the records are transferred and recorded on these forms. The cards/forms are filed according to the destruction dates assigned to the records.

Before records are destroyed, authorization to destroy is obtained. The manager of the department whose records are to be destroyed signs an authorization form that is maintained in the records center. Note that on the transmittal form in Figure 7-5, a records disposal authorization number is requested when the records are transferred. If a written authorization is already on file in the records center, the number on that form is all that is needed. Records may be destroyed by shredding, pulping (shredded and mixed with water, then bailed), sold for recycling, or other legally approved means.

Destruction File

The **destruction file** contains information on the actual destruction of inactive records. Records destruction must be witnessed or certified proof of the destruction provided. Forms held in the destruction date file are transferred to the destruction file after the records are destroyed. These records are filed by department names and dates of destruction of records.

5 Review

1. List four control files used in a records center.

2. Why do you think destruction controls are needed?

The need for controlling records in the active and inactive storage areas cannot be stressed too strongly. Through your study of *Business Records Control,* you will learn how to avoid problems resulting from failure to transfer and control records. You will know how to solve records problems before they become catastrophes.

Summary

A records retention policy is needed to prevent an overwhelming accumulation of an organization's records. Records retention is the established policy and procedure for determining what records to keep, where to keep them, and how long to keep them. In order to learn about the organization's records—what kinds of records, how many records, and where they are stored—a records inventory must be performed. From the inventory, the records manager will be able to determine the records storage needs, what filing method (alphabetic, subject, numeric, or geographic) should be used, and what records need to be destroyed or transferred to other storage.

The records inventory also will identify records that are vital, important, useful, and nonessential as well as those records that are active, inactive, or long-term. This information will form the basis for preparing a records retention and destruction schedule—an established timetable for maintaining records, transferring inactive records to storage, and destroying records that are of short-term value.

Records transfer is the process of moving inactive records from the office to inactive or archive storage areas. Records are transferred to provide more space for active files and to use less expensive storage equipment and facilities. The perpetual transfer method is a continuous process of moving records from active to inactive storage areas. The periodic transfer method is a procedure for moving records at stated intervals from active to inactive storage areas. The one-period transfer, in which one entire period of records is transferred at one time (usually once a year or once every six months), is often used.

Records transfer requires the use of transfer boxes and labels, using general folders as guides in inactive storage, and less expensive storage equipment. Control files used in the inactive storage center include an inactive records index, a charge-out and follow-up file, a destruction date file, and a destruction file.

Terminology Review

active record	(p. 114)
archives	(p. 114)
charge-out and follow-up file	(p. 122)
destruction date file	(p. 122)
destruction file	(p. 123)
important records	(p. 113)
inactive record	(p. 114)
inactive records index	(p. 122)
long-term record	(p. 114)
nonessential records	(p. 113)
one-period transfer method	(p. 118)
periodic transfer method	(p. 117)
perpetual transfer method	(p. 117)
records inventory	(p. 111)
records retention	(p. 111)
records retention and destruction schedule	(p. 115)
records series	(p. 112)
records transfer	(p. 117)
useful records	(p. 113)
vital records	(p. 113)

Questions for Discussion

1. Define *records retention*. (Obj. 1)
2. Define a *records inventory* and list information to collect during a records inventory. (Obj. 2)
3. Define *vital, important, useful,* and *nonessential* records. (Obj. 3)
4. Define *active, inactive,* and *long-term* records. (Obj. 4)
5. Describe active, inactive, and long-term records storage. (Obj. 5)
6. What are archives? (Obj. 6)
7. Define a *records retention and destruction schedule.* (Obj. 7)
8. Why do you think you will use a records retention and destruction schedule when you are responsible for a records management program? (Obj. 7)
9. Define *records transfer* and describe records transfer methods. (Obj. 8)
10. List supplies and equipment used for transferring records. (Obj. 9)
11. Describe the inactive records index. (Obj. 10)
12. Describe three control files used in an inactive records center. (Obj. 11)

► Applications

Use a separate sheet of paper to answer questions about the retention of certain records according to the records retention and destruction schedule in Figure 7-4. Assume that these questions arise at the beginning of the new year when the one-period transfer usually is done. The *Yrs. in Office* Column shows how long to retain records in the active area. (Obj. 7)

1. Two boxes of general correspondence dated January 1 to June 30 and July 1 to December 31 of last year should be retained until what date and where?

2. Bank deposits for the last two years should be retained until what date and where?

3. What should be done with deeds to property purchased three years ago?

4. The Purchasing Department has a stack of office equipment catalogs dated from three years ago to the current date. What should be done with these catalogs?

5. The Administration Department keeps telephone messages for the entire year, even after they have been answered. What needs to be done with the messages?

Practice Set Application

At this time, complete Job 9, *Transfer Procedures,* in OFFICE FILING PROCEDURES, Eighth Edition. Instructions and supplies for this job are included in the practice set.

Turn the page for Computer Applications.

Computer Applications

1. Prepare a database design sheet on a separate sheet of paper to design a database for the records retention and destruction schedule in Figure 7-4. Use the following information for the database. (Obj. 7)

Date: Current

Database filename: SCHEDULE

Database description: Records Retention and Destruction Schedule

Fields: OFFICE, RECNAME, INOFFICE, INCENTER, TOTALYRS

Field lengths: Count the longest words in each field. Be sure to count blank spaces.

Index/sort the OFFICE field.

2. If a computer is available for your use, create the SCHEDULE database on your computer. Key all information in Figure 7-4 into the database. Key leading zeros in the INOFFICE, INCENTER, and TOTAL YRS. fields so that the numbers align on the right. If a numeric field is selected in dBase III PLUS, the numbers automatically align at the right and leading zeroes are not necessary. Key three hyphens (– – –) in the INCENTER field if the records are not sent to the center. Key – – P for permanent retention. Proofread your work carefully. All data in the retention period fields should align on the right. If you are using the template, open filename **CH7AP2.DBF**. Index/sort the OFFICE field.

3. Create and print a report of the SCHEDULE (CH7AP2.DBF) database.

Title your report: RECORDS RETENTION AND DESTRUCTION SCHEDULE.

Print all fields in order: OFFICE, RECNAME, INOFFICE, INCENTER, and TOTALYRS.

Use these column headings: Office of Record (two lines), Record Name, Office, Records Center (two lines), and Total.

Compare your records retention and destruction schedule with the one in Figure 7-4. Make any corrections and print a final report to give to your teacher for checking.

4. Index/sort the SCHEDULE (CH7AP2.DBF) database by the RECNAME field. Create and print the following report:

Title your report: RECORDS RETENTION AND DESTRUCTION SCHEDULE BY RECORD NAME.

Print these fields: RECNAME, TOTALYRS, and OFFICE in that order.

Use these column headings: Record Name, Total Years (two lines), and Office of Record (two lines).

Give your report to your teacher for checking.

Chapter Eight

Use of Color in Filing Systems

Learning Objectives

After completing Chapter 8, you will be able to do the following:

1. List the reasons for using color in filing systems.

2. Define **color coding** and **color accenting**.

3. Describe the tab design and file arrangement for the following color-coded systems:
   a. Jeter Top Coder
   b. Jeter Birth Date/Alphabetical
   c. Alpha-Z® End Tab
   d. Colorscan®
   e. AlphaCode®

4. Code personal and company names for the following color-coded filing systems:
   a. Jeter Top Coder
   b. Jeter Birth Date/Alphabetical
   c. Alpha-Z® End Tab
   d. Colorscan®
   e. AlphaCode®

5. List a special feature of each of the following color-coded filing systems:
   a. Jeter Top Coder
   b. Jeter Birth Date/Alphabetical
   c. Alpha-Z® End Tab
   d. Colorscan®
   e. AlphaCode®

Why Color Is Used in Filing Systems

In this chapter you will study filing systems that are constructed around an element that is both beautiful and useful: color. You will learn *why* color is used in filing systems and *how* it is used. The conversion to color-coded systems is much simpler than it used to be. Today, labelers driven by computers prepare pressure-sensitive labels at high speed. Records and information managers recognize the advantages of color-coded systems and recommend the use of color for improving access to information in all filing systems.

While color in filing systems improves the appearance of any file, the main purpose of color-coded filing systems is not decorative but functional. The primary purpose of color is to increase the speed and the accuracy of filing and retrieving office records. The records may be optical media, microimage media, magnetic media, or, as presented in this chapter, the most common of all records media—paper records.

How does color improve filing systems?

Speed

On the highway, streetlights are more visible than street signs. We see a red light to signify a stop long before we can read a stop sign. Likewise, in the office, we see color-coded folder labels before we see the names printed on them. Color groups attract the eye from longer distances than words. TAB® Products Co. reports that substituting colors for letters and numbers improves recognition time up to 40 percent.

Accuracy

In Chapter 2 you learned that misfiling occurs with approximately 3 percent of stored documents, and the estimated cost to find each lost record is $200. Color-coded filing systems virtually eliminate these costly misfiles. Assigning colors to letters (A-Z), to numbers (0-9), or to any other kind of identifier results in a formation of color blocks. A break in the color pattern calls attention to a misfile and enables you to spot and correct a misfiled record easily and quickly. Actually, it's nearly impossible to file a record in the wrong location because a misplaced folder immediately disrupts the system's established color pattern.

How Color Is Used in Filing Systems

Almost any filing system benefits by the use of color. Color can *accent* or *code* a filing system. Although this chapter deals primarily with color-

coded filing systems, it is useful to distinguish between color accenting and color coding.

Color Accenting

Color accenting in filing is the use of color to mark a particular part of a filing system. All of the following parts of the system may carry contrasting colors simply to make them distinct from the other parts: primary, secondary, and special guides; individual folders; general folders; OUT guides; and labels. For example, primary guides may be red; general folders, yellow; and OUT guides, black. This use of color is called *color-accenting a filing system*.

Color Coding

Color coding is the assignment of a specific color to a particular letter, number, or other identifier. The following presentation of color-coded filing systems shows specifically how color functions as an organizing principle in a variety of commercially designed filing systems.

How is color accenting different from color coding?

Color-Coded Filing Systems

The filing systems presented here are by no means the only color-coded systems in use today. They are, however, widely advertised and marketed throughout the country. You may have seen one of these systems used in an office near you. More than likely, one of these systems or a similar system will be used in the office where you will work. Consequently, you need to understand the construction of color-coded systems and how color makes filing easier, faster, and more reliable.

This chapter describes and illustrates each color-coded system according to its tab design and guide arrangement, color scheme, and special features. Get ready for a vibrant topic in filing that brightens and lightens the filer's work day: color and color-coded filing systems.

Jeter Top Coder Filing System

The Jeter (pronounced Jēt′er) Top Coder, manufactured by Jeter Systems Corporation in Akron, Ohio, is shown in Figure 8-1. The illustration is of a top-access file with top-tab coding.

Tab Design and Guide Arrangement

Refer to Figure 8-1 as you study the guide arrangement of the Jeter Top Coder outlined on page 130. The eight tab label positions are described from *left to right*.

1. Solid color labels and date, numeric, or alphabetic labels occupy the first four positions on the folder tab. These labels color code a variety of useful information. For example, a solid color might code (a) a particular doctor to whom a patient has been assigned in a medical clinic, (b) an attorney to whom a client has been assigned in a law firm, (c) a specific geographic region or district, or (d) a particular department in an organization. A date label may code the date a file was opened or the date the folder was last active (this is helpful information at transfer time).

   Noticeably lacking in first position are primary guides. Although the file drawers must be labeled to show the range (AA-AW) of records in them, the color-coded alphabetic labels on each folder make separate primary guides unnecessary.

2. Name labels occupy the fifth (slightly off-center) position in the file drawer.

3. Alphabetic labels in the next position color code the first and second letters of the key unit. The highly visible color blocks created by these labels promote faster and more accurate storage and retrieval of individual folders and eliminate misfiles.

4. OUT guide tabs are clearly visible in the extreme right (eighth position) of the file drawer. The OUT guides, of course, indicate what records have been borrowed and mark the location for the return of borrowed records.

Color Scheme

Thirteen different colors are used to code letters of the alphabet. Because 26 letters in the alphabet need different coding, two different label patterns are used. Solid color labels are used for letters A through M. The same colors are used for letters N through Z, but a solid white vertical line separates the label into a two-part color label. Figure 8-2 shows the wall chart for the Jeter Top Coder. The following table lists the label patterns and the 13 colors used in Figure 8-2 to represent the letters.

Solid Label Letter	Color	Two-Part Label Letter
A	Red	N
B	Brown	O
C	White	P
D	Gray	Q
E	Orange	R
F	Beige	S
G	Yellow	T
H	Dark Blue	U
I	Light Blue	V
J	Light Green	W
K	Black	X
L	Dark Green	Y
M	Magenta	Z

JETER SYSTEMS CORPORATION

ALPHA SERIES WALL CHART

Post this color chart
in a conspicuous place near the
filing system. This will be a great aid
in the memorization and
rapid identification of color.

jeter.
systems corporation

AD-102

Figure 8-2 Jeter Top Coder Wall Chart
Source: *Jeter Systems Corporation*

Figure 8-1 Jeter Top Coder
Source: *Jeter Systems Corporation*

Notice the long, red straight line created by the labels in Figure 8-1. Red represents key units beginning with A. The second letters of the key units are color-coded to a second label—yellow (G), black (K), and then dark green (L). Names like Richard Agate, Connie Agent, and Agway, Inc., are all coded using the same color labels. A solid red label (A) and a solid yellow label (G) represent the first and second letters of the key unit in the filing segment. The straight-line color blocks keep together all filing segments with key units beginning with the same two letters. Notice the color blocks created by key units beginning with AG, AK, and AL, for example.

Jeter color-coded filing systems are available for side-access filing systems, also. Figure 8-3 on page 132 shows a side-tab folder with a similar tab design running from top to bottom. The colors used in this particular system are different and require a color chart designed for that particular system series. Color systems work as well with numeric filing systems, as you can see in Figure 8-4 on page 132.

A special feature of the Jeter Top Coder is the generous space allowed in the first four positions of the folder tab for color-coding a variety of

> **What letters in the filing segment are color-coded in the Jeter Top Coder?**

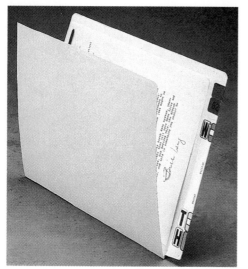

Figure 8-3
Jeter Side-Tab Folder for Side-Access Filing

Source: *Photography by Erik Von Fischer/Photonics*

Figure 8-4
Color-Coded Numeric File

Source: *Jeter Systems Corporation*

useful information. This feature was described in No. 1 of the Tab Design and Guide Arrangement section on p. 130. A unique filing system from Jeter Systems, however, is the color-coded Birth Date/Alphabetical Filing System explained next.

Jeter Birth Date/Alphabetical Filing System

How does the Birth Date/Alphabetical system reduce the number of primary search divisions?

The Birth Date/Alphabetical Filing System is a rather unique alphanumeric indexing system. **Alphanumeric indexing** is the combined usage of letters and numbers to index records in a filing system. This Birth Date/Alphabetical system provides a cross-check for personal names to be sure that you have the correct folder. The names are color-coded first by the month of birth and then by the day of birth. Finally, personal names with the same birth dates are color-coded by the first letter of the surname and then arranged in alphabetical order in the usual manner: surname, first name or initial, and middle name or initial. Instead of 26 search divisions (letters in the alphabet) required in a traditional alphabetic name file, the Birth Date/Alphabetical system requires only 12 search divisions (months of the year). Use of this system reduces the searching area by more than half!

Figure 8-5 shows an individual side-tab folder prepared for William Thomas whose birth date is March 25. Also, study the side-access system in Figure 8-6. Ideally suited to a medical office, the system works in this manner: When Jill Kenny calls for an appointment, ask her the month and day of birth—the year is not required. If her birth date is January 20, you

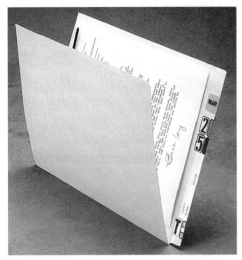

Figure 8-5
Side-Tab Individual Folder for Birth
Date/Alphabetical File
Source: *Photography by Erik Von Fischer/Photonics*

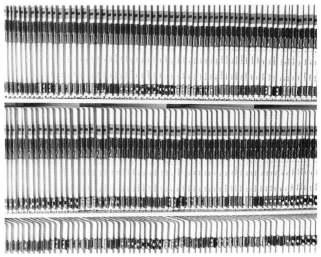

Figure 8-6
Birth Date/Alphabetical Filing System
Source: *Jeter Systems Corporation*

find Jill's folder under January, the month; 20, the day of birth; and the letter K, the first letter of her surname. Identical months create color blocks that help to detect a misfiled record. When birth dates *vary* within each month, the dates do not form large color blocks to detect misfiles. Can you spot the misfiled record in Figure 8-6?

Remember this system is primarily for personal names. When other names enter the system that do not have birth dates, Jeter systems designers recommend coding them February 30! A card or computer index listing birth dates for all individuals may be needed for times when the birth date of an individual is not readily obtainable.

Alpha-Z® End Tab Filing System

The Alpha-Z® End Tab Filing System, manufactured by the Smead Manufacturing Company of Hastings, Minnesota, is shown in Figure 8-7. Guides and folders are available for use in top-access, in side-access, and in suspended folder filing equipment. The manila folders in the side-access system illustration have 2-ply tabs for added vertical support. With double thickness at the point of greatest wear, these folders withstand heavy use. The straight-cut (or full-cut) tabs allow plenty of room for color-coded labels. The embossed lines on the folder tab make label application precise and easy. Figure 8-8 is an end-tab folder showing the tab with labeling positions.

Tab Design and Guide Arrangement

Refer to Figure 8-7, Alpha-Z® End Tab Filing System, and Figure 8-8, Alpha-Z® End Tab Folder, as you study the tab design and guide arrangement that follows.

1. Primary guides are in first position (the top position). Guides are side-tabbed with large, easily read captions.

2. A date label is in the first position on the folder tab. Similar to the Jeter system, a date label may be applied to indicate when the file was opened or when it was last active. This information is useful at transfer time.

What features make the Alpha-Z® Name Label unique?

3. A unique, patented name label color-codes the *first* letter of the key unit. The label consists of the color band, name, and alphabetic letter. The design, the preparation, and the application of the name label are shown in Figure 8-9.

   The Alpha-Z® color-coded name labels provide for all 26 letters of the alphabet on 13 distinctively colored, self-adhesive labels. A-M are color-on-white; N-Z are white-on-color. One label is used for either of two alphabetic characters by simply stripping away the end of the label not needed. These labels are scored to fold easily around the folder tab. Available in a complete alphabetic package or in individual letter packages, the labels are designed for either a top-tab or an end-tab folder arrangement.

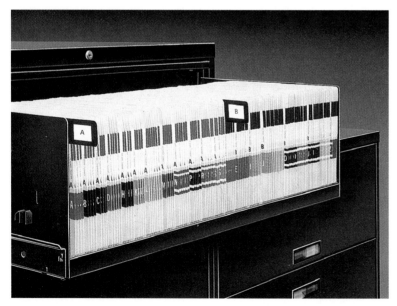

Figure 8-7 Alpha-Z® End Tab Filing System
Source: *The Smead Manufacturing Company*

Figure 8-8
Alpha-Z® End Tab Folder
Source: *The Smead Manufacturing Company*

Figure 8-9 Alpha-Z® Label Preparation
Source: *The Smead Manufacturing Company*

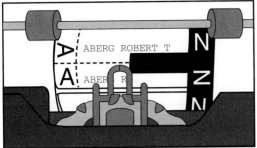 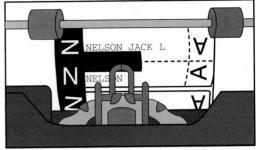

1. Insert strip of labels with letter to be used at left

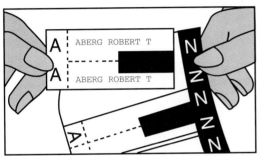 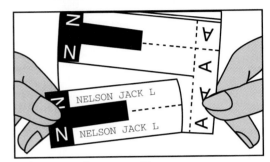

2. Remove label from backing and separate from unused letter

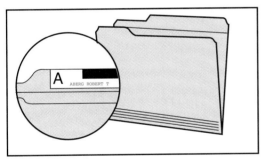 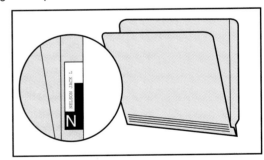

3. Labels may be used on top tab or end tab folders

4. Alphabetic labels, next in position, color-code the *second* letter of the key unit.

5. A second, smaller alphabetic label is optional and placed next in position. This label color-codes either the *third* letter of the key unit or the *first* letter of the second filing unit in large systems. The small system shown in Figure 8-7 does not make use of this additional coding option, however.

6. OUT guides occupy the last position in the system.

What three letters of the filing segment are color-coded in the Alpha-Z® End Tab system?

Color Scheme

The color scheme (plan) for the Alpha-Z® system consists of 13 colors in a solid label pattern and a three-part label pattern. The colors and patterns code letters of the alphabet as shown below:

Solid Label Letter	Color	Three-Part Label Letter
A	Red	N
B	Dark Blue	O
C	Green	P
D	Light Blue	Q
E	Purple	R
F	Orange	S
G	Gray	T
H	Dark Brown	U
I	Pink	V
J	Yellow	W
K	Light Brown	X
L	Violet	Y
M	Light Green	Z

Figures 8-10 and 8-11 illustrate Alpha-Z® name labels and alphabetic labels. They are available in either sheet or roll form and are protected by clear laminate. Note particularly the *solid* color labels used for A to M and the *three-part* label pattern used for N to Z in Figure 8-11. Although the colors are repeated once throughout the system, hash marks (white lines) separate the colors into a distinct three-part color pattern for labels N–Z. It is not necessary to memorize these color codes. Wall charts are available for reference.

Review

1. What letters of a filing segment are color-coded in the Jeter Top Coder?

2. What letters of a filing segment are color-coded in the Alpha-Z® system?

3. Why is the Birth Date/Alphabetical filing system considered an alphanumeric indexing system?

Colorscan®

Colorscan® is one of many color-coded systems by Kardex Systems, Inc., Marietta, Ohio. Colorscan® is a random access system. **Random access** is filing and retrieving records without regard for a strict alphabetic or numeric sequence. Colorscan® does not focus on a strict alphabetic arrangement of records. The first letter of the key unit and the first letter

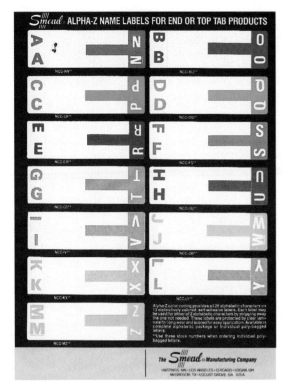

Figure 8-10 Alpha-Z® Name Labels
Source: *The Smead Manufacturing Company*

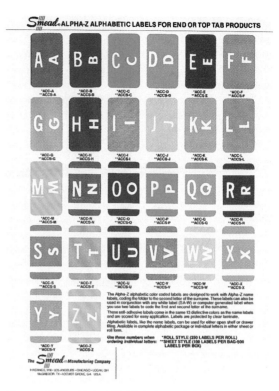

Figure 8-11 Alpha-Z® Alphabetic Labels
Source: *The Smead Manufacturing Company*

of the second indexing unit determine the location of records. Other letters in the name are disregarded.

Primary guides mark the major alphabetic sections of the file. Folders are filed first behind the appropriate primary alphabetic guides (A to Z) according to the first letter of the key unit. *Each* primary guide section (A to Z) is subdivided into ten color-coded, alphabetic subsections as follows: (1) AB, (2) C, (3) DEF, (4) GHI, (5) J, (6) KL, (7) MNO, (8) PQR, (9) ST, and (10) U-Z. These subsections follow the color wheel in Figure 8-12 on page 138 for color-coded *folders.*

Here is how the system works: All names with key units beginning with A are filed in the main section of the file. Then, all names with *second indexing units* beginning with, for example, F are filed *at the beginning* of the yellow C subsection (see color wheel). Names containing only one word, such as Xerox, are filed behind the X primary guide and placed in the X (tan folder) subdivision.

Sometimes active records account for a small percentage of the total records in a filing system. Colorscan® works well under such circumstances. With its form of random filing, Colorscan® keeps the more active records always in the front of their appropriate alphabetic subsections for faster and easier retrieval.

When is random filing useful?

Tab Design and Guide Arrangement

Figure 8-13 shows an individual folder for Nancy Carson. The name label is affixed to the top of the folder. The alphabet is printed down the side tab of the folder with the first letter of the key unit (C) blocked out with a small, self-adhesive black tab. The folder color is blue because the first letter of the second indexing unit is N (Nancy). The folder is filed in the main C section of the file and in the blue subsection (MNO). When the folder is returned to the file, it is placed *at the beginning* of the blue (MNO) subsection.

All folders in this blue subsection have only two things in common: (1) all names have key units that begin with C and (2) all names have second indexing units that begin with M, N, or O. Strict alphabetic order of the names is not observed, and the most active records are always at the beginning of a subsection.

Figure 8-14 shows a diagram of the Colorscan® filing system. The diagram illustrates (1) primary guides, (2) straight-line black blocks, (3) action guides, and (4) general folders. Refer to the diagram as you study the guide arrangement that follows on page 140.

Figure 8-13
Colorscan® Individual Folder
Source: Photography by Erik Von Fischer/Photonics

Figure 8-14
Colorscan® Arrangement

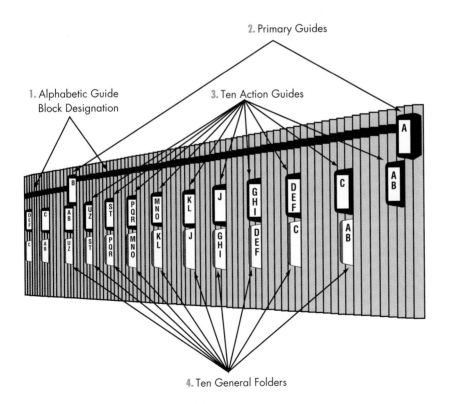

2. Primary Guides

1. Alphabetic Guide Block Designation

3. Ten Action Guides

4. Ten General Folders

1. Primary guides for A and B are clearly marked and visible in first position.

2. Notice the straight-line blocks created by the black pressure-sensitive label applied to the A box, and later the B box, on the preprinted folders. Refer to Figure 8-13 for a closer look at the preprinted individual folder. The black blocks appear at subsequently lower positions as the alphabet progresses. Misfiles are easily detected when this straight line is broken.

3. Alphabetic Action Guides subdivide each primary alphabetic section of the file and are color-coded to the *first letter of the second indexing unit*. Folders are always returned to the front of these alphabetic subsections to which they belong. Strict alphabetic order of the names is not observed. For example, when the folder for Howard Anderson is returned to the file, it is placed behind primary guide A (A̲NDERSON) and Action Guide GHI (H̲OWARD). At this moment, Howard Anderson's folder is *first* in the GHI (Green) subsection.

4. General folders are next in position. Colorscan® provides storage for correspondents who do not require individual folders. Each subdivision ends with a general folder. Alphabetic sequence must be observed in the general folders, or it becomes difficult to determine when sufficient records have accumulated for a name to warrant an individual folder.

What letter in the filing segment is color-coded in Colorscan®?

Color Scheme

All you need to know to find the general location of a record is the first letter of the key unit and the first letter of the second filing unit. Again, because other letters in the name are ignored, names do not necessarily appear in strict alphabetic order. The first letter of the key unit determines the primary alphabetic guide section behind which the folder is placed. Then color takes over: Color is used to find the first letter of the second filing unit. The first letter of the second filing unit is coded to one of ten color folders. Figure 8-12 shows the Colorscan® system and the ten colors used to code the alphabetic subdivisions. Because there are only ten colors but 26 letters of the alphabet, alphabetic subsections are divided and color-coded in this way:

Letters	Color
AB	Red
C	Yellow
DEF	Pink
GHI	Green
J	White
KL	Brown
MNO	Blue
PQR	Orange
ST	Violet
U-Z	Tan

Review the following retrieval procedures that make this random filing system unique:

1. Locate the primary alphabetic guide for the first letter of the key unit of the name.

2. Locate the appropriate Action Guide and/or COLOR subsection identifying the first letter of the second filing unit. (See the color wheel in Figure 8-12.)

3. SCAN the folders for the specific name for which you are searching. Active records are toward the front of the section; less active records are toward the back of the section.

AlphaCode® Filing System

At this point you are probably thinking, "These color systems are nice, but who's going to do the work to convert a traditional system to a color-coded one?" Good thought, because establishing a color-coded system is a time-consuming and labor-intensive task. The cost, however, is quickly offset by faster and more accurate filing.

Color-coding can be either commercially produced or done in-house. For example, TAB® Products Co., of Palo Alto, California, has developed a computer-generated system for producing numeric and alphabetic labels. Available for both top-tab and side-tab folders, the computer-generated color printing creates only the folders you need. You supply the names in the form of magnetic tape, disks, or a typed list. A computer-generated manufacturing process creates the color-coded labels that contain your file's numeric or alphabetic information—including written titles. The labels are then bonded to the folder with a hot-glue process. The long, printed label reinforces the visible folder tab with an additional 14 points thickness. This reinforcement extends the life of the folder. The printing method ensures colors that resist fading, wearing, and cracking. The position of color bars is precise and matches every other folder in the system. The folders arrive at your office in the order you need them, greatly simplifying the record conversion process.

What are the advantages of computer-generated labeling?

Tab Design and Guide Arrangement

Study Figure 8-15 on page 142. In a typical AlphaCode® system, the first two or three letters of the surname or key unit are color-coded. In addition, a full printout title appears in the white field above the color bars. A year tab may also be included in the preprinted label. Figure 8-16 on page 142 shows a section of the AlphaCode® filing system in its preferred arrangement—shelf, side-access filing. Primary guides are in the first, or top, position and mark the primary alphabetic divisions. Folders in a three-bar color format create the color blocks when folders are filed correctly.

Figure 8-15 TAB® AlphaCode® Individual Folder
Source: *TAB Products Co.*

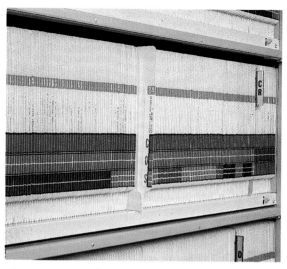

Figure 8-16 TAB® AlphaCode® Filing System
Source: *TAB Products Co.*

Although color-coded label captions can be commercially computer-generated and then applied to folders for you, handwrapping labels on individual folders is also possible for minor updating of a filing system. This is done through the use of TAB's Convert-A-Tabs. Convert-A-Tabs are applied manually when new folders enter the system. The labels are manually applied around the folder tab. The full-cut Convert-A-Tab creates a double reinforced tab on the folder. The tab is scored in eight positions for easy and precise AlphaCode® color label application.

Color Scheme

Individual color-coded, wrap-around labels are matched to TAB's computerized AlphaCode® system. Ten colors are used to code the 26 letters of the alphabet with small white horizontal bars added to distinguish letters represented by the same color. The colors used in the AlphaCode® system are these:

Solid Color		Color With One White Bar		Color with Two White Bars	
A	Red	I	Pink	S	Pink
B	Light Orange	J	Red	T	Red
C	Dark Orange	K	Light Orange	U	Light Orange
D	Emerald	L	Dark Orange	V	Dark Orange
E	Dark Green	M	Emerald	W	Dark Green
F	Blue	N	Dark Green	X	Blue
G	Purple	O	Blue	Y	Purple
H	Lilac	P	Purple	Z	Lilac
		Q	Lilac		
		R	Brown		

A barcode can also be attached to the folder. Remember what you learned in Chapter 6: Barcoding can automate the charge-out and follow-up tasks associated with manual filing systems. Folders can be scanned in and scanned out for easy tracking of file folders.

As long as paper continues to be a widely used and accepted medium for records, better and faster methods for storing and retrieving them will be needed. It appears now that color-coding and barcoding will lead manual filing systems into the 21st Century.

Review

1. Why is Colorscan® considered a random access filing system?

2. What are the advantages of a computer-generated color-coded labeling process?

Summary

There are many more color-coded systems that could have been presented in Chapter 8. Those selected, however, meet two important requirements: (1) The system is readily available and (2) the system, in some special way, illustrates how color-coded systems can be used effectively to improve filing.

In general, the standard procedure for color-coded systems color-codes the first, second, and sometimes the third letter of the key unit. However, the Jeter Top Coder demonstrated that more than the filing segment can be color-coded. Additional color-label positions make color-coding other important information possible, such as a doctor in a medical clinic, a lawyer in law offices, sales districts, or departments in an organization.

The Birth Date/Alphabetical system combined color-coded numbers (months and days) and letters (first letter of key unit) to build a personal name file with a built-in cross-check. Alpha-Z® displayed a unique color-coded *name* label. Colorscan® showed that records can be arranged by their active status in the file rather than by their strict alphabetic order. AlphaCode® introduced computer-generated color-coded labels for an easy and precise conversion to a color-coded system.

It is clear that color in filing systems has value. In manual filing systems with slow record retrieval and frequent misfiles, color-coded systems may be the only defensible and practical alternative.

Terminology Review

Questions for Discussion

1. List two important reasons for using color in filing systems. (Obj. 1)
2. Explain the difference between color-coding and color-accenting a filing system. (Obj. 2)
3. What additional color-coded features in the tab design distinguish the Jeter Top Coder from the other four systems illustrated in this chapter? (Objs. 3, 5)
4. List the three items of information color-coded in the Jeter Birth Date/Alphabetical filing system. (Obj. 3)
5. What makes the Alpha-Z® name labels different from all the other name labels used in the color-coded filing systems illustrated in this chapter? (Obj. 3)
6. What is the method for color-coding names in the Alpha-Z® system? (Objs. 3, 5)
7. Describe the use of guides and folders in the Colorscan® system. (Obj. 3)
8. What part of the filing segment is color-coded in the AlphaCode® filing system? (Obj. 3)
9. Name a special feature of each of the color-coded filing systems studied in this chapter (Obj. 5):

   Jeter Top Coder

   Jeter Birth Date/Alphabetical

   Alpha-Z® End Tab

   Colorscan®

   AlphaCode®
10. Why is Colorscan® considered a random filing system? (Obj. 5)

Applications

On a separate sheet of paper, prepare a table like those shown below. Apply your knowledge of the systems described and illustrated in this chapter to color code the names. Refer to the descriptions and photographs in this chapter as needed. Be sure to indicate when necessary whether the color label is solid, two-part, or three-part.

1. *Jeter Top Coder* (Obj. 4)

Name	1st Label Color	2d Label Color
First City National Bank		
Robert Lubbock Manufacturing Co.		
Electrical Repair Service Co.		
The Battone Sisters		

2. *Alpha-Z®* (Obj. 4)

Name	Name Label Color	Alphabetic Label
Houston Chronicle		
Schrafft Bakery, Inc.		
Van Chevrolet Co.		
Maria Lisse		
Jason Peterson		

3. *AlphaCode®.* (Obj. 4)

Name	1st Label	2d Label	3d Label
R & R Industries, Inc.			
Viacom Livestock Marketing			
Casey Alvarez			
Wayne Granger			
Margo Underhill			

4. *Jeter Birth Date/Alphabetical* (Obj. 4) On a separate sheet of paper, list the following names in correct alphabetic sequence for filing in the Birth Date/Alphabetical filing system.

Name	Birth Date
a. John Rath	March 2
b. Susan Roth	January 1
c. Katherine Lopez	April 3
d. Benjamin Larson	April 3
e. Ayako Eto	May 4

5. *Colorscan®* (Obj. 4) On a separate sheet of paper, prepare a table similar to the following sample. In the columns provided, indicate the primary guide behind which each of the following names is placed. Then in the

---

Action Guide column, specify the alphabetic subdivision for each name. Finally, indicate the color of the folder to which the name is coded.

Name	Primary Guide	Action Guide	Color Folder
Dale Campbell			
Kelly Imports			
Beverly Sing			
Chita Valero			
Retson Electronics			

Part 4

Other Filing Methods

Chapter Nine

Numeric Filing

Learning Objectives

After completing Chapter 9, you will be able to do the following:

1. Define **numeric filing** and explain when the numeric filing method should be used.

2. List advantages and disadvantages of using the numeric filing method.

3. List and describe the components of a consecutive numbered filing system.

4. Describe and use consecutive numeric filing procedures.

5. List advantages and disadvantages of consecutive number filing.

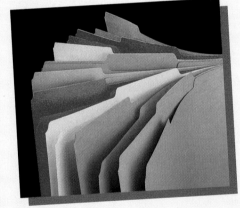

6. Describe and use terminal-digit filing.

7. Describe and use middle-digit filing.

8. List advantages and disadvantages of terminal- or middle-digit filing.

9. Define and explain **chronologic filing.**

10. List types of chronologic files.

Need for Numeric Filing

Numbers are such a part of our lives that we often memorize a list of numbers with ease. For example, you know your telephone number, your friends' telephone numbers, your student or employee ID number, and maybe your car license plate, driver's license, and social security number. These numbers can be keyed into computers to access various databases and to obtain a variety of personal information about you. For example, law enforcement officials can key in your driver's license number and obtain the number and date of any traffic citations you have received in recent years.

Can you name three numbers that you use daily?

Think of numbers that apply to your life—banking account, charge account, credit card, patient account, utility company account, ZIP Code, post office box, and safe-deposit box. The use of numbers is the quickest way to find records and information stored in computer files. Your records are stored by your numbers; accessing the information is possible by using your numbers.

In previous chapters, you have used only the alphabetic filing method. However, in this chapter you will learn how numeric filing is used for filing records. **Numeric filing** is a method of arranging records by number. In Chapter 9, you will learn the procedures for filing correspondence using consecutive numeric filing. Also, you will learn when to use numeric filing and the advantages and disadvantages of using numeric filing. You will be able to compare consecutive, terminal-digit, and middle-digit numeric filing systems and choose the appropriate system for your use and that of the organization where you work. Types of chronologic filing are presented as well.

What is numeric filing?

When to Use Numeric Filing

Generally, a numeric filing method should be used when at least one of the following characteristics of the records applies.

What are three records characteristics that indicate the need for filing by numbers?

1. Records have a unique number already assigned to them. For example, numbers are preprinted on checks, purchase orders, and invoices.

2. Records have been assigned a number that has some meaning or importance. For example, the first three digits of your gasoline credit card number may be the telephone area code number to identify your geographic location.

3. Records are confidential, and unauthorized access must be prevented. Filing by number makes it less likely that an unauthorized person can gain access to confidential records. Examples of confidential records include banking account balances and payroll information.

Advantages of Using Numeric Filing

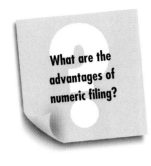

What are the advantages of numeric filing?

Large and small volumes of records may be filed by numbers. Medical offices, insurance companies, colleges and universities, the military, and many other types of organizations use numeric filing systems. Here are several advantages of using numeric filing:

1. Records can be arranged more accurately by numbers because numbers are easier to read and arrange than letters.

2. A consecutive numeric system expands quickly and easily because new numbered files can be added at the end of the system of drawers or shelves.

3. Cross-references are not filed in the numbered file. The volume of records stored in the numbered folders is kept under control because cross-references are filed in a separate alphabetic index.

4. Confidentiality is maintained because correspondent names and subjects don't appear on file labels.

5. Numeric filing systems improve efficient filing and retrieval in large-volume records systems. Because numbers are often shorter than a person's name or a company's name, they can be read, retrieved, and filed quickly. When a large number of records must be filed and retrieved daily, speed is necessary.

6. Numeric filing is useful in computerized records systems. Numbers can be keyed quickly, and the computer can search for and find a single number quickly.

Disadvantages of Using Numeric Filing

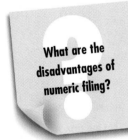

What are the disadvantages of numeric filing?

As with any filing method, numeric filing also has disadvantages. The most often identified disadvantages of using numeric filing include the following:

1. A misfile and failure to retrieve a record or file can result from one miskeyed digit.

2. Retrieval is usually a two-step process: (1) an alphabetic index must be referenced to find the number of the record or file, then (2) the record or file can be retrieved. Numeric filing is an *indirect system* because a user, unless he or she knows the number, cannot go directly to the files container to retrieve or file a record.

3. Congestion occurs when several records users at the same time need to use the alphabetic index to locate records.

4. Difficulty of remembering the correct order of digits in a large number may cause transposition of digits and misfiled or lost records.

5. Records for one correspondent name or subject may be assigned different numbers and filed in more than one location if all components

of the filing systems are not maintained carefully. Or the same number may be assigned to two different names or subjects and result in a mixture of records in one location.

6. Maintenance of the alphabetic index is time-consuming.

Review 1

1. What types of records may have numbers already assigned to them before they are sent to the records department?

2. How can a consecutive numeric filing system be expanded?

Consecutive Numbering Method

In **consecutive numeric filing** consecutively numbered records are arranged in ascending number order—from the lowest number to the highest number. Also called *serial, sequential,* and *straight numeric,* consecutive numeric filing systems often use prenumbered records such as checks, invoices, insurance policies, legal case files, medical records, and engineering drawings. In this chapter, you will learn how to use the consecutive numbering method with correspondence records.

What are other terms for consecutive numeric filing?

Components of a Consecutive Numbered System

A consecutive numeric correspondence filing system requires four components: (1) an accession log, (2) an alphabetic index, (3) a numbered file, and (4) an alphabetic file. Correspondence records are filed in a general alphabetic file until a predetermined number of records (such as five) for the same correspondent has accumulated. When enough records have accumulated, the records are removed from the alphabetic file. A number code is assigned to the name in the accession log, the number code is written on each record, and the code is written on or keyed into the alphabetic index. Finally, a numbered folder is prepared, and the records are placed in the folder, which is filed in the numbered file.

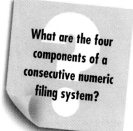

What are the four components of a consecutive numeric filing system?

Accession Log

An **accession log** is a serial listing of numbers assigned in a numeric filing system. Sometimes called a *numeric file list* or *accession book,* the accession log is used to keep track of numbers (called *number codes*) that have been assigned to records. Incoming records and copies of outgoing records received in the records department are assigned number codes in

When is a number assigned to a record?

the order received and after a sufficient number of records for the same correspondent has accumulated. A number code isn't assigned to a single record for a correspondent unless more records are anticipated. Because records are received in random order, the names recorded in the accession log are not in alphabetic order. However, they are in consecutive numeric order.

In a small filing system, the accession log may be a book as shown in Figure 9-1. The name of a correspondent or subject is written in *indexing order* on a blank line beside the next available number. The date on which the number is assigned is written in the date column on the right.

Figure 9-1
Accession Book

NUMBER	NAME	DATE
1208	Payroll Register	Feb. 1, 20--
1209	Corwin S. Adams Co.	Feb. 3, 20--
1210	Monthly Production Reports	Feb. 3, 20--
1211	Rogers Collection Agency	Feb. 4, 20--
1212	McNeil, Sara	Feb. 6, 20--
1213		

In larger numeric filing systems, numbers may be assigned automatically in an electronic accession log. The computer often is used when 1,000 or more files are in the records system or when several users must access the files at the same time. The name of the correspondent or subject title is keyed into the computer in all caps and in indexing order. The date on which the number is assigned is keyed into a date field in the computer file. A portion of a computer accession log is shown in Figure 9-2.

Figure 9-2
Computer
Accession Log

File No.	Name of Correspondent or Subject	Date
1000	RANDOLPH SCOTT AND TABOR CORP	5/09/0-
1001	123 FABULOUS TEES	5/09/0-
1002	LIANG MEILING MS	5/10/0-
1003	MR DS HAIR DESIGNERS	5/12/0-
1004	HARRISON COUNTY ROADS DEPARTMENT	5/13/0-
1005	QUEEN ANNES ANTIQUES AND COLLECTIBLES	5/15/0-

Alphabetic Index

An **alphabetic index** is a card file or a computer file of all correspondent names or subject titles arranged alphabetically. The index may contain correspondents' addresses and telephone numbers as well as a *G* code (for general alphabetic file) or a number code for each name. An alphabetic subject index to a numeric system may include subdivisions of subjects as well as the main subjects. Subject filing is discussed in Chapter 11, where you will learn that general alphabetic folders are not used in subject filing. Therefore, subject records are assigned number codes when they arrive in the records department. The *G* code is explained in detail in the Number Coding section on page 156.

The alphabetic index is used when the correspondent name or subject is known but the assigned number isn't. *Check the alphabetic index, not the accession log, for the name of the correspondent or the subject title in order to find a record number.* Checking the alphabetic index before assigning a new number prevents assigning more than one number to the same name or subject. An alphabetic index card for a numeric filing system would be prepared as shown in Figure 2-2 in Chapter 2. A printout of a computer alphabetic index, shown in Figure 9-3, serves as a handy reference when number-coding records.

Where can you find a number code for a record?

Name	File No.
123 FABULOUS TEES	1001
GEORGE ANDREA	G
HARRISON COUNTY ROADS DEPARTMENT	1004
LIANG MEILING MS	1002
MEILING LIANG MS	1002X
SEE LIANG MEILING MS	
MR DS HAIR DESIGNERS	1003
QUEEN ANNES ANTIQUES AND COLLECTIBLES	1005
RANDOLPH SCOTT AND TABOR CORP	1000
SCOTT TABOR AND RANDOLPH CORP	1000X
SEE RANDOLPH SCOTT AND TABOR CORP	
TABOR RANDOLPH AND SCOTT CORP	1000X
SEE RANDOLPH SCOTT AND TABOR CORP	

Figure 9-3
Computer Alphabetic Index

Cross-references are not needed in the numbered file in a numeric correspondence filing system. They are included only in the alphabetic index in order to refer the user to the location of the original record name and number code. As you know, in an alphabetic correspondence filing

Where are cross-references filed in a numeric filing system?

system, cross-reference sheets are used often. When cross-reference sheets are not used, filing time is saved, and congested numeric files caused by the accumulation of cross-reference sheets are avoided.

Numbered File *Individual Folder*

A numbered file contains numbered folders filed in consecutive number order, with the lowest number first. The numbered file is the main file in a numeric correspondence filing system.

Numbering of folders usually starts at an even number, such as 10, 100, or 1000, with no regard for the alphabetic order of the names or subjects. A consecutive numbered file beginning with number 2000 is shown in Figure 9-4. Numbered guides are placed in the drawer or shelf every five or ten folders. Guides may be numbered 10, 15, 20; 100, 110, 120; 1000, 1010, 1020; or 2000, 2010, 2020, and so on. Folders are numbered consecutively: 10, 11, 12; 100, 101, 102; 1000, 1001, 1002; or 2000, 2001, 2002, and so on.

Alphabetic File *General Folder*

An alphabetic file in a numeric correspondence filing system is a general alphabetic file in which guide and folder captions contain only letters of the alphabet. File records in a general alphabetic file until a predetermined number of records for a correspondent has accumulated. Each time you file a record in a general alphabetic folder, count the number of records for that correspondent. When the volume of records for a correspondent reaches a predetermined number, such as five records, assign a number code (in the accession log) to the name. Code all records for that name with the new number. Then place all the records in a numbered folder and file in the numbered file.

How are folders filed in a numbered file?

When are number codes assigned to correspondents in the general alphabetic file?

Review

1. How can you avoid assigning the same number to two different names?

2. Give two examples of consecutive numeric filing systems in organizations or offices where you work or visit.

Consecutive Number Filing Procedures

In order to maintain control in a numeric filing system, a set of procedures for filing correspondence records by numbers should be followed consistently. These procedures include the following six steps: (1) inspecting, (2) indexing, coding, and cross-referencing, (3) alphabetic sorting, (4) number coding, (5) numeric sorting, and (6) filing.

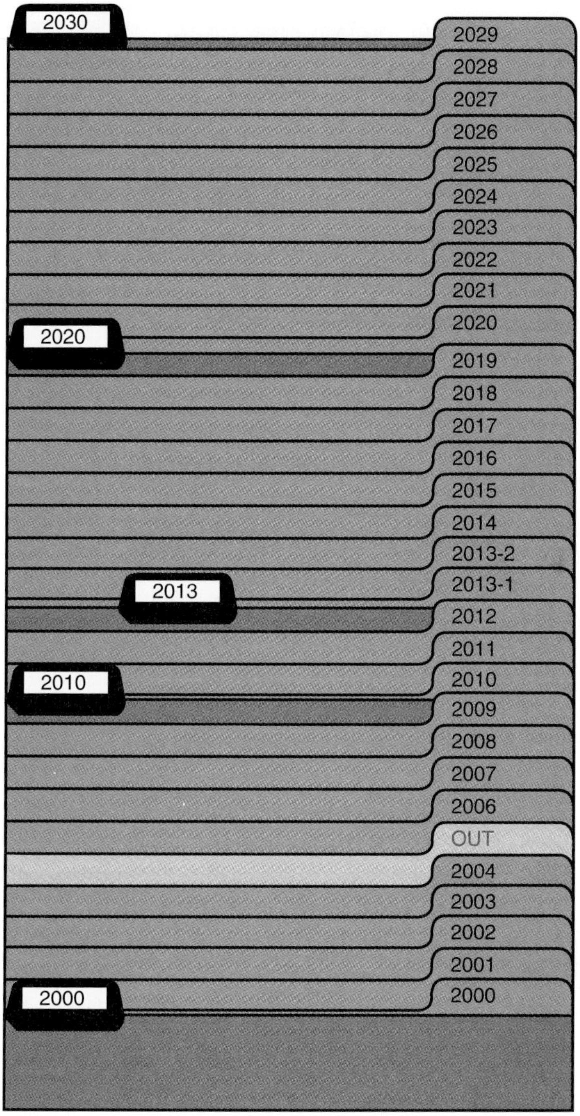

Figure 9-4
Consecutive Numbered
Correspondence File

Inspecting

Check each record for a release mark, which indicates that the record can be filed. If no release mark such as a person's initials is found, send the record back to the user to verify that the record is ready to be filed. Look for the release mark in Figure 9-5 on the next page.

Indexing, Coding, and Cross-Referencing

Select the correspondent name or subject that is the filing segment and code the units. Select and code any cross-reference names or subjects as well.

Figure 9-5
Number-Coded
Correspondence

CEI ENGINEERING CORP.
One Melrose Way
Lothian, MD 20711-7853

ȼ 324

December 15, 20—

1   2   3
MEILING / LIANG / MS   ✗

3   2
Ms./Mei-ling/Liang
1532 West Del Rio Drive
San Antonio, TX 78232-2326

Dear Ms. Liang

Thank you for accepting our invitation to visit CEI for an inter-
view on January 14 and 15, 20—. We are looking forward to
discussing in detail what we can offer you in terms of career
opportunities.

Scott Johnson will meet your plane and take you to the Broadway
Hotel. He will pick you up at 6:30 p.m. for dinner with Mike
Lever and Rhonda Blalock.

A complete agenda for the 14th and 15th is enclosed. If you
have any questions, please call me at 301/555-3400.

Sincerely yours

C. J. Ingles

C. J. Ingles

CJI/rj

Enclosure

Why are records sorted alphabetically first?

Alphabetic Sorting

First, sort the records alphabetically. Placing the records in alphabetic order speeds up the use of the alphabetic index to determine the code for each record.

Number Coding

In a manual numeric filing system with a general alphabetic file, first assign a new name a *G* (general) code and write a *G* in the upper right corner of the record. Also, write a *G* beside the name in the alphabetic index. When a predetermined number of records has accumulated for the same corre-spondent, assign the next available number in the accession log.

When a number is assigned to a name or subject, follow these five steps:

1. Find the name or subject in the alphabetic index.

2. If a number has not been assigned to a name, assign the next avail-able number in the accession log.

3. Cross out the *G* and write the number code in the upper right corner of each record for that correspondent. (See Figure 9-5.)

4. Cross out the *G* beside the name in the alphabetic index and write the number code. If a computer alphabetic index is used, delete the *G* and key the new number code into the computer index.

5. Prepare and file all cross-references in an alphabetic card index, or key all cross-references into a computer index.

Some filing systems use an **alphanumeric code**, a combination of alphabetic and numeric characters. With alphanumeric coding, the record is assigned a number code along with the first two letters of the key unit of the correspondent name or subject. For example, records for Manuel Ortega might be coded OR-1024.

What is an alphanumeric code?

Numeric Sorting

Sort all numbered records into groups of 10s, 100s, or 1000s. This rough sorting will save filing time and eliminate the need to move back and forth among drawers or shelves. Fine-sort into smaller groups of numbers if necessary. Because the records were sorted alphabetically previously, another alphabetic sort isn't necessary.

Filing

Move the sorted records to the files area. Interfile them in the alphabetic or numbered files. When color is used, filing can be completed very rapidly. Because the filers often learn the colors associated with the numbers, they are able to move to the correct files area quickly. A color-coded consecutive number file is shown on the left in Figure 9-6. A

Figure 9-6
Color-Coded Number Files
Source: *TAB Products, Co.*

color-coded terminal-digit number file, which you will study in the next major section, is shown on the right. Note the differences in the color coding.

Advantages of Consecutive Number Filing

What are the advantages of consecutive number filing?

Consecutive number filing is the most frequently used numeric filing method for a number of reasons:

1. Filing is quick and easy after records are rough-sorted.

2. Expansion of the system is easy and unlimited. The next available number is always at the end of the system.

3. File guides are prepared easily because the numbers needed are predictable.

4. Files can be moved or rearranged in sections that remain together. An entire section of records, such as records numbered 500–599, may be moved to another location and remain intact. Redistribution of the records into different files in the new location isn't necessary.

Disadvantages of Consecutive Number Filing

What are the disadvantages of consecutive number filing?

As with any method, consecutive numeric filing has some disadvantages. Being aware of the following disadvantages helps in devising ways to avoid them:

1. Congestion often is created in the last section of the files when several users need to access the newest records located at the end of the files.

2. An entire number must be read for accurate filing and retrieval. As numbers become larger, remembering them becomes more difficult.

3. Digits in long numbers are more likely to be transposed (reversed) by the person assigning the number to the file as well as by the filer who is storing or retrieving the record.

4. In manual numeric systems, maintaining a separate general alphabetic file is time-consuming. If the alphabetic index will accommodate folders, records may be filed in the index until the volume of records for the same correspondent warrants a numbered folder.

was a Indirect system

Review

1. Why are records to be filed in a numeric system sorted alphabetically first?

2. Why are numeric filing systems used so often?

Terminal-Digit and Middle-Digit Numbering Methods

As you have learned in the previous section of this chapter, longer numbers often result in transposed (reversed) digits. When the digits in a number are separated by a space, hyphen, period, or slash mark, the number is easier to read and remember. To reduce the memory load and improve accuracy in numeric filing, middle-digit or terminal-digit numbering methods sometimes are used.

Terminal-Digit Filing

Terminal-digit filing is a method of numeric filing that uses the last two or three digits of each number as the primary division under which the record is filed. Numbers are assigned consecutively; however, when filing, the numbers are read from *right to left* in small groups beginning with the terminal (final) group.

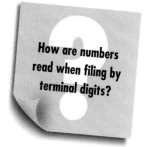

How are numbers read when filing by terminal digits?

Terminal-digit filing, primarily a manual filing method, is used in organizations with at least 10,000 files in the filing system. Hospitals, large medical clinics, and insurance companies often use terminal-digit filing to reduce congestion in the active files area. With terminal-digit filing, new files are distributed in different drawers and on different shelves rather than grouped in one location such as at the end of the file.

Numbers are divided into three groups of two or three digits each. When numbers have less than enough digits for three equal groups, zeros are added to the *left* of each number. For example, the number 23 456 789, would be written 023 456 789. The number would be read 789 456 023 (beginning with the terminal digits).

Groups of digits are identified as primary, secondary, and tertiary. The right (terminal) group is primary, the middle group is secondary, and the left group is tertiary (third). The primary number (the terminal digits) is the number of the file section, drawer, or shelf. The secondary number is the guide number. The tertiary number is the folder number and gives the order in which folders are located behind the guides. When filing, the number 50 27 54 is read from *right to left:* Drawer or shelf number (right), guide number (center), and then folder number (left) as shown below.

50	27	54
Tertiary	Secondary	Primary
(folder number)	(guide number)	(file section, drawer, or shelf number)

A portion of a computer terminal-digit accession log is shown in Figure 9-7. Numbers are assigned consecutively although the terminal digits determine the filing order. Folders in drawer or shelf 54 behind guide

27 54 are numbered 00 27 54 through 99 27 54 and are arranged in consecutive order. The next guide would be 28 54, and folder numbers behind this guide would be 00 28 54 through 99 28 54. Each folder number listed in Figure 9-7 would be filed in a different drawer or on a different shelf. They are spread throughout the filing system. Folder 50 27 54 would be filed in/on drawer/shelf 54; 50 27 55, drawer/shelf 55; 50 27 56, drawer/shelf 56; 50 27 57, drawer/shelf 57; and 50 27 58, drawer/shelf 58.

Figure 9-7
Terminal-Digit
Accession Log

File No.	Name of Correspondent or Subject	Date
502754	CHINA TOWN RESTAURANT	11/12/0-
502755	ALLEN FRANK JR	11/13/0-
502756	HOUSE OF CRAWFORD	11/14/0-
502757	ARELLANO CONCEPCION MISS	11/14/0-
502758	AT&T	11/14/0-

To file and retrieve a folder numbered 51-27-54, the filer first locates the primary digits for the drawer or shelf—54. The filer then locates the secondary digits for the guide—27. Finally, the filer locates the folder with the final or tertiary digits—51. The correct folder is between folder numbers 50-27-54 and 52-27-54, as shown in Figure 9-8. When color is used, filers quickly learn the colors associated with the primary and secondary numbers. This makes filing and retrieval faster. The sections of terminal-digit drawer and shelf files in Figure 9-8 show that folders in a drawer or shelf are numbered consecutively from 50 through 53 behind the consecutively numbered guides—25, 26, 27, and 28.

Figure 9-8
Terminal-Digit Drawer and
Shelf Files

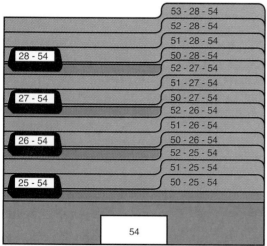

Terminal-Digit Drawer

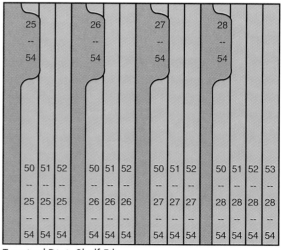

Terminal-Digit Shelf File

Middle-Digit Filing

Middle-digit filing is a method of numeric filing that uses the middle two or three digits of each number as the primary division under which the record is filed. Usually, middle-digit filing is used only in a manual filing system. Numbers are assigned consecutively; however, when filing, numbers are read from *middle to left to right*.

Again, groups of digits are identified as primary, secondary, and tertiary. The middle group is primary, the left group is secondary, and the right group is tertiary (third). When filing or retrieving a folder numbered 12 56 90, the number is read middle to left to right: drawer or shelf number (middle), guide number (left), and then folder number (right) as shown below.

12	56	90
Secondary	Primary	Tertiary
(guide number)	(file section, drawer, or shelf number)	(folder number)

A portion of a computer middle-digit accession log is shown in Figure 9-9. Folders in drawer 56 or on shelf 56 behind guide 12 56 are numbered 12 56 00 through 12 56 99 and are arranged in consecutive order. The next guide would be 13 56, and folder numbers behind this guide would be 13 56 00 through 13 56 99. Each folder number listed in the File No. column in Figure 9-9 would be filed in consecutive order behind guide 12 56 in drawer 56 or on shelf 56.

File No.	Name of Correspondent or Subject	Date
125690	INSURANCE CLAIMS	09/23/0-
125691	FIRST STATE BANK OF GEORGIA	09/24/0-
125692	TRENTON STATE COLLEGE	09/27/0-
125693	SANFRANCISCO MUSEUM OF FINE ARTS	10/03/0-
125694	CONTRACTS	10/05/0-

Figure 9-9
Computer Middle-Digit Accession Log

Review

1. How can three equal groups of numbers be created for terminal-digit filing?

2. Which group of digits determines the filing order of folders in a middle-digit filing system?

Advantages and Disadvantages of Terminal- or Middle-Digit Filing

The advantages and disadvantages described below for terminal- or middle-digit filing compare these methods to consecutive numeric filing. The primary advantages of terminal- or middle-digit filing methods include the following:

1. Fewer errors in transposition of digits occur because the numbers are divided into groups of two or three digits. The filer works with only two or three digits at a time.

2. Misreading of numbers is less likely with short groups of numbers than with one long number.

3. Congestion within the files area is avoided because records aren't filed consecutively. Current files are spread throughout the system rather than located at the end of the system.

Primary disadvantages of terminal- or middle-digit filing methods include:

1. Training of filers takes longer because of the order in which the numbers are read and folders are filed and retrieved. People are conditioned to read from left to right and to think of numbers in consecutive order. Changing this natural order may cause filers to fear a new system and think it will be confusing.

2. When a large block of consecutively numbered folders is requested, the filer must retrieve them from many locations throughout the filing system. This process can be time-consuming.

3. Transfer of inactive files also may take longer because of the various locations of files with similar activity dates.

4. Misfiled folders are hard to find unless they are color-coded.

Chronologic Filing

Chronologic filing is a method of numeric filing by which records are filed in sequence according to date. In manual filing systems, records are placed in reverse date order within file folders. In other words, the oldest records are at the back of the folder; the most recent records are at the front of the folder. Therefore, records are filed chronologically in folders.

In a chronologic filing system, the primary guide caption is the current year, such as 2004. A secondary guide for each month, January through December, is placed behind the year guide. Folder label captions also bear the months of January through December. These folders are filed behind the month guides. Records are filed and retrieved from folders by the day of the month.

Tickler, or suspense, files and transaction files may be arranged chronologically. Tickler files are used to remind someone that some type of follow-up, such as a signature or response to a request, is required. When a record is received that needs following up at a later date, the record is placed in the appropriate month folder until action is taken. When the follow-up is completed, the record is removed from the tickler or suspense folder and filed in its proper folder. A card tickler file often is used as the reminder system instead of a folder tickler file. Guides bear captions for the days of the month in a card tickler file. You studied the card follow-up/tickler file in Chapter 6. Remember that the charge-out and follow-up file and the destruction date file used in an inactive records center are tickler files as well.

Transaction files are arranged according to the dates on which the transactions occurred or are anticipated to occur. Transaction files may be used for utility customer service orders, work orders, or wherever activities occur on specific days.

Summary

Numbers are a part of our daily lives; therefore, it seems natural to use numbers whenever possible in filing systems. Numeric filing is a method of arranging records by number. A numeric filing method should be used when records have a unique number already assigned to them, when records have been assigned a meaningful number, or when records are confidential.

Advantages of using numeric filing include: (1) numbers are easier to read and arrange than letters; (2) new files can be added at the end of a numeric system making expansion easy; (3) cross-references are filed in a separate alphabetic index; (4) confidentiality of correspondent names and subjects is maintained when only numbers appear on file labels; (5) filing and retrieval in large-volume records systems are improved with numeric filing; and (6) numbers are useful in computerized records systems.

Disadvantages of numeric filing include: (1) misfiles are often caused by miskeyed digits; (2) retrieval is a two-step process because an index must be referenced before records can be accessed; (3) congestion occurs around only one alphabetic index; (4) digits in large numbers often are transposed resulting in misfiled records; (5) different numbers may be assigned to the same correspondent name or subject if the index and accession log aren't maintained properly; and (6) maintenance of the alphabetic index is time-consuming.

Consecutive numeric filing is a method by which consecutively numbered records are arranged from the lowest to highest numbers. Components of a consecutive numeric correspondence filing system include an accession log, alphabetic index, numbered file, and alphabetic file. Inspecting; indexing, coding, and cross-referencing; alphabetic sorting; number coding; numeric sorting; and filing are procedures that must be followed consistently in order to file correspondence accurately by numbers.

Numbers are assigned consecutively in terminal- and middle-digit filing; however, when filing, the numbers are grouped and are not read in natural left to right order. Terminal-digit filing uses the final two or three digits of each number as the primary division under which the record is filed. Middle-digit filing uses the middle two or three digits of each number as the primary division for filing.

Chronologic filing is a numeric filing system in which records are filed in sequence according to date. Records are filed chronologically in folders with the most recent records placed at the front of the folder. Tickler, or suspense, files and transaction files are types of chronologic files.

Terminology Review

accession log	(p. 151)
alphabetic index	(p. 153)
alphanumeric code	(p. 156)
chronologic filing	(p. 162)
consecutive numeric filing	(p. 151)
middle-digit filing	(p. 160)
numeric filing	(p. 149)
terminal-digit filing	(p. 159)

Questions for Discussion

1. Define *numeric filing* and explain when the numeric filing method should be used. (Obj. 1)
2. List two advantages and two disadvantages of using the numeric filing method. (Obj. 2)
3. List and describe the components of a consecutive numbered filing system. (Obj. 3)
4. Describe the consecutive numeric filing procedures. (Obj. 4)
5. List advantages and disadvantages of consecutive number filing. (Obj. 5)
6. Describe terminal-digit filing. (Obj. 6)
7. Describe middle-digit filing. (Obj. 7)
8. List advantages and disadvantages of terminal-digit or middle-digit filing. (Obj. 8)
9. Define and explain *chronologic filing*. (Obj. 9)
10. List three types of chronologic files. (Obj. 10)

Applications

Use a separate sheet of paper to prepare three accession logs and two alphabetic indexes as instructed below. Remember to write the names in correct indexing order and in order by the date on which each number is assigned in the accession logs.

1. Prepare an accession log for a consecutive numeric filing system. Begin with the names and assigned number code in the accession log in Figure 9-2 on page 152. Continue the numbering with 1006 and assign number codes to the following correspondents. Assign the numbers in order by the date provided in parentheses after each name. Use the current year. (Obj. 4)

   Mrs. A. J. Cummins, Jr. (6/2)

   U.S. Department of the Treasury (5/16)

   Frank Mendoza (6/18)

   Fort Howard Paper Company (6/11)

   The Detroit Free Press (6/12)

   A-1 Auto Repair (6/3)

2. Prepare an accession log for a terminal-digit filing system using the following names. The first number is 602320. Use the current year. (Obj. 6)

   G & R Mkt. (2/4)

   Colorado State Department of Motor Vehicles (3/5)

   Baker-Norton Construction Co. (2/5)

   John Bellamah's Deli (3/3)

   Samantha Smith-Davis (2/10)

3. Prepare an accession log for a middle-digit filing system using the following names. The first number is 450001. Use the current year. (Obj. 7)

   Dew-It-All Electric Co. (7/6)

   Watson's Casual Furniture (7/7)

   Transamerica Financial Services (7/1)

   Sister Margaret Chadwick (7/2)

   Day-Break Bakery (7/10)

4. Prepare an alphabetic index using the terminal-digit accession log you prepared in Application 2. Five original names and one cross-reference name will be in the index. Add to the index one cross-reference for Norton-Baker Construction Co. Use Figure 9-3 on page 153 as a guide. (Obj. 6)

5. Prepare an alphabetic index using the middle-digit accession log you prepared in Application 3. Five original names will be in the index. (Obj. 7)

Computer Applications

1. On a separate sheet of paper, create a database design sheet for an accession log, using Figure 9-2 on page 152 as an example. Use the 12 names in the accession log you prepared in Application 1 to design the database. Use the following information.

Date: Current

Database filename: ACCESLOG

Database description: Consecutive Numeric Accession Log

Fields: FILENO, NAME, DATE

Field lengths: Count the longest name, word, number, or date in each field. Count the spaces too. (NAME = 51; DATE = MM/DD/YY)

Index/sort the FILENO field.

2. If a computer is available for your use, create the ACCESLOG database in your computer. Key the names listed in the alphabetic index you prepared in Application 1 in indexing order into the database. Key the dates in the MM/DD/YY format (05/10/0–). Proofread carefully. If you are using the template, open filename **CH9AP2.DBF**. Index or sort the FILENO field.

3. Create and print a report from the ACCESLOG (CH9AP2.DBF) database.

Title your report: CONSECUTIVE NUMERIC ACCESSION LOG

Print the FILENO, NAME, and DATE fields in order.

Use these column headings: File No., Name or Subject, and Date.

Check to see that the file numbers are in correct number order. Give your printed report to your teacher for checking.

Chapter Ten

Geographic Filing

Learning Objectives

After completing Chapter 10, you will be able to do the following:

1. Define **geo-graphic filing**.

2. List types of organizations that use geographic filing.

3. Distinguish between the dictionary and the encyclopedic geographic file arrangements.

4. Distinguish between a lettered guide plan and a location name guide plan in geographic filing.

5. Inspect, code, cross-reference, sort, file, and retrieve records in a geographic file.

6. Explain the uses of an alphabetic index and a master index for a geographic file.

7. Explain when and how to expand the geographic file.

8. List advantages and disadvantages of geographic filing.

9. Prepare an alphabetic card index for a geographic file.

10. Prepare computer-generated indexes for a geographic file.

Need For Geographic Filing

Entering the "world of business" may mean just that in the office where you will work—business *of the world*, with all of its global implications. World events and high technology have brought countries of the world closer together. The collapse of communism in Eastern bloc countries, declining trade barriers, and advanced communication technology have changed the global marketplace significantly. Businesses that once operated only locally have expanded easily to city-wide, state-wide, nation-wide, and even world-wide operations. Expanding markets have provided opportunities for United States companies to move operations to foreign countries. Many foreign companies operate in the United States as well, while foreign investors continue to demonstrate super buying power in the United States.

Organizations that expect to be competitive in today's marketplace must have this new vision. A global perspective of business has influenced office-support personnel, increasing the need to maintain information and business records by location—geographic filing. When location significantly influences business operations, activities, and individuals, records are maintained by location to promote timely business decisions affecting those locations. In this chapter you will study the use of geographic filing and learn how to organize records by location when the business environment requires it.

What is geographic filing?

Geographic filing is a method of storing and retrieving records in alphabetical order by location of an individual, an organization, or a project. The need for geographic filing prevails in many areas of our social and political lives, as well as in business and industry. Political groups, social clubs, and societies with national or regional memberships use geographic filing systems. Companies that sell or buy in various regions use geographic files in their sales and purchasing departments. Large department stores with branch stores throughout the country, or even the world, find it useful to organize their records by location. Many mail-order companies, publishers, airlines, railways, wholesale houses, and real estate and travel-related agencies use geographic filing systems in one form or another.

Why is geographic filing necessary?

When business activities are spread over wide geographic areas, operational decisions in those areas need to be made: Where are the highest expenses in utilities, salaries, transportation, and materials? Where are the lowest costs? Where are profits the best? Where to expand? Where to cut back operations? Where to increase advertising? A geographic filing method allows management to make these important, necessary operational decisions that affect the success and growth of the organization.

Geographic Filing Methods

Because so many kinds of organizations make use of geographic filing, don't expect that a single design will satisfy the needs of every organization.

Geographic systems are tailored to fit the need of the organization. The expanse of business operations, from streets in a city to regions in the world, determines the scope of the file. If business activities are confined to a single city, then a file covering the districts within that city is adequate. Worldwide business activities require a file including those foreign locations.

In general, the filing segment in geographic filing includes geographic filing units first, followed by the correspondent's name. The geographic units are arranged from major to minor geographic units. Correspondents' names are arranged according to the alphabetic indexing rules already learned. When filing global activities geographically, consider the filing units in this order:

1. Country name
2. State name or state equivalent, such as provinces
3. City name
4. Correspondent name

There are two basic arrangements commonly used in *geographic* filing: (1) the dictionary arrangement and (2) the encyclopedic arrangement. You are already familiar with a dictionary and an encyclopedia. Knowing how information is arranged in these two resources helps you to understand these two basic filing arrangements.

Dictionary Geographic File Arrangement

The **dictionary arrangement** is the arrangement of records in alphabetic order (A-Z). This arrangement is used when the filing system contains a *single* geographic unit, such as a file of all streets, all cities, all states, or all countries. Study the sample files shown in Figures 10-1 and 10-2 on page 170. Both are dictionary arrangements of geographic files. Two different guide plans are used, however. The lettered guide plan is used in Figure 10-1, and the location name guide plan is used in Figure 10-2.

What is a dictionary geographic file arrangement?

Lettered Guide Plan

The lettered guide plan makes liberal use of alphabetic letter guides (A-Z) to divide the primary sections of the file. Figure 10-1 shows a reference card file for city sales districts. The file cards contain streets in the city and numbers identifying sales districts. Sales districts are easily expanded, reduced, and modified as needed. This is a simple type of geographic file in a dictionary arrangement: a file of street names arranged alphabetically from A to Z! Lettered guides, 1/5 cut in first position, divide the alphabetic sections of the file and speed up the filing process.

This reference card file easily converts to computer filing. Each card record becomes a computer database record. The record includes a data field for (1) the street name and house number, (2) the sales district number, and (3) any other useful information, such as district sales managers.

Figure 10-1
Dictionary Arrangement
of Cards
Lettered Guide Plan

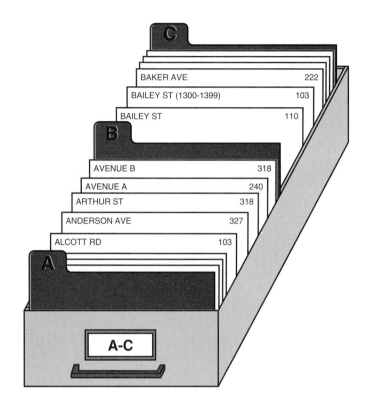

Figure 10-2
Dictionary Arrangement
of Folders
Location Name
Guide Plan

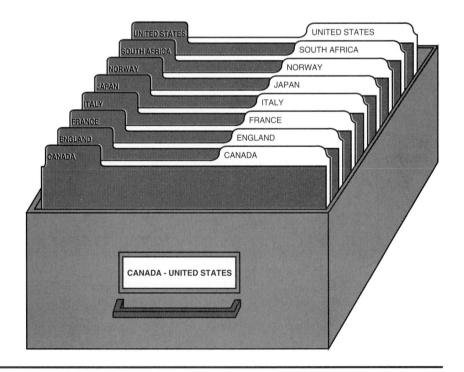

The database design sheet for the reference card file looks like this:

DATABASE DESIGN SHEET

Database name (filename) SALEDIST   **Date** 11/03/0–

Database description City Sales Districts

	Field Name	Field Description	Field Type	Field Length	Sort/Index
*1.	STREETNAME	City street name and house number	C (character)	20	Y
2.	DISTRICTNO	District number	C**	3	Y
3.	SALESMGR	Sales manager	C	18	Y
4.					

* Key field
** Only calculable numbers are considered numeric.

The data file can be sorted by STREETNAME, DISTRICTNO, or SALESMGR to produce three useful reports: (1) An alphabetic list of street names showing the sales districts to which the streets belong, (2) a list of sales districts showing the streets covered by those districts, and (3) an alphabetic list of sales managers and their assigned sales districts. All this information can be extracted from a single input of data.

Why convert card files to computer databases?

Location Name Guide Plan

The **location name guide plan** makes use of location name guides to divide primary sections of the file. A dictionary arrangement of folders by country is shown in Figure 10-2 (CANADA to UNITED STATES). Such a file might contain travel information, transportation costs, correspondence, or reports related to those countries. Additional guides and folders are prepared and added to the file as needed. Location name guides, 1/5 cut in first position, separate the main sections of the file. The location name guide plan works well in systems where location names are few and diverse.

Encyclopedic Geographic File Arrangement

The **encyclopedic arrangement** is the alphabetic arrangement of major geographic divisions *plus* one or more geographic *subdivisions* also arranged in alphabetic order. Either the lettered guide plan or the location name guide plan may be used for the subdivisions. The files shown in Figures 10-3 and 10-4 hold identical records. However, the Figure 10-3 illustration uses the *lettered guide plan* for secondary city guides; Figure 10-4 uses the *location name guide plan* for secondary city guides.

What is an encyclopedic geographic file arrangement?

Figure 10-3 Encyclopedic Arrangement of Lettered Guide Plan for Geographic File

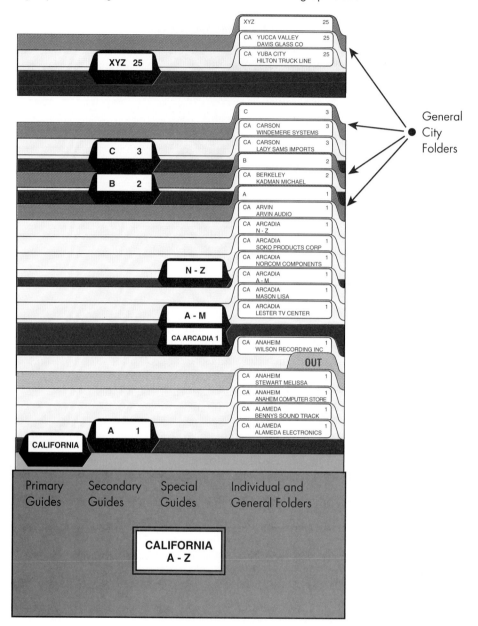

General
City
Folders

XYZ 25

C 3

B 2

N - Z

A - M

CA ARCADIA 1

A 1

CALIFORNIA

| Primary Guides | Secondary Guides | Special Guides | Individual and General Folders |

**CALIFORNIA
A - Z**

XYZ   25
CA YUCCA VALLEY   25
    DAVIS GLASS CO
CA YUBA CITY   25
    HILTON TRUCK LINE

C   3
CA CARSON   3
    WINDEMERE SYSTEMS
CA CARSON   3
    LADY SAMS IMPORTS
B   2
CA BERKELEY   2
    KADMAN MICHAEL
A   1
CA ARVIN   1
    ARVIN AUDIO
CA ARCADIA   1
    N - Z
CA ARCADIA   1
    SOKO PRODUCTS CORP
CA ARCADIA   1
    NORCOM COMPONENTS
CA ARCADIA   1
    A - M
CA ARCADIA   1
    MASON LISA
CA ARCADIA   1
    LESTER TV CENTER
CA ANAHEIM   1
    WILSON RECORDING INC
OUT
CA ANAHEIM   1
    STEWART MELISSA
CA ANAHEIM   1
    ANAHEIM COMPUTER STORE
CA ALAMEDA   1
    BENNYS SOUND TRACK
CA ALAMEDA   1
    ALAMEDA ELECTRONICS

Compare the illustrations in Figures 10-3 and 10-4 as you study the following file arrangements and guide plans.

Lettered Guide Plan

The **lettered guide plan** makes free use of alphabetic lettered guides to divide the city subdivisions. The guide plan shown in Figure 10-3

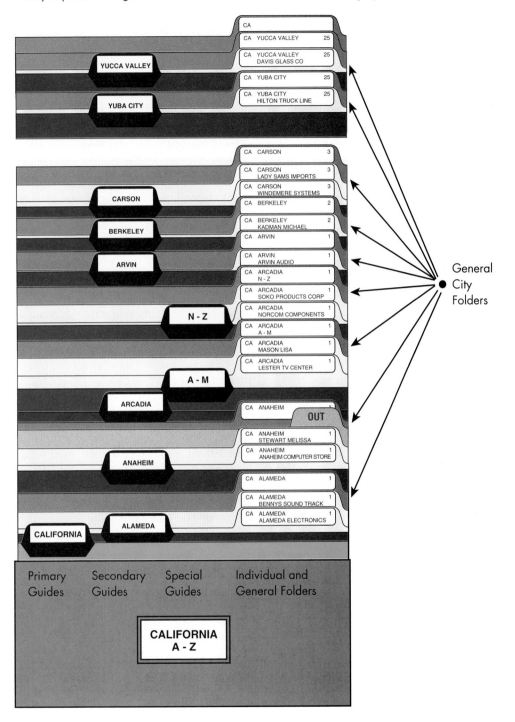

accommodates the entire filing segment—ALL filing units from the largest to the smallest geographic unit, as well as the correspondent's name. The illustration shows part of a geographic correspondence file arranged first by states. The guide plan includes (1) the state name, (2) the city name, and (3) the name of the correspondent. Although variations in guide placement are possible, this system is designed as follows:

1. Primary guides are 1/5-cut guides in first position. The primary guide in Figure 10-3 marks the key unit, which is a state name—CALIFORNIA.

2. Secondary guides are 1/5-cut guides in second position. The secondary guides are alphabetic guides and show the alphabetic range of the city names filed behind them. The guides are numbered consecutively to aid the filer in keeping them in correct alphabetic sequence.

3. Special guides, if needed, are 1/5-cut, third-position guides. Two kinds of special guides are shown in Figure 10-3: special city name guides and special lettered guides (A-M and N-Z). The special city name guides point to city names that are frequently accessed. The special lettered guides, which follow the special city name guides, provide an alphabetic subdivision of the correspondents' names in those cities.

4. Individual folders, special folders, and general folders are 1/3-cut, third-position folders and provide the straight-line filing format preferred in all filing systems.

5. OUT guides show what records have been borrowed from the files. Figures 10-3 and 10-4 illustrate OUT guides as 1/5-cut, fifth-position guides.

Study the two-line caption on the individual folder labels. The two-letter state abbreviations are keyed as close to the top of the label as possible, two spaces from the left edge of the label. The next filing designator, the city, is keyed five spaces to the right of the abbreviation. The two-letter state abbreviations are recommended because they require less label space. Other identifying information, if needed, is keyed directly under the first letter of the city name. The label looks like this:

General folders for the secondary guides carry the same lettered caption as the guide and appear at the end of the subsections. Keep all cities in California beginning with that letter in these general city folders in alphabetic order BY CITY. Within each city group, arrange correspondence alphabetically by correspondents' names. Place records with the same correspondent's name in order by date with the most recent record in front.

Examine general folders periodically. When the accumulation of documents exceeds 3/4" (19 millimeters), subdivide the general folder. For example, the A general folder can be divided AA - AK for one folder and AL - AZ for the second. Also, open individual folders for active correspondents with five or more documents.

Place general folders at the end of each subsection. If placed at the beginning of the subsection, you may overlook an individual folder prepared for the name you're filing. By placing the general folder at the end of the subsection, you first scan for an individual folder. If there is no individual folder, you do not have to backtrack to place the record in the general folder.

Location Name Guide Plan

Figure 10-3 and Figure 10-4 show the same filed records, but Figure 10-4 uses the location name guide plan. The secondary guides are location names (ALAMEDA, BERKELEY, CARSON) rather than letters (A, B, C). The location name guide plan works well with geographic files requiring a small number of subdivisions. The excessive use of lettered guides in a small system will clutter the file rather than aid in the retrieval process. Although other guide and folder positions are possible, this system is designed as follows:

1. Primary guides are 1/5-cut guides in first position. The primary guide shown in Figure 10-4 marks the key unit, which is a state name— CALIFORNIA.

2. Secondary guides are 1/5-cut guides in second position. These secondary guides point to cities from which sufficient correspondence warrants the use of a secondary city name guide. The secondary city name guides in Figure 10-4 include ALAMEDA, ANAHEIM, ARCADIA, ARVIN, BERKELEY, CARSON, YUBA CITY, and YUCCA VALLEY.

3. Special guides, if needed, are 1/5-cut guides in third position. The special lettered guides in Figure 10-4 (A-M and N-Z) provide an alphabetic subdivision of correspondents' names within those cities.

4. All individual, special, and general folders are 1/3-cut, third-position folders and provide the straight-line filing format preferred in all filing systems. Captions on the individual folders are the same as those used in the lettered guide plan. The state abbreviation and the city name, as well as the correspondent's name, are all part of the label caption and aid in returning borrowed folders to their correct file location.

General folders are provided for the primary STATE guides, the secondary CITY guides, and the special guides. They carry the same captions as the guides and are placed at the end of their file guide sections. In Figure 10-4 the general folder for the primary guide (state name) is shaded at the end of the state section of the file. Correspondence from all California cities is stored in the general state folder until individual *city* folders are needed.

The general folders for the secondary guides (city names) carry the same captions as the guides. These general city folders are shaded and appear at the end of each city section. All correspondents from that particular city are filed alphabetically in the general city folder until an individual correspondent name folder is needed.

5. OUT guides show what records have been borrowed from the files. The OUT guide illustrated is a 1/5-cut, fifth-position guide.

Although other arrangements of guides and folders exist, a thorough understanding of the two arrangements just illustrated will allow you to adapt easily to alternate arrangements. In general, records and information managers suggest that (1) primary guides be 1/5 cut in first position (far left for top-access filing; top for side-access filing), (2) secondary guides be 1/5 cut in second position, and (3) tertiary (third subdivision) guides be 1/5 cut in third position, and so on. Although one-fifth cut tabs are recommended for guides, guide tabs vary in size and must be selected to accommodate the size of the caption. One-third-cut, third-position folders (on the right side) are recommended for folders in vertical/top-access paper files. However, half-cut, second-position folders may be needed to accommodate longer folder label captions in some systems. Full-cut folders are recommended for lateral/side-access filing.

Source: *Photography by Erik Von Fischer/Photonics*

Geographic File Indexes

Filing problems sometimes arise when the correspondents' names are not used as first indexing units. Geographic files arrange records first by location and *then* by company or individual names. Therefore, location must be known to find the record. Sometimes correspondents write from a location different from their usual business address. To solve problems such as these, prepare an index. An **index** systematically guides the access to specific items contained within a larger body of information. The alphabetic index and the master index are two useful indexes when filing by location.

Alphabetic Index

An alphabetic index of all correspondents' names and their locations is needed in a geographic filing system. The filer locates the correspondent's name in the alphabetic index in order to find the address, when it is not known. The address determines the location of the record in the main geographic file. The index may be in the form of (1) a typed list, (2) a card file, or (3) a computer-generated list. However it is maintained, the index must be in an easily updated format—easy to add, delete, and change names and locations. Information in the index must include (1) the correspondent's name, (2) the state name, and (3) the city name. An alphabetic index, when needed, is used in the following manner:

What is the purpose of an alphabetic index in a geographic filing system?

1. Before filing a record, refer to the alphabetic index to see if the name of the correspondent is in the index. If not, enter the name and address of the correspondent. Because the correspondent is new, enter the letter GS (general state folder) or GC (general city folder) on the list, card, or in the database. The GS or GC code indicates that records relating to that person or company are in a general folder. Place the record in the appropriate general folder.

2. Later, when the volume of correspondence is sufficient for a particular correspondent, move all records for this correspondent from the general folder to an individual folder. Remember to remove the GS or GC code from the alphabetic index and enter an I in its place. The *I* signifies a transfer of the correspondent's records to an individual folder.

    Follow a similar procedure when correspondence from one city accumulates in a general state folder. Prepare a general city folder and transfer to it all materials to and from that city. In this example, change the GS to GC in the alphabetic index to indicate transfer of the records from a general STATE folder (GS) to a general CITY folder (GC).

Figure 10-5 shows a typical card record from an alphabetic card index. The cards are arranged by correspondents' names. Figure 10-6 shows a typical record from a geographic computer database file. A

```
NUWAY DRY CLEANERS              GS


NU-WAY DRY CLEANERS
3718 SILVER LN
LANCASTER NY 14086-3544
```

Figure 10-5 Card Record for an Alphabetic Index

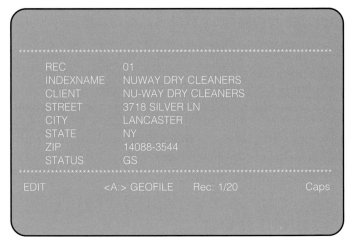

Figure 10-6 Computer Database File Record

record number field (01) and a status field (GS) are included. The record numbers help to locate records quickly when changes occur in the index. When sorted by name, the printed file (including name, status, and location) serves as the alphabetic index for the geographic file.

Master Index

What is a master index?

If the records are sorted first by state, then by city, and finally by correspondent's name, the printed report becomes a master index for the file. A **master index** is a complete listing of all filing segments in the filing system. Advantages of a computer database are apparent: Two useful indexes, a master index and an alphabetic index, can be printed from a single input of records. Folder labels and mailing labels can be prepared, as well, from the same stored data.

You learned from Chapter 5 the importance of determining the end results when planning a database. When personal and business names are mixed in a database, it is wise to have one field for a name AS INDEXED and another field for the name AS WRITTEN. The indexed field name enables accurate sorting of the entire file and preparation of folder labels. The name-as-written field simplifies the preparation of mailing labels.

Most database software programs require separate fields for items to be sorted. For example, when mailing labels are sorted by ZIP Code, the ZIP Code field must be a *separate* field; or if the file is sorted by state, then the state field needs to be a *separate* field. Fields can be joined later, as needed, to print labels, indexes, and reports.

Geographic Filing Procedures

Geographic correspondence filing follows filing procedures similar to those procedures used in alphabetic name correspondence filing: (1) inspecting, (2) coding, (3) preparing cross-references, (4) sorting, and (5) filing. Slight differences exist, however. The review that follows covers these differences. When necessary, distinctions are made also between the lettered guide plan and the location name guide plan.

What are the procedures for filing records?

Inspecting

Inspect each incoming letter to be sure that it has been released for filing. Check each paper to see that it has been dated. If no date appears on the record, write or stamp the current date on the record for filing purposes.

Coding

Geographic locations are considered the first part of the filing segment; therefore, mark the locations clearly. Circle geographic units in the name, and number them to show their rank in indexing order. See Figure 10-7.

After coding the geographic units, index the correspondent's name according to the alphabetic indexing rules already learned. Use diagonal lines to separate the filing units, and number them to show their indexing order.

Preparing Cross-References

In geographic filing, as in alphabetic filing, cross-references are sometimes necessary. For example, a compound name or an unusual name may require a cross-reference; or a letter may contain useful information about another company or person. When cross-references are

Figure 10-7
Letter Coded for
Geographic Filing

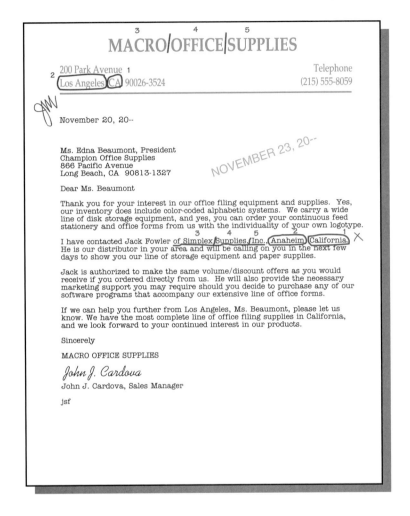

needed, code the original document and use one of the following:
(1) cross-reference sheets, (2) photocopies, or (3) cross-reference notations on guide or folder labels.

Study the cross-reference sheet in Figure 10-8 prepared for the name
Simplex Supplies, Inc., in Anaheim, California. The name is written on the
cross-reference sheet in indexing order. Refer again to Figure 10-7: Notice
that the city and state names are circled and numbered on the original
record. The name for cross-reference is underscored with a wavy line *and*
indexed in the usual manner. Remember to consider the geographic location
(state and city) before the correspondent's name in geographic filing systems.

The simplest way to prepare a cross-reference for a letter is to photocopy the coded original record. When photocopying a letter for a cross-reference, the copy of the coded letter substitutes for the cross-reference sheet.

Cross-references on guide or folder labels are useful when there is a
long-term reason for calling attention to a cross-reference, for example,
when a correspondent has offices in several locations. This type of

Figure 10-8
Cross-Reference Sheet

CROSS-REFERENCE SHEET

Name or Subject

CA/Anaheim/
Simplex/Supplies/Inc.

Date of Record

Nov. 20, 20--

Regarding

Filing equipment and
supplies

See

Name or Subject

CA Los Angeles
Macro Office Supplies

Date Filed ____*11/26/0-*____ By *JM*

cross-reference uses a permanent cross-reference notation on the folder label. If Economy Stores, Inc., has its main office in Carson, California, but has branch offices in Daly City and Alameda as well, show it on the folder label in this manner:

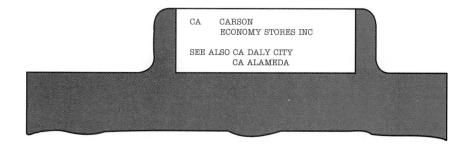

```
CA    CARSON
      ECONOMY STORES INC

SEE ALSO CA DALY CITY
         CA ALAMEDA
```

In like manner, the folder label in the CA DALY CITY section of the file would cite CA ALAMEDA and CA CARSON as alternate locations for Economy Stores, Inc. A third cross-reference would appear, as well, in the CA ALAMEDA section for Economy Stores, Inc.

Sorting

Sort letters and other records by geographic units, starting with the major geographic unit and continuing until all units in the filing segment have been used. For example, the first sorting might be by states; the second, cities; and the third, names of correspondents.

Filing

The procedures for storing and retrieving records in a geographic filing system are similar to those used in any other type of system. Locate the proper folder location by making use of labels and guides as follows:

1. Read the drawer labels to find the file drawer covering the geographic range for the record.

2. Scan the primary guides in the drawer that will point to the key unit of the filing segment.

3. Scan the secondary guides. These guides usually show either an alphabetic arrangement of letter guides or location name guides. Figure 10-3 uses lettered guides for city locations; Figure 10-4 uses location name guides for city locations.

    Look for other helpful subdivisions, such as the special city name guide and special letter guides in Figure 10-3. See also the A-M and N-Z special letter guides behind the ARCADIA city guide in Figure 10-4. From this point, the filing procedures vary according to the guide plan used.

How are records arranged in individual folders?

Lettered Guide Plan

In the lettered guide plan, locate the alphabetic section in which the city name falls. If there is an individual folder for the correspondent, place the record in it with the most recently dated record in front.

How are records arranged in general city folders?

    If there is no individual folder, or special city folder, place the record in the proper general alphabetic city folder (B for Bakersfield, P for Pasadena, etc.). Arrange letters in general folders alphabetically first by the city names and then by the names of the correspondents. If there are correspondents with identical names in the same city, follow the identical names rule, Rule 9—use street names. Finally, arrange each name group in order by date with the most recent letter in front.

Location Name Guide Plan

After locating the city section in which the correspondent is located, look for an individual folder for the correspondent. If there is a folder, file the record in the individual folder placing the most current record in front.

If there is no individual folder, look for a general city folder. If there is a city folder, place the record in the general city folder in alphabetic order by correspondent's name. Arrange records from the same correspondent with the most recent record in front.

When no general city folder is found, place the record in the general *state* folder, for example, CA. Group records in the general state folder first by city or town; next, in each city group, by correspondents' names; and finally, in each correspondent's group, by date with the most recent record in front.

How are records arranged in general state folders?

Expansion of the Geographic File

Geographic systems are readily adaptable and can be reduced and expanded with relative ease. The alert filer knows when changes in the system are necessary and how to make them. When customers are lost or vendors changed, sections of the file are simply eliminated at, or before, transfer time. Expanding the filing system, however, is more challenging.

When to Expand

As business operations continue throughout a year, changes occur that require adjustments in the records control system. For example, a business will correspond with new customers and will buy from new vendors; therefore, new names or sections will need to be added to the filing system.

The first indication of a need for expansion in a system is an increase in the volume of incoming and outgoing records processed for filing. An overcrowded folder, however, always indicates a need for expansion.

When should a filing system be expanded?

How to Expand

In efficiently managed records departments, space for expansion is anticipated at transfer time. Free space is left in every file drawer and on every shelf section. This space can be used for adding folders to the system.

For example, when general state folders become overcrowded with materials from correspondents from the same cities, add new general city folders to the system. Remove the blocks of records from the crowded general *state* folders and refile them in the new general *city* folders. In a like manner, when general *city* folders begin to bulge, look for groups of correspondents that can be transferred to newly prepared *individual* folders.

Review the file drawer positions that have been used for special guides and folders in Figures 10-3 and 10-4. These special sections help to alleviate crowding and make the system more efficient. Special sections may include a series of dated, lettered, or name guides, intended to divide crowded individual folders. Also, special guides can be used to identify sections that will hold especially active materials—records that are frequently requested.

Advantages and Disadvantages of Geographic Filing

Advantages of geographic filing have already been mentioned. They include the ability to group business activities by location; to evaluate business activities by location for the improvement of total operations; and to use a filing system that allows the addition, deletion, division, or rearrangement of territories to improve overall business operations.

Geographic filing has certain disadvantages too. The need for an alphabetic index means that time must be spent preparing and maintaining it. Filers occasionally must search through the index to locate needed records in the main file.

Another disadvantage of the geographic file is that no place is provided for filing papers relating to the internal operations of a company. Where are papers relating to the hiring of new employees filed? Some offices add appropriate primary guides to handle internal communications. For example, a primary guide is added that has been labeled with the name of the place where a company is located; then, behind this guide, other guides and folders are added, such as for Accounting, Applications, Personnel, and Purchasing.

How can internal records be stored in a geographic file?

Review

1. Explain how the filing segment is *coded* for geographic filing.

2. When preparing a cross-reference of an unusual name in geographic filing, what part of the filing segment is considered first (is the key unit)? second?

Summary

The globalization of the international economy will continue to influence American business operations. Whenever location is a primary factor in the operations of an organization—statewide, nationwide, or worldwide—some kind of geographic filing will be needed. The dictionary arrangement of records by location is used to arrange main geographic units alphabetically from A to Z. When subdivisions of geographic units are needed, the encyclopedic arrangement is used. The secondary guide captions in the encyclopedic arrangement may be letters or location names.

An alphabetic index helps to locate correspondents whose locations are not known. A master index lists all filing segments in the system and is especially useful to first-time file users who want to examine the scope, or territorial range, of the system.

When using a geographic file, familiarize yourself with the geographic breakdown of the file by either checking the master index or scanning the main file. The scope of the file depends, of course, on the territorial range of business activities. The filing procedures for inspecting, coding, preparing cross-references, sorting, and filing are similar to those procedures in other filing methods. Just remember in geographic filing that the correspondent's LOCATION is considered before the correspondent's name.

Terminology Review

dictionary arrangement	(p. 169)
encyclopedic arrangement	(p. 171)
geographic filing	(p. 168)
index	(p. 177)
lettered guide plan	(p. 172)
location name guide plan	(p. 171)
master index	(p. 178)

Questions for Discussion

1. Define *geographic filing*. (Obj. 1)
2. Name two types of organizations that would make use of geographic filing. (Obj. 2)
3. What is the primary difference between a dictionary arrangement and an encyclopedic arrangement of a geographic file? (Obj. 3)
4. What is the difference between a lettered guide plan and a location name guide plan used in geographic filing? (Obj. 4)
5. How are records arranged in individual folders in a geographic file? (Obj. 5)
6. How are records arranged in general city folders? (Obj. 5)
7. How are records arranged in general state folders? (Obj. 5)
8. What is the purpose of an alphabetic index? a master index? (Obj. 6)
9. When general city folders become crowded in your filing system, what can you do to relieve this condition? (Obj. 7)
10. When individual folders become overcrowded, how can special guides help to relieve this condition? (Obj. 7).
11. List two advantages and two disadvantages of geographic filing. (Obj. 8)

Applications

1. On a separate piece of paper, write or key the following names. Code the names according to the instructions given on pp. 179-182. Sort the names for geographic filing, and report your answer by writing the number of each name in correct order. (Obj. 5)

a. KLM Royal Dutch Airlines
P. O. Box 7700
1117 ZL Schiphol Airport
Amsterdam, Netherlands

b. Kajima Corporation
2-7, Motoakasaka, 1-Chome
Minato-Ku, Tokyo 107, Japan

c. Kuwait Petroleum Corporation
P.O. Box 26565,
13126 Safat
Kuwait

d. MTM PLC
Rudby Hall, Hutton Rudby
Yarm, Cleveland TS15 OSN
England, United Kingdom

e. Oil City Petroleum, Inc.
5579 S. Lewis
Tulsa, OK 74105-3702

f. Oxwall Tool Co.
133 - 1032nd. Ave.
Flushing, NY 11354-1921

g. Intex Corp
10, Lane 43, Fu Hsin Rd
Hsintien, Taipei Hsien
Taiwan

h. Italia Di Navigazione S. P. A.
Piazza de Ferrari, 1 16121
Genoa, Italy

i. Investment AB Cardo
Box 486
20124 Malmo, Sweden

j. Ozark-Mahoning Co.
1870 Boulder Ave.
Tulsa, OK 74119-5234

2. a. Key or write each of the following names and addresses on a 5" x 3" index card or on paper cut to that size. Follow the same format as that shown in Figure 10-5 on p. 178. These cards will be arranged later as an alphabetic index and a master index to accompany a geographic file. Place a G in the upper right corner of the card to show that the new record will be placed in a general folder. Key the name *in indexing order* at the top (ALL CAPS NO PUNCTUATION); then key the name and address below in a style acceptable for a mailing label (ALL CAPS, NO PERIODS OR COMMAS; do include hyphens and apostrophes so that the name is not altered from the way the correspondent writes it.) Number each card at the bottom left margin (1-20). You will use these numbers later to report your card order on an answer sheet. (Obj. 5)

Rec#	Client	Street	City	State	ZIP Code
01	Nu-Way Dry Cleaners	3718 Silver Ln.	Lancaster	NY	14088-3544
02	North Side Jewelers	918 Ace Ave.	Bethlehem	PA	18017-3211
03	Oliver Stoffer Electronics	230 Lark Ln.	Norristown	PA	19401-2213

Rec#	Client	Street	City	State	ZIP Code
04	Dun's Diner	23 Main St.	Johnstown	PA	15901-3328
05	Wil-Kil Pest Control Co	3602 Washington Ave.	Newberry	SC	29108-8266
06	Northside Department Store	739 W. North St.	Bethlehem	PA	18018-8355
07	North Star Car Wash	97 Copeland Ave.	Altona	NY	12910-3351
08	B & B Root Beer	18376 Hwy 12	Newburgh	NY	12550-4422
09	Bond-Well Dry Walls	415 Nelson Pl.	New Castle	PA	16101-5561
10	Larry S. Nutall	1819 E. Madison St.	Lancaster	PA	17602-3381
11	Andy's Duraclean Services	1973 A St.	Buffalo	NY	14211-1661
12	Boyd's Sporting Goods	7231 W. Salem Rd.	Williamsport	PA	17701-3577
13	Marie's Women's Wear	176 Market St.	Schenectady	NY	12302-4222
14	Rev. T. P. Bruce	527 Cass Bldg.	Charleston	SC	29401-6299
15	Bruce Termite Protection	417 Exchange Bldg.	Charleston	SC	29401-2241
16	Nut-All Peanut Shop	2615 Washington Ave.	Lancaster	PA	17603-3811
17	Wilki Leather Shop	94 Race St.	Newberry	SC	29108-2255
18	Tom Cat Hamburgers	401 Maple St.	Greenville	SC	29609-3771
19	Tom's Speedometer Shop	27 Elm Cir.	Greenville	PA	16125-3721
20	Tom Speed	4819 Jefferson Cir.	Greenville	SC	29602-5271

b. After preparing the cards, arrange them for an alphabetic index. Sort alphabetically by correspondents' names. Prepare an answer sheet by numbering 1-20 on a clean sheet of paper. Opposite each number, record the number of each name in the order you arranged the names. (Obj. 9)

c. Arrange the cards for geographic filing. Sort alphabetically first by states, then by cities, and finally by correspondents' names. Prepare an answer sheet by numbering 1-20 on a clean sheet. Opposite each number, record the number of each name in the order you arranged the names. (Obj. 5)

d. Use plain paper to simulate folder labels. Fold an 8½" x 11" paper once lengthwise so that the labels measure 4¼" wide. Then fold the paper in half, then again, and again until you have creased eight "labels" down each half the page. Two sheets of paper folded will supply you with 32 labels and 12 extra labels. Prepare a geographic individual file folder label for each name. Key the labels in correct alphabetic order. Key names from the top to the bottom of the first column of labels; then key the second column. Repeat this procedure for the second page. Use state abbreviations. Key the names in indexing order, all caps, no punctuation. Follow the folder label design shown on p. 174.

At this time, complete Job 11, *Geographic Filing,* in OFFICE FILING PROCEDURES, Eighth Edition. Instructions and supplies for this job are included in the practice set.

Computer Applications

1. If you are using the template available with this textbook, begin with No. 1.a. If you are going to design and create your own database file, begin with No. 1.b.

a. Open file CH10AP1.DBF from the template diskette and proceed to No. 2.b.

b. Prepare a Database Design Sheet for keying the names and addresses in Application 2, p. 186. Study the reports needed from the stored data (See 2.b., c., d., and e. below) before planning the field lengths. Be sure all needed data will fit on a single line of the report. Create separate fields for sorting the city, state, and ZIP Code fields. Create an indexed-name field for sorting and printing the indexes and mailing labels. Create a name-as-written field for printing mailing labels. Name the file GEOFILE and include the following fields:

REC (numbers 01-20)

INDEXNAME (the name as indexed)

CLIENT (the name as written)

STREET (street address)

CITY (city name)

STATE (state abbreviation)

ZIP (ZIP Code)

STATUS (Indicate GS for general state folder)

2.a. Use a database of your choice to create the database file [GEOFILE] that you designed above.

b. Index/sort the data for an alphabetic index. Title the report ALPHABETIC INDEX FOR GEOGRAPHIC FILE. Print only the needed data. Include in the report the column headings in the order shown below:

Client Name Indexed	State	City	Status	Rec#

3. Index/sort the data for a master index. Title the report GEOGRAPHIC MASTER INDEX. Include only the data fields needed. Group the STATE field if your database software supports this feature. Otherwise, include in the report a STATE column and the other column headings in the order shown below:

State	City	Client Name Indexed	Status	Rec#

4. (OPTIONAL) Index/sort the file by ZIP Codes; then print one set of mailing labels for all names in the database file.

5. (OPTIONAL) Index/sort the file for folder labels (same sort as the master index). Place the state and city on line one of the label. Place the client's name (as indexed) on line two as illustrated on p. 174.

Chapter Eleven

Subject Filing

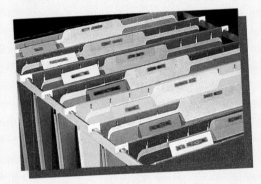

Learning Objectives

After completing Chapter 11, you will be able to do the following:

1. Define **subject filing**.
2. Describe when subject filing should be used.
3. Define and describe the **dictionary subject filing arrangement.**
4. Define and describe the **encyclopedic subject filing arrangement.**
5. Define and prepare a **subject file list/index.**
6. Explain why an alphabetic index is needed in a subject filing system.
7. Describe subject filing procedures.
8. Explain the use of subject codes and prepare a subject file list using subject codes.
9. List advantages and disadvantages of subject filing.

Need for Subject Filing

When records are requested by subject titles rather than by names of persons or organizations, subject filing is needed. **Subject filing** is a method of classifying, coding, and filing records by subject. In a *subject filing system,* information is filed primarily under subject titles.

How is information filed in a subject filing system?

You have previously studied alphabetic filing, which included some subject titles. Subject filing is used in some way in almost every office. Subject files can be arranged by geographic area: EXPENSE REPORTS SOUTHWEST REGION, for example. Subject files also can be arranged by department (EXPENSE REPORTS ADVERTISING DEPARTMENT) or functional area (EXPENSE REPORTS MANUFACTURING). Remember that a functional area refers to those operations that keep the organization functioning. Examples include accounting, administration, finance, manufacturing, marketing, records and information systems, and operations. Subjects are arranged alphabetically, and a standard set of alphabetic indexing rules are used.

Subject filing should be used whenever a series of records cannot be filed by any other filing feature or characteristic, such as a name, geographic location or area, number, or date. Records with preprinted numbers, such as invoices and checks, can be filed numerically. Employee records can be filed alphabetically by name or employee number. Sales records can be filed by date. Utility company records can be filed by geographic location. In each of these examples, the records are requested by name, number, date, or geographic location.

When records are requested most often by subject, then subject filing should be used. Subject filing is appropriate for catalogs, clippings, correspondence, inventory lists, research files, and reports. Subject or topical filing systems often use other features, such as names or numbers, to subdivide data.

When is a subject filing system needed?

After the subject filing method has been chosen, further analysis of the records determines whether a dictionary or encyclopedic arrangement should be used. You will study these two arrangements next.

Dictionary Arrangement

Records may be filed in a subject filing system in a **dictionary arrangement**—in alphabetic order by specific subject. This arrangement also is referred to as *topical arrangement* and *straight dictionary arrangement*. In the dictionary arrangement, subject folders are arranged behind A-Z guides in alphabetic order according to the subject titles.

What other terms may be used for the dictionary arrangement?

The dictionary subject arrangement should be used when the volume of records is no greater than two file drawers. As the volume of records increases, retrieval from a dictionary arrangement becomes difficult. When the volume of records is small, an index (also called a *subject file list*) is not needed because records are retrieved by *direct access*. In other words, the filer locates records by referring directly to the captions on the guides and folders. However, a subject list is helpful when indexing and coding to ensure that correct subjects are assigned. A portion of a dictionary subject file is shown in Figure 11-1.

Figure 11-1
Dictionary Subject
Arrangement

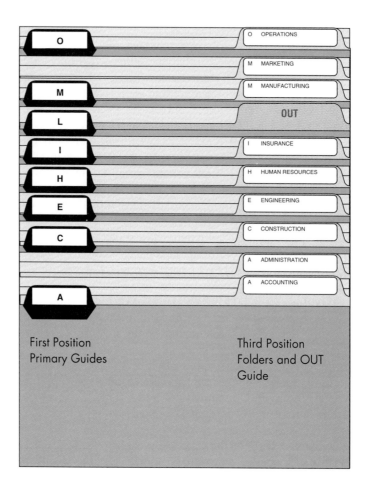

O	OPERATIONS
M	MARKETING
M	MANUFACTURING
	OUT
I	INSURANCE
H	HUMAN RESOURCES
E	ENGINEERING
C	CONSTRUCTION
A	ADMINISTRATION
A	ACCOUNTING

First Position
Primary Guides

Third Position
Folders and OUT
Guide

Encyclopedic Arrangement

How are records filed in the encyclopedic arrangement?

Records may be filed in a subject filing system in an **encyclopedic arrangement**—primary subjects and their subdivisions are arranged in alphabetic order. Records are divided into broad groups and then subdivided into more specific topics. By subdividing main topics for filing related information, the encyclopedic subject arrangement can accommodate larger volumes of records.

The flexibility of the encyclopedic arrangement allows growth and change of subjects with a minimum of revisions in the filing system. Main divisions are PRIMARY subject headings (titles or topics), or first-level headings. More specific subjects are SECONDARY, or second-level, headings. The most specific headings are the third-level, or TERTIARY, subject headings. For example, a contract for construction of a new warehouse would have the following units:

Primary: ADMINISTRATION

Secondary: BUILDING CONTRACTS

Tertiary: WAREHOUSE

The encyclopedic subject filing system is an *indirect access system.* *Indirect access* means that a filer may need to reference an index before a record can be filed or retrieved. Figure 11-2 shows a portion of an encyclopedic subject file.

Why is encyclopedic filing an indirect access system?

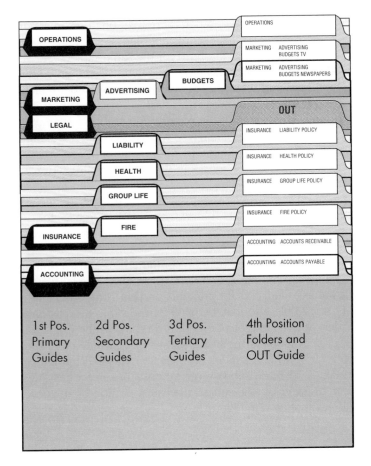

Figure 11-2
Encyclopedic
Subject File

Review

1. When should subject filing be used?
2. What two arrangements are used in subject filing?

Subject File List/Index

After choosing the dictionary or encyclopedic subject arrangement, the next step is to select the subject headings (titles). A **subject file list** (also called an index) is a complete listing of all subject headings in a subject filing system. In a small records system, the number of headings should be limited. A larger subject records system requires a longer subject list and numerous cross-references. Because subjects coded on records must match a predetermined subject, the subject file list should be available when indexing and coding records. If a filer is unsure of a subject heading, the subject list should be referenced before filing or retrieving a record.

Why should only one person assign subjects?

Only one person should be responsible for assigning subjects and maintaining the subject file list. When more than one person assigns subjects, chaos can occur if related records are filed under more than one subject and if different words are used for the same subject.

Classification is the process of analyzing and determining the subject content of a record and selecting the subject heading under which it will be filed. The person assigned the task of selecting subject headings must have a thorough knowledge of the records and records system. Subject headings should be concise (using few words), accurately descriptive of the contents, and capable of only one interpretation.

General subject cross-references in the subject file list/index will direct filers to other possible locations before searching the files for specific information. A cross-reference sheet is prepared for specific records and filed in the appropriate subject folder. Only cross-references for possible subject headings are prepared; correspondent names are not cross-referenced in a subject filing system.

The subject file list/index may be computerized and a printout used when indexing, coding, filing, and retrieving. When several filers must access the subject file list, extra printouts prevent congestion and relieve frustration. A card file also may be used for the subject file list/index.

Brief descriptions of types of records filed under the primary subject headings, or definitions of the headings, may be included in a subject file list/index. A subject file list/index for a dictionary subject arrangement is shown in Figure 11-3. All subdivisions of primary subject headings are included in an encyclopedic subject file list. A portion of an encyclopedic subject file list is shown in Figure 11-4.

Alphabetic Index

Maintaining an alphabetic index of correspondent names is essential in a subject filing system because it helps to find records for a specific correspondent. A subject file list/index is used when assigning subjects to correspondents because only those subjects on the file list can be used in the system. When the filer locates the correspondent's name in the alphabetic index, he or she will also find the subject under which the

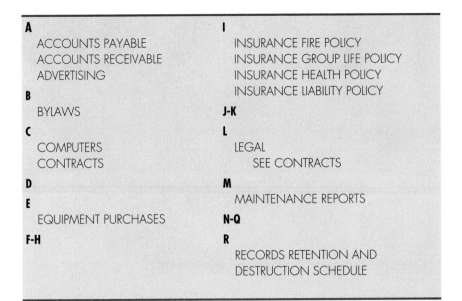

Figure 11-3
Dictionary Subject File List/Index

A
   ACCOUNTS PAYABLE
   ACCOUNTS RECEIVABLE
   ADVERTISING
B
   BYLAWS
C
   COMPUTERS
   CONTRACTS
D
E
   EQUIPMENT PURCHASES
F-H

I
   INSURANCE FIRE POLICY
   INSURANCE GROUP LIFE POLICY
   INSURANCE HEALTH POLICY
   INSURANCE LIABILITY POLICY
J-K
L
   LEGAL
      SEE CONTRACTS
M
   MAINTENANCE REPORTS
N-Q
R
   RECORDS RETENTION AND
   DESTRUCTION SCHEDULE

Figure 11-4
Encyclopedic Subject File List/Index

RECORDS MANAGEMENT
   FORMS MANAGEMENT
   MICROFILM MANAGEMENT
      MICROFICHE READERS
      MICROFILM DUPLICATORS
      MICROFILM PROCESSORS
      MICROFILM READER/PRINTERS
      MICROFILM READERS
   RECORDS DISPOSITION
      DISPOSITION SCHEDULES
   RECORDS EQUIPMENT AND SUPPLIES
   RECORDS MAINTENANCE
   RECORDS RETENTION AND DESTRUCTION
      RECORDS RETENTION AND DESTRUCTION SCHEDULE
      TRANSFER SCHEDULES
   VITAL RECORDS

Source: *General Services Administration,* Files Operations: Managing Current Records, *Washington, DC: National Archives and Records Service, Office of Federal Records Centers, 1981.*

correspondent's records are filed. The alphabetic index may be on cards or in a computer database file. Including correspondent names in a computerized subject file/index enables one to sort by subjects or by correspondent names. A printed alphabetic index may be used daily as is the subject file list.

Source: *Photography by Alan Brown/Photonics*

Subject Filing Procedures

Why aren't general folders used in subject filing?

Subject file labels, guides, and folders are similar to those used in any other filing method. Guide and folder positions and cuts are consistent with other filing methods, and either side or top tabs may be used. Primary guides are in first position, one-fifth cut. Secondary guides are in second position, one-fifth cut. Tertiary guides, if needed, are in third position, one-fifth cut. Individual folders are in third position, one-third cut. OUT guides and folders are a distinctive color, third position, one-third cut. In subject filing, every record has a subject; therefore, general folders are not necessary.

Folder label captions are prepared similarly to those in other filing methods, starting one line down from the top of the label. (See Figure 11-5.) In a dictionary subject arrangement, letters of the alphabet (A to Z) are keyed two spaces from the left edge. The complete filing segment is keyed five spaces to the right. In an encyclopedic subject arrangement, the subject is keyed in all caps two spaces from the left edge. The complete filing segment is keyed five spaces to the right of the subject.

When do color bands on subject folders change?

Color coding in subject filing speeds filing and retrieval. Color bands on guides and folders may change whenever a subject changes. Color folders may be used throughout one subject; the color of the folders changes when the subject changes.

Procedures for filing records in a subject file are similar to those used in other alphabetic filing systems. Filing a record in a subject filing system

Figure 11-5 Subject Folder Labels

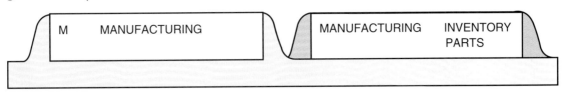

M MANUFACTURING

MANUFACTURING INVENTORY
PARTS

Dictionary Subject Label   Encyclopedic Subject Label

requires inspecting, indexing, coding, preparing cross-references, sorting, and filing procedures.

Inspecting

Check each record for a release mark. If the record has not been released for filing, send it back to the user.

Indexing and Coding

Sometimes the subject code has been identified on a record before being sent to the records management department. If a subject has not been identified, *read* the record to determine the subject. The subject must match a predetermined subject in the subject file list/index of the system. If the subject appears in the record in the same form as on the caption of the folder, the subject may be highlighted, circled, or coded with a color pencil. Preferably, the subject is printed in all caps in the top right corner of the record. In this position, the subject can be read quickly during filing and retrieval.

How is the subject of a record determined?

If the subject heading contains more than one unit, separate the units with diagonals, underline the key unit, and number all remaining units. For correspondence records, the complete filing segment includes the subject, all subject subdivisions, and the correspondent name. Review the coding in the following examples:

2   3   4   5
<u>ADVERTISING</u>/CARMEN/RIOS/ADVERTISING/AGENCY

2   3   4
<u>HUMAN</u>/RESOURCES/EMPLOYEE/GRIEVANCES

Preparing Cross-References

When more than one primary subject appears in a record, index and code the cross-reference subject on the record and place an *X* beside it. If the subject isn't on the record, write it in on the record and place an *X* beside it. Separate the units with diagonals, underline the complete cross-reference subject with a *wavy* line, and number the units. Prepare a cross-reference sheet(s) for the alternative subject(s).

³   ⁴   ⁵   ⁶
Rising/Sun/Travel/Service
716 Brennan Street
San Francisco, CA 94103-3412
415 • 555 • 7842

ANNUAL/MEETING ²

September 11, 20--

Sept. 14, 20--

Sachi Nitobe Accounting Associates
106 West Hollister
Bay City, MI 48708-8945

Annual/Meeting ²

You and your associates can start packing your bags! All plans for your
annual meeting have been finalized. Your plane leaves as scheduled on
October 15.

An itinerary, airline tickets, hotel reservations, and cruise ship tickets
for all members of the party are enclosed. Please read and sign the
authorization for travel/insurance. Trip cancellation, emergency medical,
and natural disaster travel accommodations are covered by this policy.
I recommend that you take this insurance.

We look forward to helping you plan many more business trips to Japan
in the future. Just let us know when.

Sumio Harada
Agency Manager

MC/rl

Enclosures

Study the coding in the letter in Figure 11-6. A cross-reference sheet
for this letter is shown in Figure 11-7. Notice that the cross-reference sheet
is coded as well.

Sorting

Sort the records first by the main subjects. Then sort by the subdivisions of
the main subjects, if used. Finally, sort by correspondent names, if any.

Filing

File records alphabetically by correspondent names in subject folders. File
records for the same correspondent by dates.

CROSS-REFERENCE SHEET

Name or Subject

2   3   4

Travel/Insurance/Rising/Sun
5   6
Travel/Service

Date of Record
09/11/0-

Regarding
Annual meeting held in Japan

See

Name or Subject
Annual Meeting Rising Sun

Travel Service

Date Filed *09/13/0-*   By *krg*

Figure 11-7
Subject Cross-Reference Sheet for Incoming Correspondence

Review

1. Describe how subject folder labels are prepared.
2. Where are cross-references filed in a subject filing system?

Subject Codes

Writing a long subject with subdivisions in the top right corner of a record is time-consuming. Therefore, subject codes (letters representing the subjects) often are used. For a one-word subject, the subject code may consist of the first letter of the word and the next two or three consonants in the word, such as ACC for ACCOUNTING, ADM for ADMINISTRATION, and MGMT for MANAGEMENT. The code should be recognizable as an abbreviation of the word or words in the subject.

Two or three letters should suffice in a dictionary subject filing arrangement because the subjects consist of only one to three words. As many as six letters may be needed in an encyclopedic subject filing arrangement in which there are many subdivisions of subjects. For example, HUMAN RESOURCES WAGE NEGOTIATIONS may be coded as HRWN. The code may be written as one unit or separated by a hyphen, period, or diagonal (HR-WN, HR.WN, HR/WN).

A subject code is the key unit, and the correspondent's name is coded as the remaining units in the filing segment. Cross-references are assigned subject codes also. Folder labels using subject codes are shown in Figure 11-8.

How many letters may be used in a subject code?

Figure 11-8 Subject Code Folder Labels

ADM	ADMINISTRATION
HR/WN	HUMAN RESOURCES WAGE NEGOTIATIONS

Advantages and Disadvantages of Subject Filing

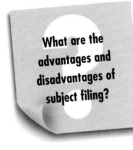

What are the advantages and disadvantages of subject filing?

The disadvantages of using a subject filing system far outweigh the advantages. But in specific applications, a subject filing system may be the most efficient filing method. For example, your personal records may be filed under CHARGE ACCOUNTS, INSURANCE, PERSONAL PROPERTY INVENTORY, TAX RETURNS, or WARRANTIES. Remember that if records can be filed by name, number, or location, subject filing isn't the method to use. Subject filing has the following advantages:

1. Most records are remembered and retrieved by subject.

2. All records on one topic are in one file or series of files and in one location.

3. Subject lists can be expanded easily by adding subdivisions to primary subjects.

The main disadvantages of subject filing are the following:

1. Subjects may overlap when subject lists become lengthy because of numerous subdivisions.

2. Selecting subject headings is difficult because headings must be concise, accurate, and similar in format (such as using one to three words or using words that end in *s*).

3. Preparing records for subject filing takes longer because each record must be read carefully; scanning isn't sufficient.

4. An incomplete or out-of-date subject file list/index prevents or delays records retrieval.

5. New personnel will have difficulty retrieving records if previous filers used their own subject headings. Subjects must be used consistently.

6. Subject filing requires experienced filers who are thoroughly familiar with the records and the organization. Consequently, salaries are higher, making subject filing more expensive than other methods.

Review

1. Why are subject codes used?
2. Why is more time required to prepare records for subject filing?

Summary

Subject filing is a method of classifying and coding records by subject. In a subject filing system, related information is filed primarily under subject titles.

In the dictionary arrangement, records are arranged in alphabetic order by specific subject. This arrangement also is referred to as *topical arrangement,* or *straight dictionary arrangement.*

In the encyclopedic arrangement, records are arranged in alphabetic order according to main subjects and their subdivisions. Primary, secondary, and tertiary headings may be included in the encyclopedic arrangement.

Classification is the process of analyzing and determining the subject content of a record and selecting the subject heading under which it will be filed. A subject file list/index is a complete listing of all subject headings in a subject filing system. To ensure consistency, only one person should be assigned the task of selecting subjects for the subject file list. Subject headings should be concise, accurately descriptive of the contents of a record, and capable of only one interpretation.

An alphabetic index containing names of correspondents in the subject file is essential for finding specific names. A computer index can include subjects and correspondent names.

Procedures used in filing records by subject include inspecting, indexing and coding, preparing cross-references, sorting, and filing. Using subject codes speeds up the indexing and coding process because only letters are written at the top of a record.

Advantages of subject filing include (1) most records are remembered and retrieved by subject; (2) all records on one topic are in one file or series of files and in one location; and (3) subject lists can be expanded easily by adding subdivisions to primary subjects. Disadvantages of subject filing include (1) subjects may overlap; (2) selecting subject headings is difficult; (3) preparing records for filing takes longer because each record must be read; (4) an out-of-date or incomplete subject file list/index prevents or delays records retrieval; (5) new personnel will have difficulty retrieving records if previous filers used their own subject headings; and (6) subject filing is more expensive because of the experience needed by the personnel.

Terminology Review

classification	(p. 194)
dictionary arrangement	(p. 191)
encyclopedic arrangement	(p. 192)
subject file list	(p. 194)
subject filing	(p. 191)

Questions for Discussion

1. Define *subject filing.* (Obj. 1)
2. When should subject filing be used? (Obj. 2)
3. Define and describe the *dictionary subject filing arrangement.* (Obj. 3)
4. Define and describe the *encyclopedic subject filing arrangement.* (Obj. 4)
5. Define and describe a *subject file list/index.* (Obj. 5)
6. Why is an alphabetic index needed in a subject filing system? (Obj. 6)
7. How can a computer database file be used for the alphabetic index and subject file list/index? (Obj. 6)
8. Describe subject filing procedures. (Obj. 7)
9. Explain the use of subject codes. (Obj. 8)
10. List the advantages and disadvantages of subject filing. (Obj. 9)

Applications

▶

1. Use a separate sheet of paper to prepare a subject file list for the human resources department of EPCON Building Contractors, Inc. The following PRIMARY subjects are used in the encyclopedic filing system. (Obj. 6)

PREEMPLOYMENT TESTING   TRAINING AND DEVELOPMENT
EMPLOYMENT AGENCIES   HIRING PROCEDURES

The following subdivisions are used in the filing system. Use Figure 11-4 on page 195 as a guide to prepare the subject file list. Arrange the primary and secondary headings in alphabetic order.

APPLICATIONS OFFICE   KEYBOARDING TESTS
APTITUDE TESTS   EMPLOYMENT INTERVIEWS
TRAINING MANUAL   EMPLOYMENT AGENCIES
   WAREHOUSE   FEE PAY
REFERENCE CHECKS   WORD PROCESSING TESTS
COMMUNITY COLLEGE   EMPLOYMENT AGENCIES
   COURSES   GOVERNMENT
DRUG TESTING   UNIVERSITY COURSES
TRAINING MANUAL   SPREADSHEET TESTS
   CUSTOMER SERVICE   TRAINING SCHEDULES
APPLICATIONS WAREHOUSE   TRAINING MANUAL OFFICE
APPLICATIONS INFORMA-
   TION SYSTEMS

2. The office manager of Wake Forrest Manufacturing Co. needs to organize the equipment, supplies, and furniture purchase files. A subject filing system will be used. Prepare a subject file list for the primary, secondary, and tertiary headings listed below on a separate sheet of paper. Arrange the headings in correct alphabetic order. (Obj. 6)

The PRIMARY headings are:

   office equipment
   office supplies
   office furniture

The SECONDARY headings are:

dictating machines   calculators
chairs   bookcases
ribbons   computers
typewriters   paper
bookends   calendars—calendar pads
copiers   binders
desks   pens
miscellaneous supplies   printers

The TERTIARY headings are:

secretarial desks
portable dictating machines
Xerography copiers
executive desks
ball-point pens
photocopy paper
address labels
laser printer paper
ring binders
felt-tip pens
correction tapes
cartridges, ball point
digital calculators
appointment calendars
tape dispensers
printing calculator ribbons
letterhead paper
computer paper
lined notepads
executive chairs
printing calculators

metal bookends
plain bond paper
typewriter ribbons
computer workstations
correction fluid
paper clips
staplers
folder labels
printing calculator paper
printer ribbons
desk calendar pads
wooden bookends
wrapping paper
ergonomic task chairs
facsimile machines
tape refills
rubber bands
color copiers
business cards
clip and spring binders

3. On a separate sheet of paper, prepare a subject filing list using subject codes. Each subject code will consist of four letters. The first two letters are separated from the last two letters by a hyphen (HR-AP). The subject codes are created from the first letter of each word in the primary subject and the first letter of each word in the secondary subject. Four codes have been done for you. Complete the list. (Obj. 6, 8)

Subject File List

Subject Codes	Subjects	
AD	ACCOUNTING DEPARTMENT	(PRIMARY subject)
AD-AP	ACCOUNTS PAYABLE	(SECONDARY subject)
	ACCOUNTS RECEIVABLE	
	GENERAL LEDGERS	
	HUMAN RESOURCES	
	ACCIDENT INSURANCE	
	DENTAL INSURANCE	
	HEALTH INSURANCE	
	LIFE INSURANCE	
	RETIREMENT PLAN	
	VISION INSURANCE	
IS	INFORMATION SYSTEMS	

Subject Codes	Subjects
IS-DP	DATA PROCESSING
	FORMS MANAGEMENT
	MICROFILM PROCESSING
	OPTICAL EQUIPMENT
	RECORDS MANAGEMENT
	MARKETING DEPARTMENT
	ADVERTISING CAMPAIGNS
	MARKET SURVEYS

Practice Set Application

At this time, complete Job 12, *Subject Filing*, in OFFICE FILING PROCEDURES, Eighth Edition. Instructions and supplies for this job are included in the practice set.

Computer Applications

1. On a separate sheet of paper, create a database design sheet. Use the ten subject records listed below to complete the design sheet. Use the following information for the database. (Obj. 5, 6)

Date: Current
Database filename: SUBJFILE
Database description: Records Filed by Subject
Fields: NAME, SUBJECT, CODE, CRSUBJ, CRCODE
Field lengths: Count the longest name or words in each field. Be sure to count blank spaces.

Index/sort the NAME and SUBJECT fields.

Subject File Records

The following records are from the ADMINISTRATION (AD), HUMAN RESOURCES (HR), MANUFACTURING (MN), and MARKETING (MR) departments.

Name	Subject	Code	CRSubj	CRCode
Dion Francis March	Application	HR-AP		
Cappers Frontier Weekly	Advertising	MR-AD		
Wakako Isako Tokuda	Contracts	AD-CN		
A K L Printers	Advertising	MR-AD	Printing	MR-PR
J.B. Hunt, Inc	Shipping	MN-SH		
Walton-Boulevard Billboard Advertisers	Advertising	MR-AD	Billboards	MR-BL
Franklin and Rivera Legal Services	Research	AD-RS	Legal	AD-LG
KRTG TV	Advertising	MR-AD	TV	MR-TV
City of Rochester	Contracts	AD-CN		
Safety Insurance Co.	Insurance	HR-IN	Liability	HR-LB

2. If a computer is available, create the SUBJFILE database in your computer. Key the records listed in Computer Application 1 in indexing order into the appropriate fields. Proofread carefully. If you are using the template, open filename **CH11AP2.DBF**. Index or sort the SUBJECT and CRSubj fields. (Obj. 5, 6, 8)

3. Create and print a report of the SUBJFILE (CH11AP2.DBF) database.

Title of report: SUBJECT FILE INDEX
Print all fields in this order: SUBJECT, CODE, CRSUBJ, CRCODE
Use these column headings: Subject, Code, C-R Subject, and C-R Code.

Check to see that all subjects have sorted correctly. Make necessary corrections if they are not in correct order. Print a report to give to your teacher for checking.

4. Using the SUBJFILE (CH11AP2.DBF) database, create and print an alphabetic index of the subject file.

Title of report: ALPHABETIC INDEX FOR SUBJECT FILE
Print all fields in this order: NAME, SUBJECT, CODE, CRSUBJ, CRCODE
Use these column headings: Correspondent Name, Subject, Code, CR Subject, and CR Code

Give your report to your teacher for checking.

Part 5

Records Storage and Control Procedures

Chapter Twelve

Paper Records Storage Supplies and Equipment

Learning Objectives

After completing Chapter 12, you will be able to do the following:

1. Defend the importance of evaluating needs, availability, and costs when selecting filing equipment and supplies.

2. List needs to consider when selecting appropriate records storage supplies and equipment.

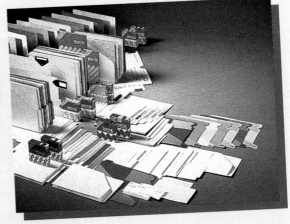

3. List advantages of rotary equipment over other types of records storage equipment.

4. List advantages of mechanical retrieval equipment over manual retrieval equipment.

5. List three design options when selecting high-density records storage equipment.

6. Identify records storage equipment and supplies by their features.

Selecting Storage Supplies and Equipment

Paper, microimage, electronic, and optical records work harmoniously to provide the mixed records media found in many offices today. Modern office designs and the volume and kinds of records stored have brought about significant changes in filing equipment. Traditional files have taken on a new look to meet the increasing demands placed on them. Ideally, records storage equipment not only stores and protects records but also conserves office space, improves file efficiency, and fits attractively into the office layout and design. Paper records haven't changed very much in the past fifty years, but equipment for storing and protecting them certainly has, as you will see.

Browse through magazines such as *Modern Office Technology, The Office, Administrative Management,* and numerous office supply catalogs. See for yourself the staggering volume of supplies and equipment for managing office records illustrated in these publications. Examine the office supply departments of discount retailers or warehouse supermarkets (box stores). Equipment in a wide range of sizes, shapes, capacities, costs, and colors is available—all designed to (1) speed up information storage and retrieval processes, (2) cut down on the number of misfiled records, (3) reduce the amount of records storage space, and (4) complement a new office design or layout.

Selecting appropriate supplies and filing equipment for controlling paper records today presents a challenge for office personnel. The selection process requires consideration of three basic selection factors: need, availability, and cost. The success of the ultimate purchase depends on the knowledge, experience, and personal taste brought to the examination of (1) the filing supply and equipment *needs* of the organization, (2) *available* supplies and equipment, and (3) the *cost* (or savings!) realized. Each organization has its own set of priorities, needs, and values. Often it is difficult to know what has been sacrificed or compromised when the ultimate purchase decision is reached. Look closely at these factors as they relate to the selection and purchase of filing supplies and equipment.

> What are three basic factors to consider when selecting filing supplies and equipment?

Need for Storage Supplies and Equipment

The selection of filing supplies and equipment begins with needs—future as well as present needs. Rarely are any two filing systems exactly alike. Organizational filing requirements differ, based on the type of records, uses of records, and anticipated growth of records. Before selecting filing supplies and equipment for any office, consider such factors as these:

1. The kinds of records to be filed and controlled.
2. The frequency of use for each kind of record during the day—constantly or infrequently.

3. The number of people working at the files at one time.
4. The volume of records to be handled in a given period of time, such as six months or a year.
5. The method of filing best suited to handling the records—alphabetic, geographic, subject, numeric, or a combination of these methods.
6. The type of charge-out and follow-up system used.
7. The transfer method used.
8. The security and retention requirements of the records.
9. The organization and distribution of records (centralized, decentralized, or a combination of these plans).
10. The manner of retrieving records (single documents or entire folders).

Refer to this list frequently as you study paper records storage supplies and equipment. An appropriate match of filing needs with supplies and equipment helps ensure a properly planned and controlled filing system.

Why examine filing supply and equipment needs?

Availability of Storage Supplies and Equipment

This chapter provides information about available equipment. Although space prohibits the coverage of every piece of filing equipment, you will learn to recognize many types of equipment used for paper records storage and retrieval. As you examine the types of equipment presented here, equipment alternative selections become evident. The more knowledgeable you are about available filing supplies and equipment, the better prepared you are to assist in making intelligent selections.

Why is knowledge of available filing supplies and equipment important?

Costs of Storage Supplies and Equipment

Cost makes a planned equipment purchase a reality. In addition, the cost of filing supplies and equipment must be justified, whether the purchase is a $200 vertical filing cabinet or a $35,000 optical filing system. Because labor accounts for about 80 percent of total filing costs, the cost justification must extend beyond the initial cost of the equipment. Some advantages and disadvantages of purchase alternatives can be expressed in terms of money. Some cannot. Will the equipment save time? Save space? Provide better client service? How will you justify the purchase expense?

Cost/benefit analysis is the process of determining the relative advantages and disadvantages of alternative solutions to a problem. The analysis helps to prepare a cost justification for an anticipated change in supplies, equipment, and procedures. If you can show a savings that is greater than the cost, the investment is probably a good one.

The cost/benefit analysis is a timely reminder that a business expects a fair return on the dollars it invests. Therefore, look for short- and long-term savings to be realized from the purchase in addition to the initial

How can spending money save money?

cost. In order to justify a more expensive piece of equipment or higher quality supplies, you will want to show significant savings through more efficient office space utilization, higher productivity, and/or reduced time and labor costs.

Review

1. Why is availability important to supplies and equipment selection?

2. Explain the value of a cost/benefit analysis when selecting records storage supplies and equipment.

Storing Correspondence

You are already familiar with correspondence filing methods. Filing correspondence by name, number, location, and subject were covered in Chapters 4, 9, 10, and 11. Electronic methods and filming methods of storing correspondence are presented in Chapter 13, where you will study how computer, laser-beam, and microfilm technology contribute to the challenge of storing correspondence and other paper records. The focus of your study now is on equipment for storing correspondence as paper records.

Surveys show that paper records make up over 90 percent of all office records. The paper records just will not go away. Ironically, a good part of the paper growth in the modern office results from the technology intended to eliminate paper records altogether—the computer! Most of what goes into a computer comes out on paper. The computer generates letters, reports, and statistical data with great ease and speed.

Because paper records are so much a part of office work, you need to know how to store and protect them. You accomplish this by learning as much as you can about records storage supplies and equipment.

Why is there a growth in office paper records?

Storage Supplies

Guides, folders, and labels were described in Chapters 4, 6, and 8. In Chapter 4, "Alphabetic Correspondence Filing," you learned about guides, folders, and labels for both top-access and side-access filing equipment. In Chapter 6, "File Maintenance and Control," you learned how to use OUT guides. The colorful Chapter 8 showed a rainbow variety of color-coded labels and file folders for color-coded systems. However, to select filing supplies, you need to know still more about them.

Folders

As you have probably suspected, ordering folders involves more than telephoning your stationery supplier and requesting "a box of folders." You will be asked whether you want Manila, kraft, pressboard, or vinyl folders. Do you want straight cut, 1/2 cut, 1/3 cut, 1/5 cut, or 2/5 cut? In what position do you want the cut (or tab)? Left position? Center position? Right position? An assortment of positions? How will you answer these questions?

Figure 4-6, p. 60 in Chapter 4, showed samples of folder tab cuts and tab positions. The guide and folder plan of your filing system dictates the tab cut and tab position of the folders you select. Top-access filing equipment requires the tab to be at the top of the folder. Side-access filing equipment requires folders with side tabs.

The thickness of the folder represents another selection factor. The thickness of a file folder stock is measured in points (pt.), with one **point** equal to .001 inch. The common folder weights are these:

What are the common folder weights?

9 1/2 pt.	mediumweight
11 pt.	heavyweight
18 pt.	tag (card or label) stock
25 pt.	pressboard

Folder *stock* refers to its construction and presents another purchase option. **Stock** is the raw material from which something is manufactured. Folder stock is available in Manila, kraft, pressboard, and vinyl. Manila is the most common folder stock and is characterized by its cream color. Typical weights of Manila folders are 9 1/2 pt. and 11 pt. Kraft is made entirely from wood pulp and is noted for its strength. The most common weight of kraft folders is also 11 pt., but you pay slightly more for their extra durability. Pressboard folders, generally 20 or 25 pt. in thickness, are recommended for bulky materials and for very active files. Vinyl folders are made of heavy plastic and are wear-resistant, tearproof, and waterproof.

Consider the factors listed on pages 209-210 when selecting stock for guides and folders. Numbers 2, 3, 6, and 7 are especially relevant: Are files active? Do many people handle the records? Are folders charged out with records? If the answers to these questions are yes, then you will select a heavier folder with a two-ply top. Two-ply-top folders have an extra thickness the full width of the tab. For rugged handling of your most active records, consider the vinyl folders.

On the other hand, less durable folders are satisfactory when (1) files are less active, (2) folders are transferred with their contents regularly, and (3) carrier folders are used at charge-out and follow-up time. In these cases, 11 pt. Manila stock folders are satisfactory and more cost effective (save money).

Be ready to specify the tab cut, tab position, and folder construction when selecting *side-tab* folders also. Side tabs come in straight cut, 1/2 cut, and 1/3 cut in top, center, or bottom positions on the side of the folder. A 4-inch-cut tab positioned 1 1/8 inches from the bottom of the folder is another option.

It's not a simple "one-size-fits-all" matter when selecting folder tab cuts. How do you determine the folder tab position (location) and tab cut (size)? The tab position depends on your guide and folder plan. For example, in straight-line filing, all folder tabs are in the same position. The tab cut is determined by the length of the folder caption. Here is a table that gives the approximate number of characters/spaces that fit the various tab cuts:

Folder Size	Tab Cut	Characters Per Inch	
		12	10
Letter	Straight-cut	135	113
	1/2 cut	68	57
	1/3 cut	43	36
	1/5 cut	26	22
Legal	Straight-cut	159	133
	1/2 cut	85	71
	1/3 cut	56	47
	1/5 cut	33	28

Suspension (Hanging) Folders

Suspension folder design includes a variety of colors, tab cuts, and tab positions. Most filers do not file correspondence directly into the suspension folder, especially when folders are carried from file to desk on a regular basis. Interior file folders are used in combination with suspension folders. Some interior file folders fit inside suspension folders without obscuring the suspension folder guide tab. Other folders are guide-height and therefore visible above the top edge of the suspension folder.

What is a box-bottom suspension folder?

Box-bottom suspension folders hold bulky records, thick reports, and manuals. The bottom is available in spreads of 1" to 4" with a pressboard floor insert to reinforce the bottom of the folder. Some box-bottom folders have sides to keep papers from falling out. All suspension folders are made of heavyweight stock or plastic.

Guides

As discussed in previous chapters, guides are designed for both top-access and side-access storage equipment. Like folders, guide stock varies according to your needs. Manila 18-pt. stock handles less active files, while rigid 25-pt. pressboard provides needed support for more active files. Guide tabs may be purchased as preprinted tabs or blank tabs for user preparation.

Guide *tabs* consist of Manila, vinyl, or metal construction. The metal guide tabs have clear plastic windows and include blank inserts. Color vinyl tabs with blank inserts are also available for suspension folders. These tabs snap in any position across the inside edge of the suspension folder.

Folder labels

Before ordering folder labels, you need to decide on the following: (1) label size, (2) label color, (3) method of preparation, and (4) method of application. The size of the label must match the length of the caption and the size of the folder tab. The color should be white unless you have a reason for choosing color. Black print on a white label produces an attractive, highly visible label. Color labels and folders should never be used to "decorate" the file. If not used in a meaningful way, such as improving file efficiency or avoiding a misfile, color labels are a distraction.

Does label preparation determine label selection?

How do you plan to prepare the labels? Most labels are designed to be keyed at a typewriter. However, if you plan to prepare them on your computer, select continuous feed (end-perforated) labels for dot matrix printers and sheet labels for laser printers.

Although water-gummed labels are less expensive, adhesive folder labels stick better and are easier to apply. Adhesive label protectors are available and useful for protecting folder tabs and labels. When applied over the folder tab, these clear protectors strengthen the folder tab and keep labels from smudging or peeling.

One final thought before leaving the subject of selecting records storage supplies: Be kind to the earth! Favor products that have been made with recycled fibers and materials. And remember to recycle your own old supplies and papers as well.

Manual Retrieval Equipment

Correspondence records storage equipment is either manual or mechanical. Manual retrieval equipment, by far more common, requires that the filer go to the record. The filer pulls out a drawer, walks to a shelf, spins a wheel, or moves a bank of shelves in order to file and retrieve records. Mechanical retrieval equipment, on the other hand, provides fingertip records access: Records are delivered to the filer or workstation by some kind of motor-driven, mechanical device.

Manual retrieval equipment includes cabinet, shelf, tub, suspension, rotary, and high-density files. Be alert to the advantages and disadvantages of each type of equipment as you study the manual retrieval equipment that follows.

Vertical File Cabinets

A **vertical file cabinet**, illustrated in Figure 4-1, page 56, in Chapter 4, is more widely used than all other filing equipment. Vertical file cabinets are rectangular shells containing a series of large, bin-like drawers. The drawers hold papers in an upright, vertical position with the writing facing forward (toward the filer).

The cabinets come in a wide variety of colors and contemporary wood veneers to fit the design of any modern office. Some cabinets are made of very heavy metal with insulated cabinet shells that provide some degree of fire protection for valuable papers and documents.

Heavy cabinets are also constructed with combination locks and necessary reinforcement to permit their use as safes for the storage of vital and valuable documents and papers.

Vertical cabinets have the added advantages of providing closed, convenient, and relatively compact storage space in drawers capable of organization under any one of a variety of guide systems. Vertical cabinets allow individual papers to be examined without removing the folders from the file drawers. Open-shelf files, on the other hand, require removal of the entire folder.

Shelf Files

Shelf files, as the name implies, are filing equipment in which records are stored on shelves. To minimize some of the disadvantages of filing records in vertical cabinets, many offices use shelf-filing equipment. The supplies used with shelf filing differ from those used with vertical filing cabinets. Folders are placed on open shelves with the visible portion of each folder along the side edge rather than across the top edge. Thus, the cut of tabs on guides and folders displays their captions vertically (down the side) rather than horizontally (across the top). Figure 12-1 pictures an open-shelf file with removable sections.

Figure 12-1
Open-Shelf File with Removable Sections
Source: *Kardex Systems, Inc.*

Open-shelf filing systems include supporting devices to secure the guides and folders in an upright position. These devices project from either the top or the bottom of the shelf unit. Figure 12-1 illustrates supporting devices with small bin-like sections that can be removed by the filer to take files where they are needed.

Is open-shelf filing better than vertical cabinet filing?

In most offices, very active papers are usually not held in shelf files, mainly because entire folders must be pulled off the shelf to file or find papers. Yet, shelf-filing equipment is used for large, active medical records systems and recommended by many records and information professionals because of the following advantages:

1. Floor space is saved because no room is needed for pulling out drawers; therefore, aisles between shelves can be narrower than aisles between vertical cabinets.
2. Direct access to visible folders is easier and faster with the elimination of file drawers.
3. Shelf-filing equipment costs much less than vertical filing cabinets because shelf equipment is relatively simple in construction.
4. Shelf filing adapts well to color-coded filing systems because the color blocks are highly visible on the open shelves.

Here are some disadvantages of shelf filing:

1. An entire folder must be withdrawn from a shelf before any action can be taken to find or file papers.
2. There is no protection from dust unless the shelf files are enclosed.
3. The highly visible records advantage may be considered a disadvantage because of a lack of file security. The files are open for all to see.
4. Notations on folders and guides are not as readable as those on the top edges of guides and folders in vertical cabinets.
5. Open shelves are not always neat in appearance.

Lateral File Cabinets

A **lateral file** is filing equipment in which folders are stored across the width of the drawer or shelf. A lateral file cabinet looks like a vertical file cabinet with drawers opening from the side rather than from the front of the cabinet. Figure 12-2 shows 2-, 3-, 4-, and 5-drawer lateral cabinets with solid drawers. In this design, the drawer front moves with the drawer as it is pulled out of the cabinet area, as in a vertical file cabinet. Folders in a lateral file may be arranged from side to side or front to back in the drawer. Figure 12-3 shows an open drawer with front-to-back folders on the left and right and suspension folders in the center in a side-to-side arrangement. The suspension folders can be installed in a front-to-back arrangement as well.

Lateral cabinets are also constructed with fronts that lift up and then slide into the cabinet to expose the contents of the drawer, as in a shelf file. Figure 12-4 on page 218 shows one open panel and two closed panels. Panels are opened by pulling up and sliding the panel into the body of the cabinet shell. In some units, not only do the panels slide up into the unit but also the drawers slide out. See Figure 12-5 on page 218. With this design of lateral cabinet, folders can be top-tabbed or side-tabbed: side-tabbed because the panel disappears into the shell and exposes the side edge of the folders; top-tabbed because the drawer slides out.

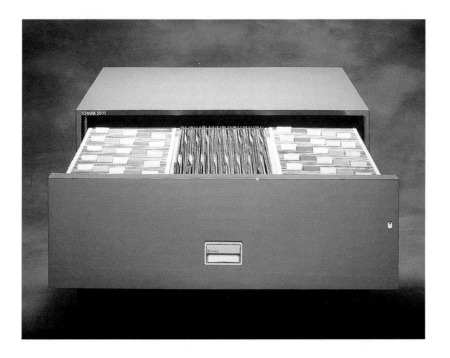

What storage
equipment uses the
least space?

A comparison of vertical cabinets, shelf units, and lateral files shows that the laterals require less aisle floor space for opening and closing drawers than do the verticals. The shelf storage units are the most economical in terms of floor area required because the units require no aisle space for drawer or panel action.

Figure 12-4
Lateral Cabinet with Sliding Front Panels
Source: *Systems Manufacturing Corporation*

Figure 12-5
Lateral Cabinet with Drawer and Sliding Panel
Source: *White Office Systems*

Tub Files

The **tub file** is an open reference file that provides instant record availability—no file drawers to open and close and no stooping and stretching. All records are visible at one time and within easy reach. An operator handles documents with ease with the aid of the handy work board. The work board rides on ball-bearing wheels with tires for silent and convenient mobility. Tub files equipped with casters become portable units movable to any office location.

Figure 12-6 shows a small open-bin file used as a sorter or temporary file. This small tub file serves as an auxiliary unit for holding current records at a ready position. The casters on this unit allow the file to be moved around the office as needed.

Suspension Files

The **suspension file** is filing equipment that makes use of metal frame parallel rods from which folders hang. The suspension folder (or hanging folder) method of holding records represents a very adaptable and widely used form of records control. Suspension folders have metal or plastic strips mounted across the top edges of the front and back folder panels. These strips extend beyond the sides of the folders and fit over the parallel rails that run along both sides of the file drawer. Figure 12-3 shows this arrangement, where side-by-side suspension folders are positioned between two sections facing the filer. The folders hang suspended over the rails. Always in a neat upright position, suspension folders are more easily

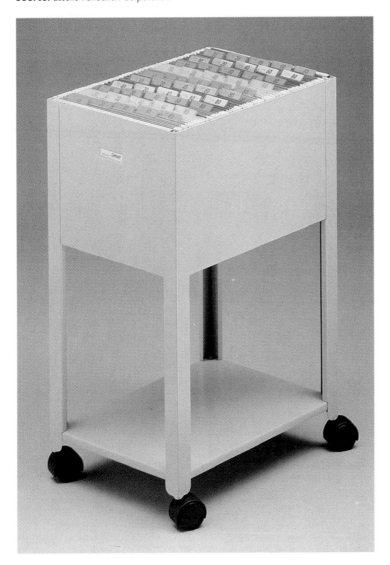

moved and more readily accessible than folders in standard vertical or lateral cabinets. Suspension folders can be placed in vertical cabinets not originally equipped for them by placing parallel rail frames inside the file drawers. Most office supply centers sell these parallel rail units.

There are many uses for suspension folders systems because of these advantages:

1. Materials of different sizes can be held more efficiently in them than in the more stationary vertical folders.

2. Different size bottoms are available for holding bulky materials, computer printouts, catalogs, and the like.

3. Folders are easily moved, opened, or replaced without disrupting other folders in the system.

4. Some types of suspension folders can be indexed more completely than is possible with other types of folders. Snap tabs that slide to reposition across the tab of a suspension folder make the suspension guide and folder plan extremely flexible.

Carrousel Files

A **carrousel file** is a rotary file in which records are accessed by turning the file. Carrousel units have a large outer shell enclosing a series of circular shelves which rotate like a lazy-Susan server. Guides and folders are placed on the rotating shelves and carried similarly to spokes on a wheel; or folders and guides are placed into rectangular bin sections formed as separate units on the "floor" of the rotating shelves.

Carrousel files are available in a variety of styles. They can be from one to six tiers high. Some are available with casters so that they can be moved to various workstations around the office. For record security, locking-cabinet enclosures are available.

Some advantages of freestanding carrousel files include the following:

1. Savings in floor space.

2. Flexibility of tiers to hold any size record from 5" x 3" cards to computer printouts.

3. Ability to add tiers or entire carrousels as needed.

4. Easy access to files by several filers because of the high visibility and independent movement of the open tiers.

High-Density Files

High density refers to the compact ability of this filing equipment to store a high volume of records in a relatively small area. High-density filing is one solution to the increased records volume and office space costs. Three types of high-density files are described and illustrated. One type of high-density file is the mobile shelf file.

A **mobile shelf file** is a series of shelf file sections mounted on rollers that glide along a fixed, embedded track in the floor. The purpose behind mobile files such as the unit shown in Figure 12-7 is elimination of the conventional, nonproductive aisle space between ranges of shelves. Figures 12-8 and 12-9 show how the number of shelf units are doubled in the same storage space by eliminating the aisles. The units may be purchased for either electric or manual operation. The operator moves the banks of shelves to create an aisle at the record location.

Although a great space saver, the mobile file may be a poor choice for an active system used by many people. Much time could be lost waiting

Figure 12-7
Mobile File Unit
Source: *Spacesaver Electric Mobile File Unit*

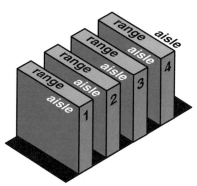

Figure 12-8
Conventional Shelving Arrangement

Figure 12-9
Spacesaver Mobile File Arrangement

to create an aisle for storage or retrieval of a particular record. Filers don't need to worry about an aisle closing on them. Safety sensors keep the file from moving when someone is standing in the aisle.

Another high-density file is the Aisle-Saver® manufactured by White Office Systems. Figure 12-10 shows this mobile storage concept. The design consists of two or three rows of files mounted in front of each other. The front-bank files are mounted on embedded tracks and slide easily left or right to expose the banks of files behind them. The file is especially suited to narrow areas, such as wall perimeters where other storage concepts might be inappropriate.

A relatively new high-density file design is the Times-2 Speed Files® shown in Figure 12-11. It has a unique cabinet-within-a-cabinet design. The inner cabinet rotates 360 degrees inside the outer shell, allowing access to two complete walls of filing from a single side. The Times-2 Speed Files® use substantially less floor space than lateral files while storing the same amount of material. Available in heights from 3 tiers to 8 tiers, the unit provides versatile solutions to a variety of space-planning problems. With laminated tops, 3-tier units become convenient work tables. Back to back, two rows of Times-2 Speed Files® function as efficiently as mobile storage units but offer greater records accessibility. They function as room dividers also—defining space while saving space. Three 8-tier units (21 sq. ft.) replace seven 5-drawer lateral files (58 sq. ft.)—a significant savings in office floor space.

Mechanical Retrieval Equipment

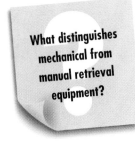

What distinguishes mechanical from manual retrieval equipment?

Mechanical retrieval equipment is file storage equipment with an engine. Sometimes referred to as "power files," this equipment operates electronically or mechanically to deliver records to a walk-up or seated workstation. Depending on the particular power equipment, a foot pedal, a pre-established code on an electronic keypad, or a microcomputer activates these systems. Two configurations of power files are common: One stores records inside the unit on shelves or in metal trays or bins. The other stores records on open shelves rotating in a room or warehouse.

Figure 12-12 shows the Lektriever by Kardex Systems, Inc. The Lektriever is capable of storing letter- and legal-size documents, computer tapes, and trays of different sizes. A pre-established index code entered on the electronic keypad activates the system, delivering records to either a walk-up or seated workstation. A computer interface (link) is a Lektriever option that provides computer-control access to records or file locations. The Lektriever stores a wide variety of records media. Trays are available to hold a combination of cards, suspension folders, cassette tapes, and microforms. Power files like the Lektriever have the following advantages over manually operated systems:

1. Storage space utilization is increased considerably because units can use space from floor to ceiling in a storage area.

2. Push-button speed in retrieval is superior to any other mechanical or manual method.

Figure 12-10
Aisle Saver Lateral Storage System
Source: *White Office Systems*

Figure 12-11
Times-2 Speed Files®
Source: *Richards-Wilcox*

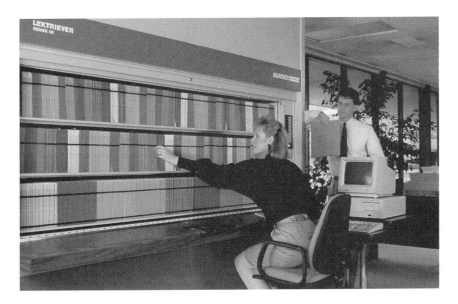

Figure 12-12
The Lektriever
Source: *Kardex Systems, Inc.*

3. Papers and documents can be kept in security control because of the completely enclosed area in which they are held and because they are accessed by a single operator.

Figure 12-13 shows the NO WALK® automated carrousels from White Office Systems. The NO WALK® automated carrousels are activated by stepping on a footpedal. Microcomputer controls are optional with this equipment. Ideal for large and small files, the NO WALK® can be designed to carry a variety of office records media, from letters to X-rays and engineering drawings. Filing productivity is increased by the automated retrieval feature of this equipment. In addition, NO WALK® manufacturers boast that up to 40 percent more filing space is possible in the same work area than with conventional file cabinets.

Storing Other Records

What other records require storage?

Up to this point, equipment and systems have been presented for document storage. There are, however, many other types of records that must be held under control programs because they are vital to the successful operation of a department or an entire organization.

Catalogs and Directories

Catalogs and directories are representative of a type of reference material used in many business, industrial, and service organizations. These records are found in bound-book form or in loose-leaf binders.

For active records of the catalog type in their original form, rotary filing units frequently hold and carry these bulky books. The rotary units handle more easily and allow easier access to records than do cabinets or book shelves. For occasional use of catalog-type material or use by a few workers, bookcases or vertical filing cabinets provide storage for this material.

Catalogs are marked and filed according to several plans: (1) by firm name—with an alphabetic index file listing the items or subjects included in each catalog, (2) by number—with an alphabetic index of firm names and the subjects included in each catalog, or (3) by subject—with an alphabetic index listing of firm names.

Large and Odd-Sized Records

Business and industrial organizations keep other types of important records. Some of these records include maps, blueprints, tracings, duplicator plates and stencils, forms, and computer printouts. These kinds of records present special storage problems. Many of these records are too large or too bulky to be held in standard filing equipment. Such records as these are stored in flat files like those shown in Figure 12-14 or in suspension files like those shown in Figure 12-15.

Figure 12-13
NO WALK® Automated Carrousels
Source: *White Office Systems*

Figure 12-14 Flat Files

Figure 12-15 Bulk Storage Suspension Files
Source: *Plan Hold Corporation*

Computer printouts can be stored in pull-out data drawers that can be removed and taken where needed. Or they can be hung in shelf units such as the mixed-media storage cabinets in Figure 12-16.

Figure 12-16
Mixed-Media
Storage Cabinet
Source: *Acme Design Technology, Co.*

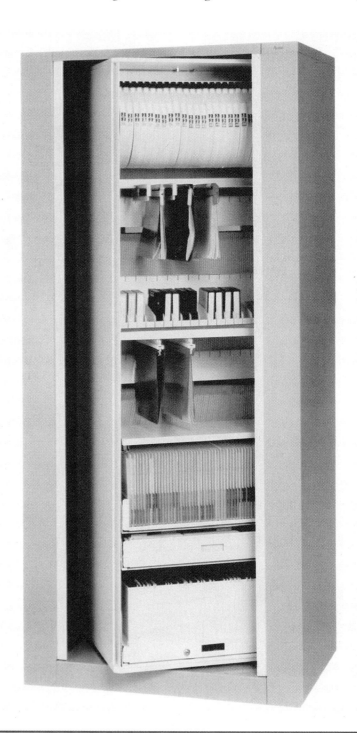

Mixed Media

A **mixed-media storage cabinet** is filing equipment in which a combination of records media is stored in one location. Mixed-media storage cabinets are available in a variety of colors, sizes, and configurations. Mixed-media cabinets are usually of a modular design with an adaptable interior to accommodate a variety of records media. Letter- and legal-size folders, computer tapes, suspension printout binders, microfilm cartridges, cassette tapes, suspension folders, disk packs, ring binders, and office supplies— all these are accommodated by the adjustable shelving in these units. The cabinets easily adapt to changing and expanding storage requirements.

When is mixed-media storage needed?

Review

1. Name three descriptive characteristics of folders that must be determined before acquiring folders for the correspondence file.

2. What advantages do suspension folder systems have over the stationary vertical folder systems?

3. Recommend storage retrieval equipment for a filing system that requires frequent access to single documents from the stored folders. Defend your choice.

Summary

Selecting paper records storage supplies and equipment requires consideration of three selection/purchase factors: need, availability, and cost. The appropriate selection of card and correspondence records storage equipment relies on how well these factors are understood and examined.

The selection of correspondence records supplies and equipment is a challenging task for any office worker. However, the more knowledge you have about folders, guides, and labels, the better equipped you will be to make suitable choices of filing supplies.

The selection of correspondence filing storage and retrieval equipment is an on-going challenge to the office worker. Although traditional filing cabinets and shelf files dominate in records storage usage, high-density filing equipment and power files are increasing in number because of their efficient use of office space and potential for rapid records storage and retrieval.

The variety of modern office records media has resulted in the construction of mixed-media storage equipment. Modular design equipment takes the shape, size, and form necessary to protect and store a records media mix. Because of easy alteration of shape and size, mixed-media storage equipment satisfies not only present storage needs but also future storage needs.

The records storage supplies and equipment business continues to grow and change to keep pace with the growth and changes taking place in records storage practices. This chapter includes basic types of equipment available for paper records storage. The topic is too immense, however, to cover in a single chapter. The professional development of every office worker should include an ongoing exploration of records storage equipment. Make browsing in current business periodicals and journals a part of your professional development. The knowledge you gain will make you a more valued office worker.

Terminology Review

carrousel file	(p. 220)
cost/benefit analysis	(p. 210)
lateral file	(p. 216)
mechanical retrieval equipment	(p. 222)
mixed-media storage cabinet	(p. 227)
mobile shelf file	(p. 220)
point (pt.)	(p. 212)
shelf file	(p. 215)
stock	(p. 212)
suspension (hanging) file	(p. 218)
tub file	(p. 218)
vertical file cabinet	(p. 214)

Questions for Discussion

1. Which is the most important factor to consider when selecting records storage supplies and equipment—needs, availability, or costs? (Obj. 1)

2. List at least five possible needs to consider when selecting records storage supplies and equipment. (Obj. 2)

3. What advantages does the rotary carrousel file have over the cabinet and shelf file equipment? (Obj. 3)

4. What advantages does mechanical retrieval equipment have over manual retrieval equipment? Any disadvantages? (Obj. 4)

5. List three designs, or configurations, of high-density file storage equipment. (Obj. 5)

6. What tab cut do you recommend for folders that carry captions up to 4½" long? 3" long? (Obj. 6)

Applications

Number from 1 to 10 on a separate sheet of paper. Write the letter of the supply or equipment in Column 2 beside the number of the description in Column 1. (Obj. 6)

Description

1. An open, top-access file for active records.
2. A rotary file that allows multiple access.
3. A correspondence file drawer cabinet requiring less aisle space than the traditional vertical file cabinet.
4. Labels for a dot matrix printer.
5. A high-density shelf file that requires minimal aisle space.
6. A storage unit for cards, letters, and computer printouts.
7. A storage unit for engineering drawings and maps.
8. Labels for a laser printer.
9. Folder storage for manuals, catalogs, and other bulky materials.
10. One type of mechanical retrieval equipment for documents.

Supply or Equipment

a. box-bottom suspension folder
b. carrousel file
c. continuous feed labels
d. flat file
e. lateral file
f. Lektriever
g. mixed-media storage cabinet
h. mobile shelf file
i. sheet labels
j. tub file

Practice Set Application

At this time, complete Job 13, *Alphabetic Correspondence Database*, and Job 14, *Numeric Records Database*, in OFFICE FILING PROCEDURES, Eighth Edition. Instructions and supplies for these jobs are included in the practice set.

Chapter Thirteen

Electronic and Image Records

Learning Objectives

After completing Chapter 13, you will be able to do the following:

1. Describe how electronic records are filed.

2. Describe types of microimage records.

3. Describe the uses for microimage records.

4. Define and describe **microfacsimile.**

5. Describe how microfilm cameras operate.

6. List indexing or coding methods used during microfilming.

7. Identify items that require a cross-reference on microfilmed records.

8. Define and describe various types of **optical disks.**

9. Define **optical character recognition.**

10. Identify equipment for an optical disk workstation.

Electronic Records

Computers are a part of the workplace, and their use will increase in the future. Therefore, the storage of records generated by computer (electronic records) are a major concern for all office workers. The selection of storage equipment is affected by the quantity of electronic records, use of the media, security required for the information, and portability (ability to move from one location to another) of the media. This section covers magnetic disks, reel-to-reel magnetic tape, and computer printout storage.

What are electronic records?

Disk Storage

Figure 13-1 shows typical desktop storage units for 3.5-inch disks. Working copy disks may be updated daily and need to be accessible from the workstation. Binders and hanging files with plastic pockets to hold these disks also are used at the workstation (see Figure 13-1). Backup copies of word processor and personal computer data usually are maintained on 8mm (millimeter) magnetic tape for long-term storage.

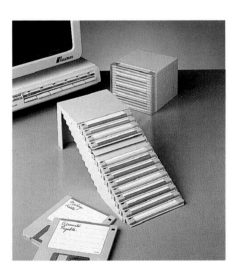

Figure 13-1
Disk Storage
Source: *Fellowes Manufacturing Company*

Compressing data on disks and tapes makes efficient use of disk space. When data is compressed, the blank spaces between words and in side, top, and bottom margins of letters and reports are reduced or eliminated. Therefore, more files can be stored on one disk or tape, which results in cost and space savings.

Tape Storage

Magnetic tape is used primarily for secondary storage—backup or archive. This tape comes in 1/2-inch open reel, 1/2-inch cartridge, 1/4-inch minicartridge, and 1/4-inch cassette. Although reel-to-reel tape has been in use for many years, the trend is toward smaller packaging. Large mainframe computer disk packs, enclosed in plastic containers, are stored flat on shelves or in cabinets. Large reels and disk packs are stored on steel shelves and in cabinets, as shown in Figure 13-2.

Printout Storage

Computer printouts can be filed in a variety of ways. Individual printouts, such as invoices that are used often, are indexed, coded, and filed in folders. Large sets of continuous printouts usually are placed in specially designed binders with a label affixed to the back or front of the binder. The binders can be placed in a file cabinet drawer, on a shelf, or in various forms of suspension equipment.

Figure 13-2
Computer Tape and Printout Storage
Source: *Dept. of Health & Human Services/Social Security Administration*

Review

1. What three media are used to store computer output?

2. What are the major uses of magnetic tape?

Microimage Records

Microimage records, as you learned in Chapter 1, are reduced in size when photographed. An estimated 3.9 billion pages of data are converted to microforms each year. The primary purposes for converting paper records to microimage records are to reduce the amount of floor space and filing equipment required for filing paper records. A cabinet equal in size to a four-drawer vertical paper file can store 1,000 rolls of 16mm (millimeter) microfilm—equivalent to almost 1,750 drawers of paper documents. The benefits of microfilm are numerous. It is easy to use, is inexpensive to operate, can be used as evidence in legal cases, and produces quality images and outstanding print copies. **Micrographics** is the full range of services for creating, storing, retrieving, using, and protecting microimage records.

What are microimage records?

What is micrographics?

Types of Microimage Records

Microfilm rolls and flat forms are the two basic microimage media formats. Each microform has its own applications. All microforms begin as roll film but may be formatted into aperture cards, microfiche, microfilm jackets, card jackets, micro-opaques, ultrafiche, and ultrastrips, which are also known as *unitized microforms.* A **unitized microform** contains one unit of information. The unit may be a file folder of related correspondence, computer printout, engineering drawing, report, or other multi-page document set. One unitized microform contains one record. Unitized microforms are well suited for applications involving small record units such as one file. Common microforms are shown in Figure 13-3.

What are unitized microforms?

Figure 13-3
Common Microforms

Roll Microfilm

Roll microfilm is a length of microfilm that is or can be put on a reel, spool, or core. Generally, microfilm is produced on 16mm, 35mm, or 105mm film, in 100-foot or 215-foot lengths. The 16mm reels are used primarily for financial data, government files, educational files, and similar data. The 35mm reels commonly are used for graphics and large documents such as engineering drawings.

What microforms are used in most active records systems?

Most active records systems utilize microfilm cartridges and cassettes, while inactive records systems frequently include microfilm reels. A **cartridge** is a single-core (one loop) plastic container used for protection and retrieval of microfilm images. A **cassette** is a double-core (two loops for feed and take-up) plastic container used for protection and retrieval of microfilm images. When mounted on an appropriate reader or reader-printer, microfilm from a cartridge or cassette loads automatically.

Microfilm is suited to recording lengthy documents that do not need updating frequently. Correspondence, checks, invoices, complete computer runs, and other daily transactions often are stored on roll film. A roll of film cannot be updated. To do so requires filming the entire roll again. And because paper records usually are destroyed after filming, updating an entire roll is not possible in all cases. Splicing (cutting and pasting) new microfilm into an existing roll destroys its legal quality.

Aperture Card

An **aperture card** contains a rectangular hole (aperture) specifically designed as a carrier for a microfilm image or images. (See Figure 13-4.) Each card contains one or more images considered as a record unit. A *mounter* is a device that simultaneously cuts, positions, and fastens film frames in aperture cards. Identifying data may be keypunched into the card, permitting automatic sorting and retrieval.

Aperture cards originally were developed and continue to be used extensively for engineering drawings. They are used most often in applications involving large documents that are difficult to handle in paper form. Some business forms and X-rays may be stored on aperture cards.

Microfiche

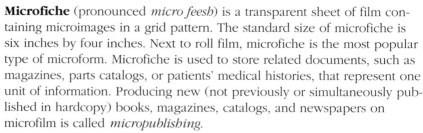

What two microforms are most popular?

Microfiche (pronounced *micro feesh*) is a transparent sheet of film containing microimages in a grid pattern. The standard size of microfiche is six inches by four inches. Next to roll film, microfiche is the most popular type of microform. Microfiche is used to store related documents, such as magazines, parts catalogs, or patients' medical histories, that represent one unit of information. Producing new (not previously or simultaneously published in hardcopy) books, magazines, catalogs, and newspapers on microfilm is called *micropublishing*.

Updatable microfiche is very useful in active and growing records systems. A previously exposed microfiche can be reinserted into the camera

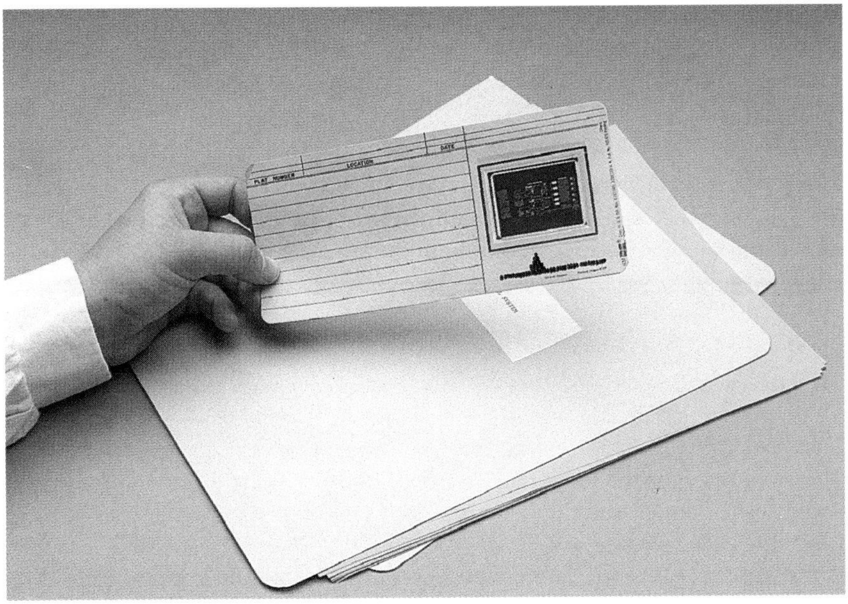

Figure 13-4
Aperture Card

and new images added to any blank areas remaining on the film. Some cameras will erase previously recorded images and record new images in their place.

Jackets

A **microfilm jacket** consists of two thin pieces of rectangular transparent polyester material sealed together in channels, usually 16mm or 35mm wide, with a header strip across the top for the file title. A **card jacket** is a paper card containing one or more transparent channels into which strips of microfilm can be inserted. The card portion is used for recording eye-readable information. Microfilm rolls are cut into strips to fit the jacket channels and inserted by hand or by machine (called a *loader*). Jackets may be updated by removing outdated strips and inserting new strips. Jackets are usually 6" x 4" and hold 60 film frames. A hard copy may be made from a jacket by using a reader-printer. Jackets are widely used to unitize and update case files maintained by insurance companies, police departments, hospitals, and banks.

Computer-Output Microfilm

Computer-output microfilm (COM) is a microform produced by converting and recording data from a computer onto microfilm in human-readable language. The paper printout (hard copy) is eliminated—actually bypassed. Computer-output microfilm (COM) uses 105mm film, which may be in roll or flat format. COM recorders can print data 10 to 15 times faster than standard impact (computer) printers. Consequently, reports are produced and distributed sooner. Business applications for COM include accounts payable and receivable, audit reports, customer name/number/ address, customer statements, general ledger, inventory, market research, parts lists, payroll, shareholder records, and numerous other uses.

Other Microforms

For specialized applications, microfilm chips, micro-opaques, ultrafiche, and ultrastrips may be used. These microforms are not readily available because they require special reading equipment and often require a two-step filming and refilming process.

Microfacsimile

Why is the microfacsimile useful in some applications?

Microfacsimile is a method of converting microimages to computer-readable data, which are transmitted electronically and recreated at the other end, locally or at some remote location. A scanner converts the microimages to computer-readable data. A computer fax modem transmits and recreates the microform at the other end. The electronic image can also be output to a laser printer.

Film image scanners have been designed for roll film, microfiche, and aperture cards. Diagrams as well as printed or written material can be transmitted by microfacsimile. Engineering drawings in aperture cards can be faxed to remote construction locations for immediate use.

Review

1. List three common types of microforms.

2. Which microform is computer-generated?

Filming and Processing Microimage Records

In what order are records microfilmed?

Microfilming is a process of photographing documents to reduce the original document to a very small (micro) size. Records are prepared for microfilming in the same manner as they are for filing in cabinets and shelves. They must be indexed, coded, and arranged in correct order according to the filing systems used before they are filmed. Types of cameras used for microfilming include rotary, planetary, and step-and-repeat.

Rotary Camera

A **rotary camera** is a type of microfilm camera that photographs documents while they are being moved by some form of transport mechanism. Documents may be inserted manually or with automatic document stackers that provide for faster filming. Rotary cameras are used most often because of the speed at which documents can be filmed. All staples, paper clips, or other fasteners must be removed, and all torn papers must be repaired before inserting the documents into the camera. Correspondence, checks, invoices, and school transcripts usually are microfilmed with a rotary camera and remain in a roll format. A rotary camera is shown in Figure 13-5, page 238.

Planetary Camera

A **planetary camera** is a type of microfilm camera in which the document being photographed and the film remain in a stationary position during exposure. The document is on a plane (flat) surface at the time of filming. A planetary camera is also known as a *flatbed camera*. Although documents are usually fed one sheet at a time, a greater variety of document sizes can be photographed, and the quality of the images is higher than with a rotary camera. Blueprints, engineering drawings, bound books, newspapers, and magazines are filmed with planetary cameras. Smaller planetary cameras are used for smaller documents requiring the filming of fine detail. Figure 13-6, page 238, shows a planetary camera.

Step-and-Repeat Camera

A **step-and-repeat camera** is a type of microfilm camera that can expose a series of separate images on an area of film according to a predetermined format, usually in orderly rows and columns, such as is needed for producing microfiche. As each document is exposed by the camera, a mechanism moves (or *steps*) the film into the next position on the grid format to accept the next exposure. This pattern is repeated until a complete microfiche is produced. A step-and-repeat camera is shown in Figure 13-7.

Why isn't the master copy used daily?

All microfilm must be processed after it is removed from the camera. The quality of the images (clarity of the print or photographic material) is checked carefully before the film is packaged into the desired microform. The original microform is called a *master copy* and never is used as a daily working copy. The master copy is used for making duplicate copies for daily use and for charging out. Master copies are stored in an archival-quality vault according to the records retention and destruction schedule.

Equipment and Supplies for Microimage Records

Microfilm rolls and flat microforms usually are stored in vertical/top-access storage equipment. Trays, drawer dividers, and binders are used for specific microforms. Portable trays and binders are used at individual workstations. Carrousel storage units, trays, and binders are available for flat forms. Microfilm cartridges also are stored in carrousels. Microform storage equipment is shown in Figure 13-8, page 238.

Retrieval of requested microrecords may be accomplished by searching a computer database of indexed information, which will identify the exact roll and frame location of the desired information. **Computer-assisted retrieval (CAR)** is the capability of locating or identifying

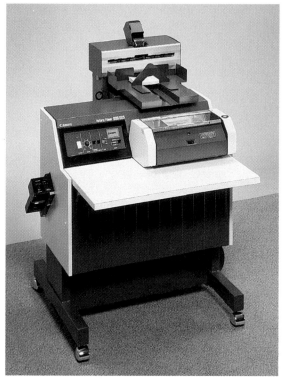

Figure 13-5 Rotary Camera
Source: *Canon U.S.A., Inc.*

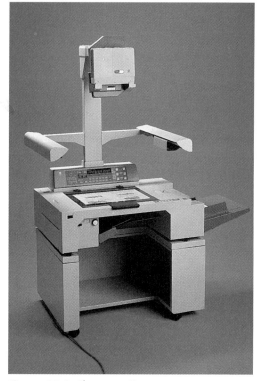

Figure 13-6 Planetary Camera
Source: *Minolta Corporation*

Figure 13-7 Step-and-Repeat Camera
Source: *Courtesy of Anacomp, Inc.*

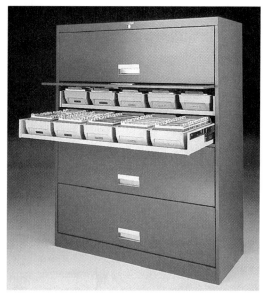

Figure 13-8 Microform Storage Equipment
Source: *Taylor-Merchant Corp. N.Y.C. 10001*

microimages by commands initiated through a computer terminal. CAR is a combination system that uses the speed and indexing capability of the computer and the storage and retrieval efficiencies of microfilm.

A reader that will enlarge (magnify) the microimage is needed for using all microforms. A print copy may be made when using a reader-printer. A microform reader-printer is shown in Figure 13-9.

Figure 13-9
Microfiche and Jacket Reader-Printer
Source: *InfoGraphix Corp.*

Labels

Labels are affixed to the outside of microimage media storage units to identify the contents of each drawer, shelf, or entire unit. Guide labels used in microimage media drawers, trays, binders, and shelves to separate microforms are prepared according to the filing method used.

Labels or headings may be hand-printed, typed, or computer-generated. The title of the records series and department name should appear on all labels. The beginning and ending dates or the beginning and ending records numbers, whichever applies to the records series, also should be included. Arabic numbers should be used in headings, except when a Roman numeral is part of a records series or title.

Roll-film reels are placed in small boxes the size of the film. Each roll of film is assigned a unique identifier, which appears on both the film and the box label. A microfilm roll box may have preprinted labels on the edge and front for writing the information. A separate adhesive label also may be affixed. Labels are affixed to microfilm cartridges and cassettes. Color accenting on drawer, shelf, guide, cartridge, cassette, and box labels facilitates storage and retrieval.

Flat forms of microfilm have an eye-readable heading or caption. This heading may be created during filming or on an adhesive label affixed after filming. Flat microform labels should include the department or company name on the left side, records series and coding information in the center, and microform number on the right. (See Figure 13-10.) Adhesive labels may be used on aperture cards, microfilm and card jackets, and copies of microfiche that have a short retention.

Figure 13-10
Microfiche
Heading/Label

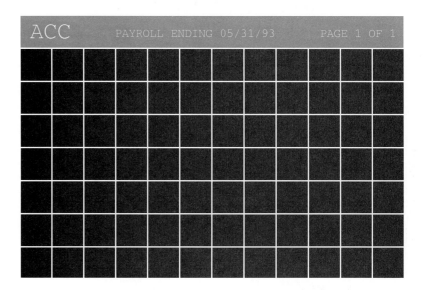

ACC   PAYROLL ENDING 05/31/93   PAGE 1 OF 1

Envelopes

Envelopes are used to protect microfiche and jackets from scratches, dirt, and abrasion. Several microfiche on the same subject may be stored in one envelope.

What procedures are followed for filing and retrieving microimage records?

Filing and Retrieval Procedures for Microimage Records

Accurate retrieval of records from microforms requires the same care during indexing and coding as is used for paper records. Records are filmed in a specific order, and they stay in that order. Consequently, correct coding and arrangement of records is essential.

Indexing and Coding

Coding of microimage media occurs when any identifying information is added to or made a part of the microform to help retrieve a specific image record. The type of records or the way in which they are used determines the coding system. Most often, coding is alphabetic, numeric, or alphanumeric.

Roll film may have numbers, blips, bar codes, or lines placed on the film as identifiers. **Targets,** or **flash targets,** are guides used during filming to identify the contents of a microfilm roll and facilitate indexing. Targets serve the same purpose as guide and folder captions in a paper filing system and may contain alphabetic, numeric, or subject titles and dates. (See Figure 13-11.)

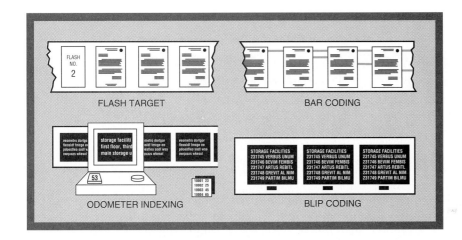

Figure 13-11

Forms of Microfilm Indexing and Coding

Other indexing and coding systems used to retrieve records include electronic devices for counting the images, counting the feet of film run through a reader (odometer indexing), and reading magnetic codes. In each retrieval system, you can enlarge and read the microimage on any reader or reader-printer that has the proper magnification without using the coding or indexing system. You can find the correct image by checking each frame, which takes more time. Flat microforms may be edge-notched, colored, or color-striped to speed up filing and retrieval.

Cross-Referencing Microfilm Rolls

Cross-references for microfilm usually are written on the container labels. Retakes, omissions, and misfiles that appear on another roll need a cross-reference. If a records series is on more than one roll, a cross-reference may be made to other rolls. A card file or an automated index contains the cross-references in large microrecord storage centers.

Sorting and Filing

Microimage media are sorted according to the filing method used. Filing of microimage media is in a front-to-back arrangement with the most recent microforms in the back.

Charging Out

The master copies of microforms are not charged out. A copy of the original roll, microfiche, jacket, or other microform is used to fulfill a request for a microform. These copies may be marked *duplicate* and destroyed after use. OUT cards replace microforms removed from storage units for local use. When microforms are combined in folders with paper records, the entire folder is charged out. Charge-out and follow-up procedures for microimage records are similar to those used for paper records.

Review

1. Describe how two microfilm cameras photograph records.
2. What microforms can be charged out?

Optical Technology

What is an optical disk?

The quantity of stored computer data doubles about every two years. The advances made in optical disk technology make electronic imaging a cost-effective alternative to computer disk and tape storage. An **optical data disk,** or *optical disk,* is an information storage medium in which a laser beam burns or etches holes to form a dot pattern of the letters, numbers, lines, and drawings as it copies from the original document onto the disk. Optical disks are available in 2.5-inch, 3.5-inch, 4.75-inch, 5.25-inch, 12-inch, and 14-inch sizes. They are packaged in plastic cartridges to protect their surfaces. The storage capacity of one double-sided disk is estimated to be 40,000 pages or 800 reams of documents. A single 12-inch optical disk stores as much as 80 file cabinets.

What is OCR?

Optical character recognition (OCR) is a technique by which printed or photographically recorded characters can be rapidly recognized by scanning and converted to digital (computer) codes for storage. By using OCR, higher density (compressed) storage and full-text (entire document) retrieval are possible.

Full-text storage, rapid file retrieval, and high-density storage are the primary advantages of optical disk technology. Electronic and optical technologies are advancing at such a rapid pace that this text can only touch the surface of the currently available technology.

Types of Optical Technology

Computer system users have a broad range of optical storage methods available to solve massive storage problems. Included in the choices are: CD-ROM (Compact Disk, Read-Only Memory), WORM (Write Once, Read Many) technology, MO (Magneto-Optical) disks, mixed-media systems, multifunction drives, and autochangers.

Compact disk, read-only memory (CD-ROM) is a 5.25-inch optical disk on which data and photographs are recorded for reading only. CD-ROM technology is ideally suited to the personal computer (PC) and to applications that require storage of large amounts of information for periodic referral. It is primarily used for catalogs, online manuals, education, and training packages that are mass produced for mass distribution for short-term usage. Production of the initial disk is expensive and, therefore, makes CD-ROM technology too expensive for most records applications.

Write once, read many (WORM) is a nonerasable, nonrewritable optical storage media. WORM is used most frequently for optical storage because it provides permanent storage that cannot be overwritten. Because WORM disks have an estimated 30-year life, they are a favorite choice for archive applications where data security is essential.

WORM is the most secure optical technology because it is not affected by magnetic forces, accidental erasure, or tampering. However, a file change requires rewriting the entire file. WORM is generally the best storage medium when file entries are not extremely large and require a permanent track record of changes. WORM is the technology of choice for document image management systems for medical records. It is also used for bank credit card application files.

Which is the most secure optical technology and why?

A laser card is a credit card with WORM optical data storage instead of a magnetic strip. The laser card may hold 1,100 typed pages. Where a credit card is portable identification, the laser card is a portable database. Applications include storage of truck and auto maintenance records and health care records. In Japan, laser cards are used as medical record cards in a health and welfare program for the elderly. In London, laser cards are used in a prenatal care program for keeping track of pregnant women.

Magneto-optical (MO) disks are rewritable optical disks. Magneto-optical technology requires two or three phases—erasing, rewriting, and sometimes verifying—to create an updated disk. With new technology, known as *phase-change rewritable,* an optical disk can be rewritten in a single pass. Rewritable technologies are subject to human error and data loss through magnetic forces, erasure, or tampering. Consequently, data on rewritable optical disks should be backed up on rewritable optical disks or 8mm magnetic tape. Because you must scan magnetic tape, access is slower; but it is less expensive than rewritable optical disks.

Mixed-media or *multimedia* mass-storage systems provide flexibility through a combination of hard disks, optical disks (including CDs), and tapes. With mixed-media systems, users can take advantage of all technologies with *multifunction drives. Computer Output to Laser Disk (COLD)* is widely used by large mainframe data centers to replace computer-generated paper reports, COM, and magnetic disk storage.

Autochangers, also known as *jukeboxes,* often are used to store large libraries of optical disks. The device searches the vertical columns of disks and retrieves and positions the requested disk for reading. Storing files on more than one disk or requesting files from different time periods slows retrieval time.

Optical Equipment and Procedures

What equipment is necessary for an optical disk workstation?

Optical technology is essentially an online paper processing system. Records are scanned into the computer; then they are viewed on a monitor, indexed, and stored on an optical disk. The necessary equipment for an optical disk workstation includes an OCR scanner, a high-resolution monitor, and a laser printer. Departmental optical systems are used most often. The emphasis is on using personal computer local-area network (PC-LAN) imaging software.

The optical disk system shown in Figure 13-12 is the Canonfile 250. With a unique design in which the scanner is under the monitor, the Canonfile 250 requires less desktop space. Two-sided scanning allows both the front and back sides of a document to be scanned simultaneously. A 5.25-inch magneto-optical disk and two storage modes are used in the Canonfile. In the nonerasable mode, original information cannot be changed or deleted. The erasable mode allows revisions or deletions of old information. Documents are retrieved on screen, where they can be enlarged, both sides can be viewed, and they can be rotated by as much as 90 degrees before printing a hard copy on the laser printer. The scanner and the disk are shown in Figure 13-13.

Optical Technology Applications

Some of the largest users of optical imaging are in the federal government. The Internal Revenue Service has undertaken a massive modernization project that will completely automate the filing, retrieving, and processing of the 1040 federal income tax form. Optical technology will be used to convert over 200 million annual tax returns to an electronic format.

The FBI is converting fingerprint file cards to fingerprint imaging. The retrieval and fingerprint matching process can now be done on a screen, verified, and a print copy made much more rapidly than by the manual system.

The U.S. Postal Service is using PC-based CD-ROM workstations. A massive database that contains millions of ZIP+4 numbers is being installed at postal facilities throughout the country to enable users to look up ZIP+4 codes.

Technology for use in records systems is advancing at high speed. You will work with a variety of new technologies throughout your career in records control. Embrace technology as a medium for improving records control.

Figure 13-12 Canonfile 250 Optical Disk Workstation
Source: *Photography by Mimi Ostendorf-Smith/Photonics*

Figure 13-13 Canonfile 250 Scanner and Disk
Source: *Photography by Mimi Ostendorf-Smith/Photonics*

Review

1. What are the steps for recording documents on optical disk?

2. Why are WORM optical disks used most often?

Summary

Storage of electronic records (computer disks, tapes, and print-outs) is affected by the quantity, use, security, and the need to move the records to various locations. Desktop storage units, units accessible at an office workstation, and large multimedia storage units are available.

Photographing microimage records reduces their size. A unitized microform contains one unit of information such as a computer printout or a report. Commonly used microforms include roll microfilm (reels, cartridges, and cassettes), aperture cards, microfiche, microfilm and card jackets, and computer-output microfilm (COM). Microforms for very specialized applications include microfilm chips, micro-opaques, ultrafiche, and ultrastrips.

Microfacsimile converts microimages to computer-readable data, transmits it electronically, and recreates the microform image at the other end. Microfacsimile can transmit roll film, microfiche, and aperture cards that contain diagrams, printed, or written material.

Records may be microfilmed with a rotary camera, a planetary camera, or a step-and-repeat camera. The type of records being filmed and the resulting microform determines which camera will be used. Microfilm is processed, the quality of the images is checked, and the film is packaged into the desired microfilm.

Vertical/top- and lateral/side-access storage units are used for microforms. Computer-assisted retrieval (CAR) can be used to search a computer database and identify a microfilm roll and the exact frame containing the desired information. All microforms need a reader to enlarge the microimages for reading and using. A reader-printer is used when a print copy of a microimage is needed.

All microforms are labeled, either on the microform or on its container. Guides used in microimage media drawers, trays, binders, and shelves are prepared according to the filing method used. Envelopes are used to protect microfiche and jackets from scratches, dirt, and abrasion.

Filing and retrieval procedures for microimage records include indexing and coding, cross-referencing of microfilm rolls, sorting, and filing. Duplicate copies of microforms may be charged out, and proper follow-up procedures ensure their return.

Terminology Review

aperture card	(p. 234)
card jacket	(p. 235)
cartridge	(p. 234)
cassette	(p. 234)
compact disk, read-only memory (CD-ROM)	(p. 243)
computer-assisted retrieval (CAR)	(p. 237)
computer-output microfilm (COM)	(p. 235)
magneto-optical (MO) disk	(p. 243)
microfacsimile	(p. 236)
microfiche	(p. 234)
microfilm jacket	(p. 235)
microfilming	(p. 236)
micrographics	(p. 233)
optical character recognition (OCR)	(p. 242)
optical data disk	(p. 242)
planetary camera	(p. 237)
roll microfilm	(p. 234)
rotary camera	(p. 236)
step-and-repeat camera	(p. 237)
targets/flash targets	(p. 241)
unitized microform	(p. 233)
write once, read many (WORM)	(p. 243)

An optical disk is an information storage medium in which a laser beam burns holes to form a dot pattern of the letters, numbers, lines, and drawings as it copies from the original document onto the disk. Printed or graphically recorded characters may be converted to digital codes using optical character recognition (OCR). Optical disk technology includes compact disk, read-only memory (CD-ROM); write once, read many (WORM); and magneto-optical (MO) disks.

Questions for Discussion

1. Describe the storage containers used for electronic records. (Obj. 1)
2. Describe the following microimage records: roll microfilm, aperture card, microfiche, microfilm jacket, card jacket, computer-output microfilm. (Obj. 2)
3. What types of records often are stored on roll microfilm, aperture cards, microfiche, jackets, and COM records? (Obj. 3)
4. Define and describe *microfacsimile*. (Obj. 4)
5. Describe how records are filmed with rotary, planetary, and step-and-repeat microfilm cameras. (Obj. 5)
6. List four indexing or coding methods used during microfilming. (Obj. 6)
7. What items require a cross-reference on microfilmed records? (Obj. 7)
8. Define and describe an *optical disk, CD-ROM, WORM,* and *MO* disks. (Obj. 8)
9. Define *OCR*. (Obj. 9)
10. What equipment is necessary for an optical disk workstation? (Obj. 10)

▶ Applications

On a separate sheet of paper, write your answers to the following questions.

1. Which microform is the best choice for the following types of records? The choices are roll microfilm, aperture card, microfiche, and jackets (either microfilm or card).

   engineering drawings   checks
   accounts receivables   parts catalogs
   patients' medical histories   X-rays
   insurance company case files   correspondence

2. Which type of camera should be used to microfilm each of the records listed in No. 1?

Practice Set Application

At this time, complete Job 15, *Geographic Records Database,* and Job 16, *Subject Records Database,* in OFFICE FILING PROCEDURES, Eighth Edition. Instructions and supplies for these jobs are included in the practice set.

Chapter Fourteen

Records Control and Disaster Prevention

Learning Objectives

After completing Chapter 14, you will be able to do the following:

1. Explain why planning is essential in records control.

2. Describe the contents of a records management manual.

3. Discuss the uses of a records management manual.

4. Identify and describe common information disasters.

5. Define and describe a **disaster recovery plan.**

6. List the components of a disaster recovery plan.

7. Explain ways that paper, electronic, and image records can be protected from disaster.

8. Describe disaster recovery procedures for paper, electronic, and image records.

Records Control Planning

Your study of *Business Records Control* has included alphabetic indexing rules; procedures for filing records by alphabetic, numeric, geographic, and subject filing methods; computer records database procedures; records maintenance procedures; and how to select equipment and supplies to establish and control all records media in a records system. In order to establish policies and procedures for a records system that will run smoothly and efficiently, extensive planning and coordination are required. Without planning and coordination of the records function, disaster will occur.

Each component of the records system from the filing method selected to the method of destruction requires long-range planning. The decisions of which records media, storage equipment, and procedures to use in the system must be based on anticipated growth of the company and, therefore, the records function. Planning is used to add records to the system, protect them while in the system, and remove them from the system.

You will be involved in solving records problems from your first job throughout your entire work life. Most office jobs and many other jobs include creating, using, storing, and retrieving information. Even if your job is not directly in the records area, you will probably be (1) a user of a filing system that may be inefficient or (2) you will be expected to file and find records.

In this chapter, you will learn to document policies and procedures in a records management manual. The manual is a primary tool for controlling and coordinating the records system and preventing disasters. It also provides the documentation resulting from planning and establishing the records system. You will learn also how to plan for the possibility of a records disaster and, therefore, how to prevent loss of information.

Records Management Manual

Why is a records management manual needed?

You may be fortunate and begin working in an office where a good records control program has been developed. If so, a records management manual should be available for your use. A **records management manual** is a guide to how the records system works. Employees in the records department and others in the organization who use the services of the records department are provided copies of the manual. The recommended contents and uses of a records management manual are discussed in the following paragraphs.

Contents of the Manual

The contents and organization of the information in the records management manual determine whether or not it is used effectively. It should contain essential information for running an efficient and effective records management program. Three main sections should be included in the manual: (1) an introduction, (2) the body, and (3) the closing.

Introduction

The introduction should include a title page, preface, and table of contents. The title of the manual, organization name, authorship of the manual, and publication date should appear on the title page. The preface includes the reasons for the manual, a definition of records management, and a description of the contents of the manual. The table of contents lists all subjects covered in the manual along with their page numbers.

Body

The body of the records management manual includes all records management policies and procedures for each task. Typical policies and procedures cover creation and distribution of correspondence; creation, distribution, and use of forms and reports; storage and retrieval of records (including alphabetic indexing rules); records transfer; records retention; records destruction; disaster plans; selection of equipment and supplies; and microimage and optical applications.

Closing

The closing consists of a glossary of terms used in the manual and an index to the contents. An appendix of additional illustrations may be included. Terms such as *record, active record, inactive record, vital record,* and various microforms are defined in the glossary.

Effective use of the manual makes an alphabetic index of key words essential. The more thorough the indexing process, the more easily and quickly users can locate information. Placing the index in the front of the manual, after the table of contents, makes accessing information even easier. Figure 14-1 illustrates a sample table of contents.

Uses of the Manual

A records management manual generally increases the efficiency of the records department. The records management manual has four main uses: (1) to standardize procedures, (2) to establish responsibility, (3) to assist in employee training, and (4) to provide procedures for updates.

Standardizes Procedures

Records control procedures established by the records department must be followed consistently by other departments. Only when everyone performs the same tasks consistently will the records control system be efficient. Procedures such as selecting supplies and equipment, transferring records, and establishing records retention periods are procedures that must be consistent.

What are the main uses of a records management manual?

Figure 14-1

Records Management
Manual Table of
Contents

Table of Contents

If an organization has a central active files area for filing records from all departments, these records need to be coded correctly before they are sent to central files. Consistency and accuracy in filing and retrieval makes the use of a standard set of indexing rules essential. These rules should be printed in the records management manual.

Establishes Responsibility

Each organization needs to determine the person responsible for performing each records-related task. With specific written instructions for tasks (for example, records transfer), responsibility or blame cannot be passed to others when these tasks are late or not completed. Knowing the right person to contact with records-related questions or problems prevents the distribution of inaccurate information.

Assists in Employee Training

The records management manual is not intended to take the place of on-the-job training. It is used to supplement and reinforce training. Written procedures not only help train new employees in the records department, but they also help long-term employees who need to review procedures from time to time.

Brief records and information management job descriptions were presented in Chapter 1. A records management manual would include more detailed job descriptions and procedures for performing specific assigned tasks, with illustrations. For example, preparation of file folder labels follows a standard procedure. All folder labels should look the same and be affixed in the same position on each folder. Instructions and illustrations help those responsible for performing such tasks.

Provides Updates to Procedures

When records policies change in any way, all users of records services must be notified to ensure consistency. Updates can be prepared quickly and efficiently when the manual is stored in a word processor or computer. A records management manual in a three-ring binder can be updated quickly. The number of pages that need to be revised, reprinted, and distributed can be controlled through the use of a three-ring binder.

Review 1

1. Who uses a records management manual?
2. What records control procedures should be standardized?

Records and Information Disasters

What is an information disaster?

A **disaster** is a sudden and unexpected event that produces adverse results, a sudden or great misfortune. An **information disaster** is a sudden and unexpected event that results in the loss of records essential to an organization's continued operation (vital records). Historical records also are included in disaster planning, prevention, and recovery procedures.

Disaster causes are categorized as natural disasters, building/equipment failure or malfunction, acts of deliberate destructiveness, and human error or carelessness. Natural disasters include cyclones, earthquakes, hail, heavy storms, hurricanes, lightning, snow, and tornadoes, which vary among geographic locations. Good weather forecasting and careful planning can reduce the adverse effects of natural disasters.

Building/equipment failure or malfunction includes fire and flooding caused by leaking roofs, broken pipes, defective wiring and switches, faulty machinery and equipment, and broken heating or cooling systems. Electrical malfunctions such as defective wiring, faulty switch boxes, and overheated motors cause most business fires. Proper maintenance procedures prevent many of these disasters.

Acts of deliberate destructiveness include theft, espionage, vandalism, terrorism, and war. Theft is the most common problem in organizations. The threat of these disasters can be reduced through awareness and planning.

Records destruction or damage also results from human error or carelessness. Smoldering cigarettes, unattended stoves, open windows, unlocked doors, careless handling of flammable materials, data entry errors, and many similar examples present hazards to vital records.

Disaster Planning, Prevention, and Recovery

Why is a disaster recovery plan necessary?

A disaster recovery plan can restore order after a disaster and save an organization considerable money. A **disaster recovery plan** is a written, approved, implemented, and periodically tested program to reconstruct and/or salvage an organization's vital and historical records. The plan also establishes procedures for the immediate resumption of business operations after a disaster. Step-by-step procedures must be written for recovering vital records and other priority information. The disaster recovery plan should include all the items listed in Figure 14-2.

The Association of Records Managers and Administrators, Inc. (ARMA) publishes materials helpful in disaster prevention and recovery planning. These ARMA publications—*Disaster Prevention and Recovery,* by Susan L. Bulgawicz and Charles E. Nolan; *Handbook for the Recovery of Water Damaged Business Records,* by Julia Niebuhr Eulenberg; and the *Vital Records Guideline*—are the sources for much of the information in this chapter.

What are the results of information disasters?

Information disasters most often result in fire-damaged records, water-damaged records, or missing records due to theft, error, or carelessness. In all cases, disaster-recovery procedures must begin immediately or at least within 24 hours.

Underground storage facilities provide secure offsite storage for many organizations. Cold sites—full computer rooms without the hardware—provide immediate disaster recovery. If an organization loses a computer

Figure 14-2 Components of a Disaster Recovery Plan

Recovery Procedures Manual	Detailed procedures for handling specific types of disasters and recovering data from various media should be in writing.
Disaster Recovery Team	A disaster team should be formed to initiate the disaster plan and direct the recovery process. The team should be comprised of representatives from the records area, building emergency and security personnel, building maintenance personnel, and someone knowledgeable in archives storage procedures. All other personnel who will assist during the recovery process are identified also.
Priority Record Schedule	Each type of records media should be identified and prioritized in terms of recovery. Immediate and follow-up salvage techniques for each media should be identified.
Disaster Recovery Kit	Supplies have to be available to begin recovery procedures while waiting for additional supplies. The supply list might include absorbent paper, plastic sheeting and drop cloths, blotting paper, flashlights, identification tags, chemicals (alcohol and disinfectants), rubber gloves, protective clothing, rubber boots, and hand tools. A complete list of supplies and supply outlets, a copy of the disaster plan, an emergency telephone list, and recovery handbooks also are included in the disaster recovery kit. Several kits should be available so that the recovery procedures can begin immediately.
Equipment	Reproduction equipment for microform and data/word processing records should be available. Extra equipment can be stored at another location, leased, or borrowed.
Computer Program and Application Documentation	Backup copies (disks or tapes) of the computer programs should be stored at another location. Printed directions for running the programs can be backed up on paper or microform.

Source: *Association of Records Managers and Administrators, Inc., adapted from* Vital Records Guidelines, *Prairie Village, KS, 1984.*

operation because of a disaster, records stored underground can be accessed quickly, and the business can be running again with minimum disruption. One such facility, Iron Mountain, is shown in Figure 14-3.

Fire-Damaged Records

According to the National Fire Protection Association, 40 percent of all companies that lose their records in a fire are forced to close within a year. Buildings and equipment are usually adequately insured; the information they house, however, often is not adequately protected.

Storing records in fire-resistant vaults, safes, cabinets, rooms, and boxes provides fire protection. Fire resistance is measured by the length of time it takes for the interior of the container to reach 350 degrees.

Steel file cabinets will not burn but have a fire resistance of only about five minutes. Insulated safes are rated fire resistant for up to four

What storage containers are recommended for fire protection?

Figure 14-3 Underground Storage Facility

Source: *Reprinted by permission, Iron Mountain, America's largest records management company.*

hours. Separate fire-resistance ratings should be provided on each insulated safe or cabinet used for storing microimage and electronic media. An insulated file drawer is shown in Figure 14-4.

Some paper records damaged by fire can be reconstructed. Readable pieces can be placed together and laminated (sealed between two pieces of plastic) or photocopied. In some cases, they may be microfilmed. Fire-damaged microforms and electronic media usually cannot be recovered. However, smoke-damaged microimage and electronic media usually can be recovered.

Water-Damaged Records

What recovery processes may be used on paper records?

Water is just as damaging to records as fire. For this reason, overhead sprinkler systems are not recommended for computer and records storage areas. **Halon gas** is a fire-fighting agent that is effective and safe in a records environment. When triggered, the gas is emitted from sprinkler-type devices in the ceiling. It leaves no residue.

Wet paper records should be handled as little as possible, but taken care of immediately. Mold and mildew will appear within 48 hours. **Blast freezing**, a process that freezes material very quickly, is recommended for preventing mold and mildew on water-damaged paper records.

Freeze drying is a method of evaporating moisture before it returns to a liquid state and is recommended for recovering frozen paper records.

Figure 14-4
Insulated File Drawer

Source: *Schwab Corporation*

Records should be inventoried as they are packed for freezing so that they can be relocated after they have been dried. Numerous disaster-recovery companies have mobile environmental chambers for freeze-drying records. These chambers may be sent to disaster locations. Some disaster-recovery companies anticipate the demand for records recovery before a weather disaster, such as a hurricane, arrives and send the mobile chambers to the area before disaster strikes. Consequently, damaged businesses can obtain disaster-recovery assistance quickly.

The best protection against loss of electronic records is a good backup system with backups stored in another location. All equipment and media should be protected with plastic covers. However, most wet electronic

---

What is the best protection for electronic records?

equipment and magnetic media can be cleaned and dried. After magnetic disks have been cleaned and dried and the data recovered, the damaged media should be discarded. Electronic media should not be stored in places where water damage is likely to occur, such as on the floor, on floor-level shelves, or in basements. Waterproof and fireproof storage units that are rated for microfilm and electronic media should be used.

Water-damaged microfilm should be left in their storage boxes and submerged in room-temperature water in a plastic container until recovery. The boxes should be placed under the water until all air is forced out so that the film is kept uniformly wet. The film is then reprocessed using chemical-free water.

Missing Records

What forms of protection can be taken against unauthorized computer access?

Billions of dollars are spent annually by organizations trying to prevent theft and vandalism of information. Specific security, maintenance, and disaster prevention training programs reduce these risks.

Electronic access devices, passwords, and procedures are often used to prevent unauthorized access to computer rooms and computer information. Computer users must key their passwords before they can get into the computer to access records. Punch-codes and card keys may be used to prevent unauthorized access to computer and records storage areas.

Using the manual and barcoding records control procedures discussed in Chapters 6 and 7 helps to reduce the number of disasters caused by employee errors in filing and charging out records. Well-designed procedures and responsible staff who carry out the procedures are the best protection against errors and carelessness.

Review

1. List three fire-resistant storage devices.
2. How are water-damaged microimage records recovered?

Summary

An efficient and effective records system results from extensive planning when establishing policies and procedures for operating the system. The records media and storage equipment must be selected with consideration for growth of the company and of the records system.

A major tool in the planning of the records system is a records management manual. The manual serves as a guide to how the records system works and is used to standardize procedures, establish responsibility for tasks, assist in employee training, and provide procedures for policy updates. It should include three main sections—an introduction, the body, and the closing. A title page, preface, and table of contents are included in the introduction. Policies and procedures for each records management task are included in the body. The closing includes a glossary of terms and an index.

Good planning and development of the records management manual are important for records and information disaster prevention and recovery. Disasters may be natural disasters, building/equipment failure or malfunction, acts of deliberate destructiveness, and human error or carelessness. A disaster recovery plan establishes procedures for the immediate resumption of business operations after a disaster. Through careful planning and preparation, fire- and water-damaged records may be recovered after a disaster. Electronic-access devices, passwords, and barcodes often are used to prevent the loss of records and information.

Throughout your study of *Business Records Control,* you have learned the essential components necessary for planning, establishing, and documenting a records system. The records management manual and a disaster recovery plan are the final components that complete your study of records control. You now have a strong basis for entering the field of records management.

Terminology Review

blast freezing	(p. 256)
disaster	(p. 253)
disaster recovery plan	(p. 254)
freeze drying	(p. 256)
halon gas	(p. 256)
information disaster	(p. 253)
records management manual	(p. 250)

Questions for Discussion

1. Why is planning essential in records control? (Obj. 1)
2. What should be included in a records management manual? (Obj. 2)
3. What are the primary uses of a records management manual? (Obj. 3)
4. Identify three types of disasters. (Obj. 4)
5. Define and describe a *disaster recovery plan.* (Obj. 5)
6. List the components of a disaster recovery plan. (Obj. 6)
7. Explain storage equipment and procedures that may be used to protect paper, electronic, and image records from disaster. (Obj. 7)
8. Describe how water-damaged paper records can be recovered. (Obj. 8)
9. What is the best recovery method for electronic media? (Obj. 8)
10. What procedures are used to recover water-damaged microimage records? (Obj. 8)

Computer Applications

Chapter 5

1. On a separate sheet of paper, create a database design sheet, using Figure 5-2 as an example. Ask your teacher for a new database design sheet found on page 15 in the Teacher's Manual. Use the names listed in Computer Application 2 to complete the design sheet. Use the following information to plan and design the database.

   Date created: Current
   Database filename: Customers
   Database description: List of current customers
   Field names: Name, Title
   Field captions: Customer Name, Title/Suffix
   Field descriptions: Customer's full names, Seniority titles or professional suffixes
   Field types: All fields are text fields.
   Field sizes: Count the longest name or title to be keyed into each field. Be sure to count spaces.
   Sort/Index: Name and Title fields

2. Create the Customers database that you designed in Computer Application 1, using available software. Key the following names into the database. Sort the Customer Name and Title/Suffix fields in that order. Print the table for the Customers database correctly sorted. (Obj. 8)

Mrs. Jonetta DeSalvo	John R. McGovern, Sr.
John R. McGovern, Jr.	Baxter Edward Manheim II
Ms. Jonetta DeSalvo	John R. McGovern, Attorney
Baxter Edward Manheim III	Professor Baxter Edward Manheim
Jonetta DeSalvo, MD	Miss Jonetta DeSalvo

3. On a separate sheet of paper, design a database for the names listed in Computer Application 4. Use the following information to plan and design the database.
   Database filename: Delivery Customers
   Database description: Customers who receive daily deliveries
   Field names: Name, Address, City, State, Postal Code
   Field captions: Name, Address, City, State, Postal Code
   Field descriptions: Company name, Full street address, City name, 2-letter state abbrev., ZIP + 4
   Field types: All fields are text fields.
   Field sizes: Count the longest item to be keyed into each field. Be sure to count spaces.
   Sort/Index: Name and Address fields

4. Create the database that you designed in Computer Application 3, using available software. Key the following names and addresses into the data-

base. Remember to add leading zeros to numbers of unequal length that will be sorted. Sort the Name and Address fields. Print the table for the Delivery Customers database correctly sorted. (Obj. 8)

18th Street Bagels
1543 18th Street
Butte, MT 59701-1543

Carlson Real Estate Co.
7841 Madison Road
Butte, MT 59702-7841

Carlson Real Estate Co.
900 Madison Road
Butte, MT 59702-1900

Catucci Computer Hardware
75 Riverside Parkway
Butte, MT 59702-1175

Cawood Funeral Home
One East 18th Street
Butte, MT 59750-1201

Carlson Real Estate Co.
2335 W. Court
Butte, MT 59703-2335

Carlson Real Estate Co.
10 E 24th Street
Butte, MT 59707-1100

Cawood Funeral Home
905 Madison Road
Butte, MT 59701-1905

Catucci Computer Hardware
9809 Riverside Parkway
Butte, MT 59703-9809

6th Street Bagels
34 6th Street
Butte, MT 59707-4534

Why are the Carlson Real Estate Co. offices located at 2335 W. Court and 7841 Madison Road out of order by street addresses? What can you do to correct the order of the street addresses?

Chapter 7

1. On a separate sheet of paper, create a database design sheet for the records retention and destruction schedule shown in Computer Application 2. Use the following information to plan and design the database. (Obj. 8)

Database filename: Retention Schedule
Database description: Records Retention and Destruction Schedule
Field names: Office, Record Name, Years in Office, Years in Center, Total Years
Fields captions: Office of Record, Record Name, Yrs./Office, Yrs./Center, Total Yrs.
Field types: All fields are text fields.
Field sizes: Count the longest item to be keyed into each field. Be sure to count spaces.
Sort/Index: Office and Record Name fields

2. Create the database you designed in Computer Application 1, using available software. Key the following information into the database. Key leading zeros in the Yrs./Office, Yrs./Center, and Total Yrs. columns to align the numbers in these columns on the right. Key three hyphens (---) in the Yrs./Center column if the records are not sent to the center. Key P for permanent retention. Proofread your work carefully. Sort the Office of

Record field. Print a copy of the Retention Schedule database table. Make any corrections and print a final copy to give to your teacher for checking

RECORDS RETENTION AND DESTRUCTION SCHEDULE

| | | Retention Periods | | |
Office of Record	Record Name	Yrs. in Office	Yrs. in Center	Total Years
Accounting	Accounts Payable	03	03	06
Accounting	Accounts Receivable	03	03	06
Accounting	General Journals	03	03	06
Accounting	Payroll Records	03	03	06
Administration	Deeds	03	P	P
Administration	General Correspondence	01	—	01
Administration	Maintenance Records	01	—	01
Administration	Telephone Messages	30D	—	30D
Corporate	Certificates of Incorporation	IND	IND	IND
Corporate	Incorporation Records	IND	IND	IND
Finance	Audit Reports	03	—	03
Finance	Bank Deposits	03	03	06
Finance	Bank Reconciliations	01	03	04
Human Resources	Attendance Records	01	—	01
Human Resources	Retirement Benefits	03	P	P
Legal	General Contracts	03	17	20
Legal	Product Warranties	03	17	20
Public Relations	Advertising	01	—	01
Purchasing	Catalogs	ACT	—	ACT
Purchasing	Purchase Orders	03	03	06
Sales	Orders	03	—	03
Sales	Price Lists	ACT	—	ACT

Chapter 9

1. On a separate sheet of paper, create a database design sheet for an accession log, using Figure 9-2 as an example. Use the names in the accession log in Computer Application 2 to design the database. Use the following information.

Database filename: Accession Log

Database description: Accession log for consecutive numeric filing system

Field names: File#, Name, Date

Field captions: File #, Name, Date

Field descriptions: File No., Name of correspondent/subject, Date number assigned

Field types: All fields are text fields.

Field sizes: Count the longest item to be keyed into each field. Be sure to count spaces.

Sort/Index: All fields

2. Create the database you designed in Computer Application 1, using available software. Key the following names and dates into the database. Assign number codes to the names beginning with 2315. Assign numbers in order by date. Use the current year. Key the names in indexing order into the database. Key the dates in the MM/DD/YYYY format (03/06/----). Proofread carefully. Sort the File # field. Print the database table for the Accession Log and give it to your teacher for checking. (Obj. 4)

Prof. Carole A. Rios (8/3)
Arkansas Fish and Game Commission (3/16)
Sr. Silva's de Cantina (3/18)
Kraus Plumbing and Supply Co. (2/11)
U.S. Department of State (6/12)
The Bell-Tone Communications Corp. (7/23)

3. On a separate sheet of paper, create a database design sheet for an alphabetic index for a terminal-digit filing system, using Figure 9-3 as a guide. Names for the index are in Computer Application 4. Use the following information.

Database filename: Alphabetic Index
Database description: Alphabetic index for a terminal-digit filing system
Field names: File#, Name
Field captions: File #, Name
Field descriptions: File No., Name of correspondent/subject
Field types: All fields are text fields.
Field sizes: Count the longest item to be keyed into each field. Be sure to count spaces.
Sort/Index: All fields

4. Create the database you designed in Computer Application 3, using available software. Key the following names in indexing order into the database. Begin numbering with 230120. Use the current year. Be sure to include any necessary cross-references. Proofread carefully. Sort the Name field. Print the database table for the Alphabetic Index and give it to your teacher for checking. (Obj. 6)

Ms. Alicia Gardner (12/14)
Miss A. K. Hillenmeyer, M.D. (12/5)
Trent Rios, Attorney (12/15)
Saundra Brown-Gardner (12/3)
Mr. Henry J. Smith (12/10)

Chapter 10

1. On a separate sheet of paper, create a database design sheet for the names listed in Application 2, page 186. Use the following information.

Database filename: Geographic File
Database description: Client list with addresses

Field names: Rec#, Client, Street, City, State, ZIP Code
Field captions: Rec #, Client, Street, City, State, ZIP Code
Field descriptions: Record No., Client name, Street address, City, State, ZIP Code
Field types: All fields are text fields.
Field sizes: Count the longest item to be keyed into each field. Be sure to count spaces.
Sort/Index: Client, City, State

2. Create the database that you designed in Computer Application 1, using available software. Key the client names in indexing order into the database. Proofread carefully. Sort the Client field. Print the database table and give it to your teacher for checking. All fields will not print on one page.

3. Sort the Geographic File database by the City and State fields. Print the database table and give it to your teacher for checking. All fields will not print on one page.

4. Sort the Geographic File database by the State field. Print the database table and give it to your teacher for checking. All fields will not print on one page.

Chapter 11

1. On a separate sheet of paper, create a database design sheet for a subject file list, using Figure 11-3 as a guide. Key the letter of the alphabet under which each subject heading is listed (location) along with the subject heading. Use the following information. (Objs. 5, 6)

Database filename: Subject File List 1
Database description: Subject file list for dictionary subject filing system
Field names: Location, Subject
Field captions: File Location, Subject Heading
Field descriptions: Alphabetic section of files, Subject heading
Field types: All fields are text fields.
Field sizes: Count the longest item to be keyed into each field. Be sure to count spaces.
Sort/Index: All fields

2. Create the database you designed in Computer Application 1, using available software. Use the following subjects. Some File Locations (E-H, L, and Q) may have subject headings in the future; key them into the database now. Proofread carefully. Sort the File Location and Subject Heading fields in that order. Print the database table for Subject File List 1 and give it to your teacher for checking. (Obj. 5)

depreciation schedules	petty cash records
travel expenses	credit card statements
amortization records	invoices

payroll records	mortgage payments
credit applications	partnership agreements
articles of incorporation	bank statements
records inventory	maintenance records
board of directors meeting minutes	wire transfers
shareholders meeting minutes	budgets five year
voting records	agreements

3. On a separate sheet of paper, create a database design sheet for an encyclopedic subject file index. The subject headings and subject codes that you will use are listed in Computer Application 4. Use the following information. (Obj. 5)

Database filename: Subject File List 2
Database description: Subject file list for encyclopedic subject filing system
Field names: Code, Subject
Field captions: Code, Subject
Field descriptions: Subject code, Tertiary subject heading
Field types: All fields are text fields.
Field sizes: Count the longest item to be keyed into each field. Be sure to count spaces.
Sort/Index: All fields

4. Create the database that you designed in Computer Application 3, using available software. Arrange the tertiary headings under the appropriate primary and secondary subject headings. Then assign subject codes to the primary and secondary headings. Key the list into your database. Proofread carefully. Sort the Code and Subject fields in that order. Print the database table for the Subject File List 2 and give it to your teacher for checking. (Obj. 5, 8)

PRIMARY	SECONDARY
CORPORATE	INCORPORATION
ADMINISTRATION	SECURITY
	GENERAL
	RECORDS MANAGEMENT
	PROPERTY FACILITIES
FINANCE	INVESTMENTS
	BANKING

TERTIARY

stockholders dividend records	employee clearances
stockholders meeting minutes	building permits
deposit slips	bond investments
correspondence	incorporation records
reading files	stockholders proxies
annual stockholders meeting minutes	bank deposits
bank reconciliations	stock investments

records inventory	badge lists
bylaws	certificates of incorporation
board of directors meeting notices	records management procedures
electronic mail policy	water rights
check registers	proxies signed
office layout	stock investments
bank reconciliations	visitor registration
property title	computer tape indexes

Each subject code will consist of six letters. The first three letters are separated from the last three letters by a diagonal. The subject codes are created from the first three letters of the primary subject and the first three letters of the secondary subject (CORPORATE INCORPORATION = COR/INC). Two codes have been done for you. (Objs. 5, 8)

SUBJECT FILE LIST

Subject	Subject Code
ADMINISTRATION	
GENERAL	ADM/GEN
CORPORATE	
INCORPORATION	COR/INC

Chapter 13

1. On a separate sheet of paper, create a database design sheet for a microfilm database index. Use the following information to plan and design the database.

Date created: Current
Database filename: Microfilm Index
Database description: Terminated employees
Field names: Name, Termination Date, SS#, Roll#, Batch#, Frame#
Field captions: Name, Term Date, SS #, Roll #, Batch #, Frame #
Field descriptions: Supply appropriate descriptions.
Field types: All fields are text fields.
Field sizes: Count the longest item to be keyed into each field. Be sure to count spaces.
Sort/Index: Name, Termination Date, Roll #, Batch #.

2. Create the Microfilm Index database that you designed in Computer Application 1, using available software. Key the following information into the database. Sort the Name field and print the table. Sort the Roll # and Batch # fields and print the table. Proofread the tables carefully and correct any errors and reprint them if necessary. Give the two tables to your teacher for checking.

Name	Term Date	SS #	Roll #	Batch #	Frame #
Thelma J. Haskell	08-26-1998	019-000-6755	0001	0010	0131-0140
William A. Johnson	08-14-1998	555-300-0900	0001	0100	1236-1248
Anthony L. Fresquez	01-04-1999	402-555-4265	0050	0035	0210-0225
Mary S. Brown-Duncan	10-15-1998	375-000-6341	0039	0253	2057-2068
Richard T. Plakidas	07-15-1998	700-555-3255	0045	0125	1043-1054
Nikki S. Wong	11-10-1998	655-025-7600	0025	0165	1430-1441
Emily K. Mendes	09-07-1998	265-001-5726	0001	0001	0001-0012
Charles R. Edwards	06-30-1998	026-000-3077	0001	0009	0120-0130
Miguel Q. Figuroa	07-10-1998	855-666-0760	0001	0036	0281-0293
Brian D. Beasley	01-04-1999	155-333-1663	0001	0025	0211-0223

Answers to Reviews

Chapter 1, Review 1 (Page 5)

1. Records are used by most workers in every type of organization. Examples are factory workers, corporate presidents, and building contractors.

2. Organizations keep records for their administrative value, fiscal value, legal value, or historical value.

Chapter 1, Review 2 (Page 6)

1. The phases of the records cycle are creation, distribution, use, maintenance, and disposition.

2. Finding records that have been filed is the goal of a filing system.

Chapter 1, Review 3 (Page 9)

1. Three media used for records are paper, electronic, and image.

2. Paper media include letters, forms, faxes, printed voice and e-mail messages, and computer printouts. Electronic media consist of computer and word processor disks and tapes. Optical disks, CD-ROM, and microforms are examples of image media.

Chapter 1, Review 4 (Page 12)

1. Any two job titles. Answers will vary.

2. The Association of Records Managers and Administrators, Inc. (ARMA), and the Association of Information and Image Management (AIIM) serve the records areas.

Chapter 2, Review 1 (Page 22)

Number	Name Indexed
3	ALICIA BENAVIDES TRAVEL AGENCY
4	BANK OF AMERICA
9	BANKERS TRUST COMPANY
6	BANKORAMA
8	BANKS AND BANKS PLUMBING
1	BANKS GEORGE R
5	BANKS M
2	BANKS PORTABLE COACHES
10	BANKS WINDOW REPAIRS
7	BANKTOWN CREDIT UNION THE

Chapter 2, Review 2 (Page 25)

Number	Name Indexed
1	A AND W VIDEO RENTALS
10	ANN WALKER AND JOEL BIEZ MOTOR CO
8	ATANDT
11	BENNETT PATRICK II
3	BENNETT PATRICK SR
12	BENNETTJONES GWYN MRS
5	BENNETTMARKS INC
2	DR BENS HEALTH SPA
7	JOHNSON SUSAN CRM MS
9	JOHNSON SUSAN DR
6	WENCO
4	WSNY RADIO

Chapter 3, Review 1 (Page 41)

Number	Name Indexed
3	007 HOUR PHOTO
7	007 STORE
2	008 AVENUE DELI AND FLOWERS
9	711 PLUMBING CORP
10	ASSOCIATION OF MANAGEMENT CONSULTING FIRMS
12	BANK OF RALEIGH
6	ELEVENTH AVENUE CAMERA STORE
1	ELSOL TAILORS SHOP INC
5	FRAMINGHAM STATE COLLEGE
11	FT LAUDERDALE NEWS
8	SANANA DESIGNS LTD
4	SANCARLOS HOTEL

Chapter 3, Review 2 (Pages 46-47)

Number	Name Indexed
10	JOHNSON ALEX 2020 AVENUE D DENVER CO 80207-4121
1	JOHNSON ALEX 2979 AVENUE D DENVER CO 80207-2114
4	JOHNSON ALEX 22 WEST MAIN ST DENVER CO 80207-3422

8   PAKISTAN REPUBLIC OF
     FINANCE MINISTRY OF

2   PAKISTAN REPUBLIC OF
     INTERIOR MINISTRY

11   RITTER JOHN
     HWY 59
     ALBANY TX 76430-1099

12   RITTER JOHN JR
     50 ROCKLINE RD
     ALBANY NY 12237-2121

6   U S STEEL CORP
     130 LINCOLN AVENUE
     VANDERGRIFT PA 15690-1210

9   UNITED STATES GOVERNMENT
     DEFENSE DEPARTMENT OF
     THE PENTAGON
     WASHINGTON DC 20301-0999

3   UNIVERSITY OF WYOMING
     BOX 3434 UNIVERSITY STATION
     LARAMIE WY 82071-3434

7   WYOMING COUNTY OF
     AGING OFFICE OF THE
     COURTHOUSE SQUARE
     TUNKHANNOCK PA 18657-7634

5   WYOMING RESOURCES CORP
     CLAYDESTA TOWER EAST
     MIDLAND TX 79705-2112

Chapter 4, Review 1 (Page 63)

1. In the geographic method, correspondence is arranged alphabetically by location first and then by correspondents' names. In the subject method, correspondence is arranged alphabetically by subject first and then by correspondents' names. In the name method, correspondence is arranged alphabetically by correspondents' names.

2. One reason for selecting the shelf file is the savings in office floor space. Another reason is the convenient access of the open-shelf, side-access files. Finally, color-coding is highly effective because large bands of color are readily discernible on open shelves.

3. An open caption shows the beginning alphabetic range of stored records behind a guide, in a drawer, or on a shelf. A closed caption shows the beginning and ending ranges of the stored records.

Chapter 4, Review 2 (Page 71)

1. In straight-line filing, the guide tabs and folder tabs occupy horizontal positions in the file that are readable in a straight line from front to back in a top-access file or from top to bottom in a side-access file.

2. Correspondence is arranged in individual folders by the letter date, with the most current date filed in front. Correspondence in the general folder is arranged first by correspondent's name. If more than one record for the same correspondent is filed, the more current record is filed in front.

      5   2   3   4
3. Dr./William/J./Burns,/Jr.

Chapter 5, Review 1 (Page 76)

1. Using a database for records control allows for rapid access of records and information.

2. Five types of computer fields are character, date, numeric, logical, and text or memo fields.

Chapter 5, Review 2 (Page 79)

1. A database design sheet shows the database structure and provides the history of changes made in the database structure.

2. ASCII stands for American Standard Code for Information Interchange—the internal coding system used by most computers.

Chapter 5, Review 3 (Page 82)

1. Leading zeros are zeros that must be added to the front of numbers so that all numbers align at the right and are the same length. Numbers will sort correctly when they are of the same length.

2. When house/building numbers and street names are in the same field, the computer will sort the house/building numbers first. Separate fields are needed for the street names to be in order, in accordance with Indexing Rule 9.

Chapter 5, Review 4 (Page 84)

1. Backup copies of program or data files provide recovery of data if original files are lost or damaged.

2. Any three of the following precautions help preserve external disks: avoiding extreme temperatures and direct sunlight; keeping disks away from magnetic fields; keeping disks dust free; not allowing disks to rub together; not bending disks; not writing on disks; and not touching the disk surface.

Chapter 6, Review 1 (Page 100)

1. When using the OUT guide with printed lines, *one* copy of the requisition is prepared. Information from the requisition is copied to the printed lines of the OUT guide. The requisition is saved for follow-up. When using the OUT guide with a pocket, *two* copies of the requisition are prepared. One copy is placed in the pocket of the OUT guide and the duplicate copy is saved for follow-up.

2. When using an OUT folder to charge out records, the OUT folder is substituted for the original folder in the main file. When using a carrier folder to charge out records, the records are placed in the carrier folder and the original folder is maintained in the main file.

Chapter 6, Review 2 (Page 105)

1. The three methods to follow up on borrowed records include (1) scanning the file, (2) maintaining a charge-out log, and (3) using a follow-up file.

2. A follow-up is not necessary when *copies* of the original records are sent to borrowers.

3. An additional step is taken when reserving records for use at a future date to keep others from borrowing those records during the reserved times. Place an OUT guide or requisition sheet in the main file to show when the records are needed. In addition to placing a requisition in the follow-up file behind the date the records are needed, this additional step keeps others from borrowing those records during the reserved period.

Chapter 7, Review 1 (Page 114)

1. Records retention policies are necessary in order to control the growth of records in the active and inactive storage areas.

2. Records values are determined by the information contained in the records and the usefulness of that information to the organization.

Chapter 7, Review 2 (Page 117)

1. Records are accessible when they are near the records user. Active records should be easily accessible to users. Inactive and archive records are less accessible because they are used less often than active records.

2. Another term for archival is life expectancy.

Chapter 7, Review 3 (Page 118)

1. Records are transferred to free additional space for storing active records. Inactive records storage is also less expensive storage.

2. The volume and use of the active records determines which transfer method to use..

Chapter 7, Review 4 (Page 121)

1. A transmittal form is needed to identify box contents, location, retention, and destruction information as well as ownership of the records.

2. Active records storage uses file folders and guides, sometimes hanging folders, and file cabinets or shelves. Inactive storage uses folders but doesn't need guides or cabinets. Boxes stored on steel shelving is used in inactive storage and archives. Vaults also may be used in archives.

Chapter 7, Review 5 (Page 123)

1. Four control files used in a records center are an inactive records index, a charge-out and follow-up file, a destruction date file, and a destruction file.

2. Records destruction controls are needed to ensure that records are destroyed on schedule. Timely destruction prevents the accumulation of records that are no longer necessary. Records destruction controls also ensure that the destruction is conducted properly.

Chapter 8, Review 1 (Page 136)

1. The first two letters of the key unit are color-coded in the Jeter Top Coder.

2. In the Alpha-Z® system, the first two letters of the key unit are color-coded. In larger systems, the third letter of the key unit or the first letter of the second filing unit may also be color-coded.

3. The Birth Date/Alphabetical filing system is considered alphanumeric because it uses a combination of letters and numbers to index records in the filing system.

Chapter 8, Review 2 (Page 143)

1. Colorscan® is considered a random access filing system because records are filed and retrieved without regard for strict alphabetic or numeric sequence.

2. The advantages of a computer-generated labeling process include (1) the speed of converting to a color-coded system because the folders arrive ready for use, (2) the accuracy of color-coding the names, (3) the precise and uniform application of folder labels, and (4) the added durability of the laminated label and reinforced folder tab.

Chapter 9, Review 1 (Page 151)

1. Numbers are preprinted on checks, purchase orders, and invoices.

2. New numbers can be added at the end of a consecutive filing system.

Chapter 9, Review 2 (Page 154)

1. Be sure that you write the name or subject beside the number in the accession log each time a new number is assigned.

2. Examples will vary.

Chapter 9, Review 3 (Page 158)

1. The alphabetic index must be checked for each name or subject when coding the records so that the correct code can be used on each record. When the records are in alphabetic order, this is a quicker process.

2. Answers may include: Numbers are quicker to sort and file; the filing system may be easily expanded at the end of the system; and so on.

Chapter 9, Review 4 (Page 161)

1. Zeros are added to the left of any number having less than enough digits for three equal groups.

2. The tertiary digits on the right.

Chapter 10, Review 1 (Page 179)

1. The number and diversity of the names will determine which guide plan to use. Use the lettered guide plan when similar names are numerous. Use the location name guide plan for location names that are diverse and few in number.

2. The alphabetic index is an alphabetic list of correspondents' names with their locations. The master index is an alphabetic list of all filing segments by location first and then by correspondents' names.

Chapter 10, Review 2 (Page 184)

1. Filing segments in a geographic file are coded by circling the geographic units and numbering them in the order they will be considered. Then the filing units in the name are separated with diagonals and numbered in the order they are considered.

2. The key unit in the filing segment is the largest geographic unit used in the system. Consider each geographic unit first; look to the correspondent's name second.

Chapter 11, Review 1 (Page 193)

1. Subject filing should be used whenever records cannot be filed by any other filing feature or characteristic, such as a name, number, or geographic location.

2. Two arrangements used in subject filing are the dictionary and encyclopedic arrangements.

Chapter 11, Review 2 (Page 199)

1. For a dictionary subject file folder, the letter of the alphabet (A to Z) is keyed one line from the top and two spaces from the left edge. The subject is keyed five spaces to the right. For an encyclopedic subject file folder, the subject or subject code is keyed one line from the top and two spaces from the left edge. The complete filing segment is keyed five spaces to the right.

2. General cross-references are in the subject file list. Cross-reference sheets are used for specific record cross-references. Cross-reference sheets are filed under the second primary subject heading to refer the filer to the record which is filed under the first primary subject heading.

Chapter 11, Review 3 (Page 201)

1. Subject codes are used to simplify and speed up the indexing, coding, and filing processes.

2. Each record must be read to determine the subject; scanning isn't sufficient.

Chapter 12, Review 1 (Page 211)

1. The more knowledge you have about records storage supplies and equipment availability, the better equipped you will be to make appropriate supplies and equipment selections.

2. The advantages of a cost/benefit analysis come from comparing advantages—short- and long-term benefits—against cost and any disadvantages. A more expensive investment initially may save money ultimately. The analysis helps to determine whether or not the investment is a good one.

Chapter 12, Review 2 (Page 227)

1. You will need to specify folder tab cut, tab position, and folder stock. Folders are either letter size or legal size. Correspondence filing requires letter-size folders.

2. Suspension folders stay upright in the file and are easily moved, opened, or replaced without disrupting other folders in the system. They store different-size materials more efficiently than the stationary vertical folders. Snap tabs that slide easily to reposition the tabs across the back of the folder make a flexible guide plan possible.

3. Because single documents are retrieved from the folders, you will want to select retrieval equipment that does not require the removal of the entire folder. The vertical and lateral drawer file cabinets offer this feature.

Chapter 13, Review 1 (Page 232)

1. Computer output is stored on disks, tapes, or printouts.

2. The major uses of magnetic tape are backing up and archiving.

Chapter 13, Review 2 (Page 236)

1. Roll microfilm, aperture cards, microfiche, or jackets are common microforms.

2. Computer-output microfilm (COM) is a computer-generated microform.

Chapter 13, Review 3 (Page 242)

1. (Any two) A rotary camera photographs records while they are moving. A planetary camera photographs records while they are stationary. A step-and-repeat camera photographs records in a grid pattern for microfiche.

2. Copies or duplicates of microforms may be charged out.

Chapter 13, Review 4 (Page 245)

1. Documents are scanned, indexed, and saved to the optical disk.

2. WORM optical disks cannot be overwritten and are the most secure.

Chapter 14, Review 1 (Page 253)

1. Employees in the records department and others in the organization who use the services of the records department use a records management manual.

2. The following records control procedures should be standardized: selecting supplies and equipment, transferring records, establishing records retention periods, and coding according to a standard set of alphabetic indexing rules.

Chapter 14, Review 2 (Page 258)

1. Fire-resistant storage devices include fire-resistant vaults, safes, cabinets, rooms, or boxes.

2. Water-damaged microimage records are recovered by reprocessing the microfilm in chemical-free water.

Index

Follow-up
  defined, 101
  eliminating, 103-104
Follow-up file
  charge-up and, 122
  illustrated, 104
  using, 102-103
Follow-up methods, manual, 102-104
Freeze drying, for water-damaged records, 256

G

General folders, 65
Geographic file indexes, 177-179
Geographic filing, 54, 167-189
  advantages and disadvantages of, 184
  defined, 168
  dictionary arrangement in, 169-171
  encyclopedic arrangement in, 171-176
  expansion of, 183-184
  letter coded for, 180
  master index in, 177-179
  methods of, 168-176
  need for, 168
  procedures for, 179-183
Government names
  federal, 44
  foreign, 44
  indexing rules for, 43-46
  state and local, 44
Guide, defined, 26
Guides, 58
  arranging folders and, 63-66
  for correspondence storage, 213
  labels for, 61
  OUT. *See* OUT guide
  primary, 29, 64-66
  secondary, 29, 65
  third-level, 29
  top-tab and side-tab, 58

H

Halon gas, 256
Hanging folders. *See* suspension folders
Hard copy, 55
High density files, 220

I

Identical names, indexing rules for, 42-43, 81-82
Image media, 8
  storage equipment for, 9
Important records, 113
Inactive records, 114
  index for, 122
Index cards, preparing, 30
Indexing
  in consecutive numeric filing, 155
  defined, 18, 67
  in microimage filing, 241
  in subject filing, 197
Indexing order, 19
Indexing rules
  for abbreviations, 22
  adopting, 17
  alphabetic, 17-52
  for business names, 20
  defined, 17
  for government names, 43-46
  for identical names, 42-43, 81-82
  for numbers in business names, 81
  for personal names, 17-36
  for possessives, 21
  for prefixes, 38
  for punctuation, 21
  for single letters, 22
  studying, 19
  for subjects as primary titles, 47-48
  for titles and suffixes, 23, 80
Individual folders, 65-66
Information disaster, 253
Input, 79
Inspecting
  in consecutive numeric filing, 155
  defined, 67
  in geographic filing, 179
  in subject filing, 197
Insulated safe, illustrated, 257

J

Jeter Birth Date/Alphabetical Filing system, 132-133
Jeter Top Coder Filing system, 129-132

K

Key unit, 18, 68

L

Label
  drawer, 61
  folder, 62, 214
  guide, 61
  in microimage media storage, 239
  shelf, 61
Lateral file, 57
  cabinets for correspondence storage, 216-218
Leading zero, 80
Lektriever, The, 223
Lettered guide plan
  in encyclopedic geographic filing, 172-175
  in geographic filing, 182
Location name guide plan, 171
  in encyclopedic geographic filing, 172-175
  in geographic filing, 183
Long-term records, 114

M

Magneto-optical (MO) disks, 243
Maintenance of records, 6
Manual, records management, 250-254
Manual retrieval equipment, for correspondence storage, 214-222
Master control file, 122
Master index, in geographic filing, 177-179
Mechanical retrieval equipment, 222-224
Media
  electronic, 8
  image, 8
  paper, 7
Microfacsimile, 236
Microfiche, 234
  heading for, 240
  and jacket reader-printer, illustrated, 239
Microfilm
  computer-output, 235
  jacket, 235